D0063135

THE QUOTABLE CHESTERTON

THE
QUOTABLE
CHESTERTON

A Topical Compilation of the Wit, Wisdom and
Satire of G. K. Chesterton

Edited by

GEORGE J. MARLIN, RICHARD P. RABATIN
and JOHN L. SWAN

With a Foreword by
JOSEPH SOBRAN

IGNATIUS PRESS   SAN FRANCISCO

Cover and jacket by Marcia Ryan

© 1986 Ignatius Press, San Francisco
All rights reserved
ISBN 0-89870-102-3 (HB)
0-89870-122-8 (SB)
Library of Congress catalogue number 86-80788
Printed in the United States of America

Our Efforts Are Dedicated
To Our Fathers

JOHN G. MARLIN

GEORGE F. RABATIN

DANIEL J. SWAN, M.D.
(1890–1969)

CONTENTS

FOREWORD

The main defect of the present volume is its brevity. But it could be many times as long and suffer from the same fault. Chesterton always leaves the reader wanting more Chesterton.

It is hard to think of another author so intensely loved by those who know him yet so widely neglected by the reading public. Some people, it's true, find him unreadable. One critic sneers that Chesterton "makes verbal mountains out of intellectual molehills". This is nearly the opposite of the truth, but one knows why it's possible to feel that way: the verbal density of Chesterton is so overwhelming that until you get the hang of him, you may suspect, in some irritation, that it may be all nonsense.

That verbal density, however, proceeds from a habit of extreme intellectual concentration. Chesterton has a way of coming to the point almost too swiftly. He knocks us off balance with sudden insights and doesn't give us time to recover. He is the Shakespeare of the aphorism, delighting us with an astounding fertility that defies comprehension at a first reading, and rewards endless rereading.

For this reason, although he—like Shakespeare—invites anthologizing, he—like Shakespeare—eludes it. In his books and essays the witticisms pour forth, but they interlock. The anthologist never has to look far for material, but when he finds it he also finds pain in cutting it.

Consider this: "Tradition may be defined as an extension of the franchise. Tradition means giving votes to the most obscure of all classes, our ancestors." That is excellent, and it has the finality of a good aphorism. But dare we omit the very next sentence? "It is the democracy of the dead." The idea is deepened, and given a solemn note. Still he continues: "Tradition refuses to submit to the small and arrogant oligarchy of those who merely happen to be walking about." Again, memorable. And yet Chesterton is *still* not through playing with the insight for all it is worth: "All democrats object to men being disqualified by the accident of birth; tradition objects to their being disqualified by the accident of death." This, I think, is best of all. Maybe he should have stopped there; what follows isn't quite as brilliant. But who else could even have matched this: "Democracy tells us not to neglect a good man's opinion, even if he is our groom; tradition asks us not to neglect a good man's opinion, even if he is our father."

Chesterton has a passion for coming to the point, and he comes to an infinite number of points. He always defines things without reducing them to abstractions. They keep their mystery even when they are known. There is lightning in his logic: it flashes and illuminates, but without dissolving the solidity of the objects under his observation. Unlike Max Weber, Chesterton doesn't live in a world that has lost its enchantment. He rushes to enjoy, and in the fullest sense to *appreciate,* the glory and beauty of sheer being. He takes in more than most of us, and yet there is still too much for him. His mode of appreciation and criticism is to try to imagine the realities around him. This makes him the most sympathetic of critics. Imagination, for Chesterton, is not fantasy, creating something more colorful though more insubstantial than life: imagination is the faculty through which we begin to know the real world that only God can know fully.

It is because there is an inexhaustible amount to know that we can never know it all, and that is why Chesterton's mind is always in a sort of happy hurry. In him the intellectual verges on the mystical. He offers his aphorisms without vanity, as shortcuts to realization. They are little paths he has made through life's mysteries.

He is notoriously disorderly. Maybe he is having too much fun exploring the world to stop and make a map of it. No writer except P. G. Wodehouse manages to combine hilarity and kindness as Chesterton does. He might seem sentimental, except that he is always discovering something genuinely and unsuspectedly real wherever he turns. He teaches us too much to allow us to accuse him of blind optimism. He achieves order—the order of lucidity and style—in those wonderful epigrams. They show a mind too sharp to yield to emotional sloppiness.

It's because that mind always beats ours to the punch that we react as we do, with awe or antagonism. But eventually we realize that humble awe is a more worthy and intelligent response than belligerence. In the first place, Chesterton himself is so generous. In the second, he sees so much: the world discloses itself to his sympathy. To deny that he sees it is to deny ourselves a share in the sight of it. That would be self-stunting. Our victory lies in surrender.

"If a thing is worth doing, it is worth doing badly." "There is more simplicity in the man who eats caviar on impulse than in the man who eats grape-nuts on principle." "As for the general view that the Church was discredited by the War—they might as well say that the Ark was discredited by the Flood." The wisdom of these remarks is nearly obscured by their wit. But they hold up. We remember them for their elegance, and as we ponder them we come to realize the profundity behind the apparent flippancy. That is what makes them durable jokes, of course. And Chesterton not only loves jokes, he trusts them. His faith in humanity takes the form of faith in humor. He doesn't insult us by explaining everything. He honors us by joking about everything.

This also accounts for his love of Dickens. "Dickens did not write what the people wanted," he tells us. "He wanted what the people wanted." That is why Chesterton prefers the demagogue to the mystagogue. At least the demagogue doesn't affect superiority to human nature. At least he isn't a snob. And the snob is Chesterton's *bête noire*. This man of superior gifts seems to have hated the air of superiority more than anything else. He excuses the violence of Samuel Johnson because he thinks it reveals how little Johnson took his own superiority for granted: even the great Johnson knew keenly that he could lose any argument to any contender. He was anything but a "literary dictator". Johnson could fight unfairly because he was fundamentally too humble to think his mere word could settle any dispute. It may seem strained to find democracy in disputatiousness, but once Chesterton has planted the idea we can never quite dismiss it.

Like his friend Hilaire Belloc, Chesterton talked about the great and departed as real people, not as statues and monuments. He saw no reason to stop arguing with them just because they were dead. He took them seriously; that is why he always has something fresh to say about them. He is not finished talking about them for the same reason he is not through listening to them. It is his argument for tradition applied to individuals.

In the same spirit he rejects the cult of art for art's sake. At the conclusion of *Heretics* he pleads that "men such as these of whom I have spoken should not be insulted by being taken for artists. No man has any right whatever merely to enjoy the work of Mr. Bernard Shaw; he might as well enjoy the invasion of his country by the French. Mr. Shaw writes either to convince or to enrage us." He feels that the "esthetic" approach is really anesthetic: it shields us from direct contact with real sentiment, and he calls "that miserable fear of being sentimental" "the meanest of all the modern terrors". He explains: "Everywhere the robust and uproarious humor has come from the men who were capable not merely of senti-mentalism, but of a very silly sentimentalism. There has been no humor so robust or uproarious as that of the sentimentalist Steele or the sentimentalist Sterne or the sentimentalist Dickens. These creatures who wept like women were the creatures who laughed like men. It is true that the humor of Micawber is good literature and that the pathos of little Nell is bad. But the kind of man who had the courage to write so badly in the one case is the kind of man who would have had the courage to write so well in the other. . . . And herein is especially shown the frigid and feeble limitations of our modern wits. They make violent efforts, they make heroic and almost pathetic efforts, but they cannot really write badly. There are moments when we almost think that they are achieving the effect, but our hope shrivels to nothing the moment we compare their little failures with the enormous imbecilities of Byron or Shakespeare."

And there is the key to Chesterton, the conviction that underlies his special warm audacity. He was willing to write badly, because writing was a thing worth doing. Whether he ever wrote badly I can't say. But he is constantly willing to risk it by saying what he really feels about important subjects. His epigrams aren't small and polished things. They are large enough to be bawled in a crowded street. They are about God and the human soul, about the things men have killed and died for. Even their elegance is more boisterous than pretty. They ring with challenge; they demand assent or disagreement. We are not invited to savor them as verbal displays. Chesterton is writing not only for us, but about us.

This is why Chesterton has never settled into a comfortable place in the curriculum. He has to be taken personally. He never lends himself to disinterested contemplation. He is still alive. He proves with his own voice that the most viable democracy is the democracy of the dead.

Joseph Sobran

PREFACE

In 1986 we observe the fiftieth anniversary of the death of Gilbert Keith Chesterton. On his death, T. S. Eliot writing of Chesterton's role as the Champion of Orthodoxy stated: "He did more, I think, than any man of his time and was able to do more than anyone else, because of his particular background, development and abilities as a public performer to maintain the existence of the important minority in the modern world. He leaves behind a permanent claim upon our loyalty, to see that the work that he did in his time is continued in ours." Since 1936, the world has trembled at the brink of devastation many times yet the words of G. K. C. continue to live on and inspire us.

For us, Chesterton lives in his inverness cape, in his sword cane, in his pince-nez. He lives because his words are timeless. His battle against atheistic humanism and scientism continues today. The scope and breadth of his knowledge is amazing. His commentaries and views on the continuing dehumanization of man, the so-called social sciences, the idealistic movements and totalitarian ideologies and the intellectual fashions of his day continue to be relevant in our own age.

In *A Handful of Authors* Chesterton wrote:

> We have all heard of prophets and poets being unpopular; and also of unpopularity as a thing that may purify the soul. But there is this further and rather odd fact—that every great man must go through a period of unpopularity, not while he is alive, but shortly after he is dead. That after eclipse is essential because in that is settled the difference between temporary and eternal oblivion. The prophet and the quack are alike admired for a generation, and admired for the wrong reasons. Then they are both forgotten, for no reason at all. But if the man is a mere quack he never returns. If he is a great man he returns, and he returns for the right reasons.

These words were prophetic because Chesterton truly returns for the right reasons.

In recent years the growth of the G. K. Chesterton Society and *The Chesterton Review* have signaled his renascent influence. There is a large demand for material on G. K. C. His out of print books command a premium. To the delight of many, Ignatius Press has begun the republication of all of his works. Notables, including President Ronald Reagan, quote G. K. C. frequently.

13

This revival in Chesterton gave us the idea for this volume of quotes topically arranged. Many people quote G. K. C., but due to the unavailability of his words to date it is difficult to know exact wordings or origins of citations.

In compiling this volume we read and edited 73 of G. K. C.'s books consisting of 16,667 pages. We extracted and assigned topics to several thousand quotes. For the purpose of this book we selected 1,200 passages which we thought represented the best of G. K. C. Regretably, we may have overlooked some favorite quotes of many of Chesterton's readers. For that we apologize, with an apology G. K. C. would recognize: "If a thing is worth doing, it is worth doing badly."

We are grateful to those who assisted and guided us in the preparation of this volume. Very special thanks to Barbara Dyson Marlin, whose contribution to the assembling of this volume was invaluable. Also our thanks to Donna Albertus Rabatin for proofreading and putting up with us during the last two years. We are grateful to the following for their guidance: Mr. Joseph Sobran, Senior Editor of the *National Review;* Ian Boyd, C.S.B., Editor of *The Chesterton Review;* Kenneth Baker, S.J., Editor of the *Homiletic and Pastoral Review;* Miss Eleanor Schlafly, Executive Director of the Cardinal Mindzenty Foundation; and noted authors Father Enrique T. Rueda and Father Vincent Miceli.

Also, we want to thank Joseph A. Bierbauer, Vincent Bologna, Gary S. Casino, Rev. Msgr. Eugene V. Clark, Michael C. Crofton, Joseph E. Darden, Ann Deans, John P. DeMaio, Lisa DeSantis, Kevin Fitzgerald, Lynn Kelly, Lisa Offenborn, John J. Reilly, Rev. Bro. George Schuster, S.M., Thomas Walsh and James S. Wilson.

One of us would like particularly to thank Alan Chase and Guy Mastrion for being excellent educators who have never failed to be sources of inspiration.

Finally, special thanks to Dr. Larry Azar, Professor of Philosophy at Iona College, for introducing one of us to Chesterton.

We acknowledge our indebtedness to all of the individuals who kindly helped us in the preparation of this volume, yet we alone take full responsibility for any inaccuracies of the work herein.

January 1986   George J. Marlin
New York City   Richard P. Rabatin
                                                                      John L. Swan

Absent-mindedness

We have read of some celebrated philosopher who was so absent-minded that he paid a call at his own house. My own absent-mindedness is extreme, and my philosophy, of course, is the marvel of men and angels. But, I never quite managed to be so absent-minded as that.

—MM, 83

It would be well to understand the quality, for there are several types of absence of mind, including that of some pretentious poets and intellectuals, in whom the mind has never been noticeably present.

—STA, 124

Absurdity

Perfect absurdity is a direct thing, like physical pain, or a strong smell. A joke is a fact. However indefensible it is it cannot be attacked. However defensible it is it cannot be defended.

—CD, 85

Accidents

This world and all our powers in it are far more awful and beautiful than even we know until some accident reminds us.

—TT, 56

Act of Faith

The greatest act of faith that a man can perform is the act that we perform every night. We abandon our identity, we turn our soul and body into chaos and old night. We uncreate ourselves as if at the end of the world: for all practical purposes we become dead men, in the sure and certain hope of a glorious resurrection.

—L & L, 30

Adventurers

It is the apologia of a political adventurer, and a political adventurer of a kind peculiarly open to popular condemnation. Mankind has always been somewhat inclined to forgive the adventurer who destroys or re-creates, but there is nothing inspiring about the adventurer who merely preserves. We have sympathy with the rebel who aims at reconstruction, but there is something repugnant to the imagination in the rebel who rebels in the name of compromise.

—RB, 121

Advertisements

It is really not so repulsive to see the poor asking for money as to see the rich asking for more money. And advertisement is the rich asking for more money.

—NJ, 70

The Aesthetic

... the definition of an aesthetic is a man who is experienced enough to admire a good picture, but not inexperienced enough to see it.

—L & L, 119

Aging

The advantage of advancing years lies in discovering that traditions are true, and therefore alive; indeed, a tradition is not even traditional except when it is alive. It is great fun to find out that the world has not repeated proverbs because they are proverbial, but because they are practical.

—AIG, 52

Agnosticism

It is very good for a man to talk about what he does not understand; as long as he understands that he does not understand it.

—HA, 163

Agnostics

There is still a notion that the agnostic can remain secure of this world, so long as he does not wish to be what is called "other-worldly." He can be content with common sense about men and women, so long as he is not curious of mysteries about angels and archangels. It is not true. The questions of the sceptic strike direct at the heart of this our human life; they disturb this world, quite apart from the other world; and it is exactly common sense that they disturb most. There could not be a better example than this queer appearance, in my youth, of the determinist as a demagogue; shouting to a mob of millions that no man ought to be blamed for anything he did, because it was all heredity and environment. Logically, it would stop a man in the act of saying "Thank you" to somebody for passing the mustard. For how could he be praised for passing the mustard, if he could not be blamed for not passing the mustard?

—*Bio,* 182

The word agnostic has ceased to be a polite word for atheist. It has become a real word for a very real state of mind, conscious of many possibilities beyond that of the atheist, and not excluding that of the polytheist. It is no longer a question of defining or denying a simple central power, but of balancing the brain in a bewilderment of new powers which seem to overlap and might even conflict. Nature herself has become unnatural.

—*NJ,* 156

Agreement (Practical)

It is a very unpractical thing to trust to practical agreement. Two people may agree to keep a cat; but if they only agree because one is a lover of animals, and the other has a fiendish pleasure in watching cruelty to birds, it is probable that the practical agreement will not last very long.

—*Survey,* 100

Alcohol

If it is true, as I surmise, that "alcohol" is a word of the Arabs, it is interesting to realise that our general word for the essence of wine and beer and such things comes from a people which has made particular war upon them. I suppose that some aged Moslem chieftain sat one day at the opening of his tent and, brooding with black brows and cursing in his black beard over wine as the symbol of Christianity, racked his brains for some word ugly enough to express his racial and religious antipathy, and suddenly spat out the horrible word "alcohol."

—*ATC,* 169

Amateurs

A man must love a thing very much if he not only practises it without any hope of fame or money, but even practises it without any hope of doing it well. Such a man must love the toils of the work more than any other man can love the rewards of it.

—RB, 84

America

It has long been recognized that America was an asylum. It is only since Prohibition that it has looked a little like a lunatic Asylum.

—Amer, 14

. . . America has a genius for the encouragement of fame. . . .

—FBO, 455

Whilst I was in America, I often lingered in small towns and wayside places; and in a curious and almost creepy fashion the great presence of Abraham Lincoln continually grew upon me. I think it is necessary to linger a little in America, and especially in what many would call the most uninteresting or unpleasing parts of America, before this strong sense of a strange kind of greatness can grow upon the soul.

—S, 168

Americans

I fancy that the American, quite apart from any love of money, has a great love of measurement. He will mention the exact size or weight of things, in a way which appears to us as irrelevant. It is as if we were to say that a man came to see us carrying three feet of walking stick and four inches of cigar.

—Amer, 104

There is one thing, at any rate, that must strike all Englishmen who have the good fortune to have American friends; that is, that while there is no materialism so crude or so material as American materialism, there is also no idealism so crude or so ideal as American idealism.

—*CD,* 102

Nothing would be more American than to expect a genius to be too high-toned for trade.

—*CD,* 102–103

For it is quite unjust to say that the Americans worship the dollar. They really do worship intellect—another of the passing superstitions of our time.

—*CD,* 103

Americans have a great power, which Europeans do not always appreciate, of creating institutions from below; that is by popular initiative. Like every other good thing, it has its lighter aspects; one of which, as has been remarked by Mr. Wells and others, is that a person may become a public institution without becoming an official institution.

—*FBO,* 815

The real, natural Americans are candid, generous, capable of a beautiful wonder and gratitude; enthusiastic about things external to themselves; easily contented and not particularly conceited. They have been deliberately and dogmatically thought to be conceited. They have been systematically educated in a theory of enthusiasm which degrades it into mere egotism.

—*S,* 83

I do not think that bragging and go-getting are American faults. I hate them as American virtues; I think the quarrel is not so much with the men as with the goods: the false gods they have been taught to worship and still only worship with half their hearts. And these gods of the heathen are stone and brass, but especially brass; and there is an external struggle in that half-hearted idolatry; for often, while the gods are of brass, the hearts are of gold.

—S, 90–91

Americans do not need drink to inspire them to do anything; though they do sometimes, I think, need a little for the deeper and more delicate purpose of teaching them how to do nothing.

—S, 150

Americans (and Work)

Americans really respect work, rather as Europeans respect war. There is a halo of heroism about it; and he who shrinks from it is less than a man.

—FBO, 532

Anachronisms

An anachronism is often simply an ellipsis; and an ellipsis is often simply a necessity.

—RLS, 156

Anecdotes

Again, few people would object to that general privilege whereby it is permitted to a person in narrating even a true anecdote to work up the climax by any exaggerative touches which really tend to bring it out. The reason of this is that the telling of the anecdote has become, like the telling of fairy-tale, almost a distinct artistic creation;

21

to offer to tell a story is in ordinary society like offering to recite or play the violin.

—RB, 194

Animals (and Man)

It is exactly when we do regard man as an animal that we know he is not an animal. It is precisely when we do try to picture him as a sort of horse on its hind legs, that we suddenly realize that he must be something as miraculous as the winged horse that towered up into the clouds of heaven.

—EM, XXII

Monkeys did not begin pictures and men finish them. . . . The higher animals did not draw better and better portraits; the dog did not paint better in his best period than in his early bad manner as a jackal; the wild horse was not an Impressionist and the race horse a Post-Impressionist. All we can say of this notion of reproducing things in shadow or representative shape is that it exists nowhere in nature except in man; and that we cannot even talk about it without treating man as something separate from nature. In other words, every sane sort of history must begin with man as man, a thing standing absolute and alone.

—EM, 17–18

Anthropologists (Modern)

Now the modern Anthropologists, who call themselves Agnostics, completely failed to be Anthropologists at all. Under their limitations, they could not get a complete theory of Man, let alone a complete theory of nature. They begin by ruling out something which they called the Unknowable. The incomprehensibility was almost comprehensible, if we could really understand the Unknowable in the sense of the Ultimate. But it rapidly became apparent that all sorts of things were

Unknowable, which were exactly the things that a man has got to know. It is necessary to know whether he is responsible or irresponsible, perfect or imperfect, perfectible or unperfectible, mortal or immortal, doomed or free, not in order to understand God, but in order to understand Man.

—*STA*, 161–162

Anthropology (Modern)

It is a pity that the word Anthropology has been degraded to the study of Anthropoids. It is now incurably associated with squabbles between pre-historic professors (in more senses than one) about whether a chip of stone is the tooth of a man or an ape; sometimes settled as in that famous case, when it was found to be the tooth of a pig. It is very right that there should be a purely physical science of such things; but the name commonly used might well, by analogy, have been dedicated to things not only wider and deeper, but rather more relevant.

—*STA*, 159

Nothing that leaves these things under a cloud of religious doubt can possibly pretend to be a Science of Man; it shrinks from anthropology as complete as from theology: has a man free will; or is his sense of choice an illusion? Has he a conscience, or has his conscience any authority; or is it only the prejudice of the tribal past? Is there any real hope of settling these things by human reason; and has *that* any authority? Is he to regard death as final; and is he to regard miraculous help as possible? Now it is all nonsense to say that these things are unknowable. . . . Nothing calling itself a complete Science of Man can shirk them.

—*STA*, 162

Anthropomorphism

Possibly the most pathetic of all the delusions of the modern students of primitive belief is the notion they have about the thing they call anthropomorphism. They believe that primitive men attributed phenom-

23

ena to a god in human form in order to explain them, because his mind in its sullen limitation could not reach any further than his own clownish existence. . . . The final cure for all this kind of philosophy is to walk down a lane at night. Anyone who does so will discover very quickly that men pictured something semi-human at the back of all things, not because such a thought was natural, but because it was supernatural; not because it made things more comprehensible, but because it made them a hundred times more incomprehensible and mysterious. For a man walking down a lane at night can see the conspicuous fact that as long as nature keeps to her own course, she has no power with us at all. . . . so long as a tree is a tree it does not frighten at all. It begins to be something alien . . . only when it looks like ourselves. When a tree really looks like a man our knees knock under us. And when the whole universe looks like a man we fall on our faces.

—H, 149–150

Anthropophagy

As a fact, anthropophagy is certainly a decadent thing, not a primitive one. It is much more likely that modern men will eat human flesh out of affectation than that primitive men ever ate it out of ignorance. I am here only following the outlines of their argument, which consists in maintaining that man has been progressively more lenient, first to citizens, then to slaves, then to animals, and then (presumably) to plants. I think it wrong to sit on a man. Soon, I shall think it wrong to sit on a horse. Eventually (I suppose) I shall think it wrong to sit on a chair.

—O, 205–206

Aquinas, St. Thomas

He is arguing for a common sense which would even now commend itself to most of the common people. He is arguing for the popular proverbs that seeing is believing; that the proof of the pudding is in the eating; that a man cannot jump down his own throat or deny the fact of his own existence. He often maintains the view by the use of abstractions; but the abstractions are no more abstract than Energy or Evolution or Space-

24

Time; and they do not land us, as the others often do, in hopeless contradictions about common life.

—STA, 156–157

Arabs

The Arab out of the desert, crying the terrible truism that God is God, was of all men the wildest worshipper of simplicity. He came out of the golden glare of sand and sunlight, to proclaim that all religion must be as single as the sun and as naked as the drawn sword. Yet it is curious that even the most perfect sword blade of his own forging is famous for being "damascened"; and that the one word which art has gathered from the Arab is Arabesque.

—Rome, 145–146

Archeologists

The other day a scientific summary of the state of a prehistoric tribe began confidently with the words "They wore no clothes." Not one reader in a hundred probably stopped to ask himself how we should come to know, whether clothes had once been worn by people of whom everything has perished except a few chips of bone and stone. It was doubtless hoped that we should find a stone hat as well as a stone hatchet. It was evidently anticipated that we might discover an everlasting pair of trousers of the same substance as the everlasting rock.

—EM, 29–30

Architecture

A building is akin to dogma; it is insolent, like a dogma. Whether or no it is permanent, it claims permanence like a dogma.

—TT, 68

When people have finally got into the horrible habit of preserving buildings, they have got out of the habit of building them.

—TT, 69

Architecture (Permanence of)

You can tear a poem to pieces; it is only in moments of very sincere emotion that you tear a town-hall to pieces.

—TT, 68

Argument

It is generally the man who is not ready to argue, who is ready to sneer.

—STA, 126

Aristocracy

The evil of aristocracy is not that it necessarily leads to the infliction of bad things or the suffering of sad ones; the evil of aristocracy is that it places everything in the hands of a class of people who can always inflict what they can never suffer. . . . The case against them simply is that when they legislate for all men, they always omit themselves.

—H, 278

Aristocracy, as it has flourished in England since the Reformation, with not a little national glory and commercial success, is in its very nature built up of broken and desecrated homes. It has to destroy a hundred poor relations to keep up a family. It has to destroy a hundred families to keep up a class.

—Irish, 63

Aristocracy is not an institution: aristocracy is a sin; generally a very venial one. It is merely the drift or slide of men into a sort of natural pomposity and praise of the powerful, which is the most easy and obvious affair in the world.

—O, 222

Aristocrats

Few except the poor preserve traditions. Aristocrats live not in traditions but in fashions.

—FBO, 158

Men living a life of leisure and luxury are always eager for new things; we might fairly say they would be fools if they weren't. And the English aristocrats are by no mean fools. They can proudly claim to have played a great part in every stage of the intellectual progress that has brought us to our present ruin.

—Outline, 109

Art

Art indeed copies life in not copying life, for life copies nothing.

—CD, 14

Exaggeration is the definition of Art.

—CD, 14

Whichever side may be really right in the question of art ... the whole modern world is verbally prepared to regard the new artist as right and the old artist as wrong. It is prepared to do so by the whole progressive philosophy. ... The language which comes most readily to everyone's mind is the language of innovation; but it is a language that is rather exercised than examined.

—CM, 112

Art is born when the temporary touches the eternal; the shock of beauty is when the irresistible force hits the immovable post.

—*FVF*, 122

It is not so much the fact that there is no such thing as allegorical art, but rather the fact that there is no art that is not allegorical.

—*GFW*, 57

But the whole essence of art is that it contracts and reduces itself to scale. Those who talk of the artist nature swelling and expanding, those who talk of the outbreak, licence and overflowing of art are people with no sort of feeling of what art is. Art means diminution. If what you want is largeness, the universe as it is is large enough for anybody. Art exists solely in order to create a miniature universe, a working model of the universe, a toy universe which we can play with as a child plays with a toy theater.

—*HA*, 148

For all art is sensational, since it aims at producing some sort of sensation.

—*Rome*, 32

Art for Art's Sake

The idea of following art through everything for itself alone, through extravagance, through cruelty, through morbidity, is just exactly as superstitious as the idea of following theology for itself alone through extravagance and cruelty and morbidity. To deny that Baudelaire is loathsome, or Nietzsche inhuman, because we stand in awe of beauty, is just the same thing as denying that the Court of Pope Julius was loathsome, or the rack inhuman, because we stand in awe of religion.

—*GFW*, 17

If the principle of "art for art's sake" means simply that there is a solely technical view of painting, and that it must be supreme on its own ground, it appears a piece of pure madness to suppose it other than true. Surely there never was really a man who held that a picture that was vile in colour and weak in drawing was a good picture because it was a picture of Florence Nightingale!

—GFW, 55–56

Art (Morality and)

If art could be unmoral it might be all very well. But the truth is that unless art is moral, art is not only immoral, but immoral in the most commonplace, slangy, and prosaic way. In the future, the fastidious artists who refuse to be anything but artists will go down to history as the embodiment of all the vulgarities and banalities of their time.

—Blake, 63

Art (Revolutionary)

Just as the French Revolution claimed to have a new and special revolutionary art, so the Russian Revolution still claims to have a new and special revolutionary art. In both cases, the art is as narrow as it is new; or a great deal more narrow than it is new. That is, perhaps, the one and only characteristic that is common to the two. It seems as if there were simply no chance for a young Bolshevist artist, unless he wants to draw horrible pictures of huge oppressive machines, just a little too dull to be merely instruments of torture. Exactly in the same way, there once seemed to be no chance for a young French artist, unless he happened to want to draw the draperies of Cato as he stabbed himself with the expression of a Stoic, or the hard profile of Scaevola as he stretched an extremely muscular arm over the fire of Lars Porsena.

—Avowals, 65

Art Schools

An art school is a place where about three people work with feverish energy and everybody else idles to a degree that I should have conceived unattainable by human nature.

—Bio, 86

An art school is different from almost all other schools or colleges in this respect: that, being of new and crude creation and of lax discipline, it presents a specially strong contrast between the industrious and the idle. People at an art school either do an atrocious amount of work or do no work at all.

—TT, 269

The Artist-Advertiser

And no one who knows the small minded cynicism of our plutocracy, its secrecy, its gambling spirit, its contempt of conscience, can doubt that the artist-advertiser will often be assisting enterprises over which he will have no moral control, and of which he could feel no moral approval. He will be working to spread quack medicines, queer investments; and will work for Marconi instead of Medici.

—UU, 7

Artistic Individualism

. . . Artistic Individualism, which is so much crueller, so much blinder and so much more irrational even than commercial individualism. The decay of society was praised by artists as the decay of a corpse is praised by worms.

—GBS, 87

Artists

Cockney artists profess to find the bourgeoisie dull; as if artists had any business to find anything dull.

—CD, 71

Food and fire and such things should always be the symbols of the man entertaining men; because they are the things which all men beyond question have in common. But something more than this is needed from the man who is imagining and making men, the artist, the man who is not receiving men, but rather sending them forth.

—CD, 190

A man cannot have the energy to produce good art without having the energy to wish to pass beyond it.

—H, 291

A small artist is content with art; a great artist is content with nothing except everything.

—H, 291

Artists as Teachers

The narrow notion that an artist may not teach is pretty well exploded by now. But the truth of the matter is, that an artist teaches far more by his mere background and properties, his landscape, his costume, his idiom and technique—all the part of his work, in short, of which he is probably entirely unconscious, than by the elaborate and pompous moral dicta which he fondly imagines to be his opinions.

— Types, 131

Artists (Modern)

The modern artist, only too often, loses himself in seeking to find and fix himself; he imposes a fictitious self upon that unthinking real self which otherwise would be expressed freely. He has become an individualist, and ceased to be an individual. Nay, he has even become a madman in the most frightful and vivid meaning of the term. He has become conscious of his subconsciousness.

—L & L, 92

Asceticism (Catholic)

Because it is uncommon for an alderman to fast forty days, or a politician to take a Trappist vow of silence, or a man about town to live a life of strict celibacy, the average outsider is convinced, not only that Catholicism is nothing except asceticism, but that asceticism is nothing except pessimism. He is so obliging as to explain to Catholics why they hold this heroic virtue in respect; and is ever ready to point out that the philosophy behind it is an Oriental hatred of anything connected with Nature, and a purely Schopenhauerian disgust with the Will to Live.

—STA, 103

Asceticism (Christian)

The essential difference between Christian and Pagan asceticism lies in the fact that Paganism in renouncing pleasure gives up something which it does not think desirable; whereas Christianity in giving up pleasure gives up something which it thinks very desirable indeed. Thus there is a frenzy in Christian asceticism; its follies and renunciations are like those of first love.

—GFW, 32

Atheism

"What we all dread most," said the priest, in a low voice, "is a maze with *no* centre. That is why atheism is only a nightmare."

—FBO, 319

Atheism is indeed the most daring of all dogmas, more daring than the vision of a palpable day of judgment. For it is the assertion of a universal negative; for a man to say that there is no God in the universe is like saying that there are no insects in any of the stars.

—Five Types, 59

Authority

Authority ruling men must be respected; it must even be loved. Men must in the last resort love it; for the simple reason that men must in the last resort die for it.

—Well, 198

Autobiography (on the "True")

If it is really to tell the truth, it must at all costs profess not to. No man dare say of himself, over his own name, how badly he has behaved. No man dare say of himself, over his own name, how well he has behaved. Moreover, of course, a touch of fiction is almost always essential to the real conveying of fact, because fact, as experienced, has a fragmentariness which is bewildering at first hand and quite blinding at second hand. Facts have at least to be sorted into compartments and the proper head and tail given to each. The perfection and pointedness of art are a sort of substitute for the pungency of actuality. Without this selection and completion our life seems a tangle of unfinished tales, a heap of novels, all volume one.

—CD, 139–140

B

Bacon, Sir Francis

Bacon was a public man of wide renown and national scientific philosophy; and out of him have come riddles and oracles and fantastic cryptograms and a lifelong hobby for lunatics.

—Gen S, 260

Barbarians

There is above all this supreme stamp of the barbarian; the sacrifice of the permanent to the temporary.

—NJ, 57

Barbarism

Never be merely on the side of barbarism, for it always means the destruction of all that men have ever understood, by men who do not understand it.

—Avowals, 43

Barbarism (Rise of Rationalism)

That Great wave of barbarism that swept over Western Europe in the nineteenth century, and which has been called the Rise of Rationalism, has this note in it even more savage than its other notes of savagery: that it sought to make a man's soul the slave of his body. It did not say that the spirit was willing but the flesh was weak—the free and generous doctrine of religion. It said that the spirit was unwilling because the flesh was strong.

—L & L, 154

Becket, St. Thomas

Becket wore a hair shirt under his gold and crimson, and there is much to be said for the combination; for Becket got the benefit of the hair shirt while the people in the street got the benefit of the crimson and gold. It is at least better than the manner of the modern millionaire, who has the black and the drab outwardly for others, and the gold next to his heart.

—O, 182

Beggars

I happen to think the whole modern attitude towards beggars is entirely heathen and inhuman. I should be prepared to maintain, as a matter of general morality, that it is intrinsically indefensible to punish human beings for asking for human assistance. I should say that it is intrinsically insane to urge people to give charity and forbid people to accept charity. . . . Everyone would expect to have to help a man to save his life in a shipwreck; why not a man who has suffered a shipwreck of his life?

—FVF, 156

Behaviourists

Everybody knows that a new school of sceptics has recently appeared, especially in America; they call themselves the Behaviourists, and the late Mr. Harvey Wickham called them the Misbehaviourists.

—AIG, 45

So far as I can understand, their philosophy is rooted in a theory of physiology: the theory that thought is originally a sort of movement of the body rather than the brain. "There is nothing in the brain," I think one of them has written, "except a lot of neurons. We do not think with our minds. We think with our muscles. . . . " The new scientific theory never does really deny the old religious theory. What it does do is to deny . . . the old scientific theory. And it was precisely in the name of that old theory that religion was once to have been destroyed. The heretics never attack orthodoxy; the heretics only avenge orthodoxy on each other. . . . It does not matter to any Christian whether God has made man to think with his brain or his big toe. But it did matter very much to the recent type of Materialist that a man could only think with his brains. . . . There is no question of his touching the soul . . . for that escapes him as completely as it does every other kind of material analysis, including that of the old Materialist himself. What he abolishes is not the soul, but the cells on which his predecessor depended for the denial of the soul.

—AIG, 45-46

The psychologists may present us with a series of subtle and fascinating states of mind, without our being morbidly curious to enquire whose mind. They in turn may yield to some other school; such as those bright and breezy Americans who call themselves behaviourists. They declare with some warmth that there is really nothing in their minds and that they only think with their muscles; which in the case of some thinking, we might well believe.

—RLS, 171

Being an Old Bean

I cannot imagine anybody except an aged and very lean vegetarian positively dancing with joy at being called an old bean; and I am not a very lean vegetarian.

—FVF, 66

Bias

It is useless to argue at all, if all our conclusions are warped by our conditions. Nobody can correct anybody's bias, if all mind is all bias.

—Bio, 27

Bigness

It is well known that I am an unreasonable reactionary, who refuses to face the great facts of the modern world. I have never been convinced that a giraffe is a better fireside playmate than a kitten. . . . An invincible prejudice prevents me from admitting that whales served on toast are more appetizing than sardines. Nay, I cannot even persuade myself that the larger sort of sharks are, as drawing-room ornaments, necessarily improvements upon goldfish. . . . In short, I am lamentably lacking in that reverence for largeness, or for things on a Big Scale, which is apparently the religion of the Age of Big Business.

—Come, 200

Bigotry

It is not bigotry to be certain we are right; but it is bigotry to be unable to imagine how we might possibly have gone wrong.

—CCC, 27

Bigotry may be roughly defined as the anger of men who have no opinions. It is the resistance offered to definite ideas by that vague bulk of people whose ideas are indefinite to excess. Bigotry may be called the appalling frenzy of the indifferent.

—*H*, 298

Bigotry is an incapacity to conceive seriously the alternative to a proposition.

—*L & L*, 151

Bigots

In real life the people who are most bigoted are the people who have no convictions at all. . . . it is the hard-headed stockbroker, who knows no history and believes no religion, who is, nevertheless, perfectly convinced that all . . . the priests are knaves.

—*H*, 297

A man may be sure enough of something to be burned for it or to make war on the world, and yet be no inch nearer to being a bigot. He is only a bigot if he cannot understand that his dogma is a dogma, even if it is true.

—*L & L*, 151

Biographers

. . . it is, indeed, the sin and snare of biographers that they tend to see significance in everything; characteristic carelessness if the hero drops his pipe, and characteristic carefulness if he picks it up again.

—*RB*, 5

Biography

Once a man is dead, if it be only yesterday, the newcomer must piece him together from descriptions really as much at random as if he were describing Caesar or Henry II.

—*CD,* 151

Birds

The very fact that a bird can get as far as building a nest, and cannot get any farther, proves that he has not a mind as man has a mind; it proves it more completely than if he built nothing at all. If he built nothing at all, he might possibly be a philosopher of the Quietist or Buddhistic school, indifferent to all but the mind within.

—*EM,* 21

Blake, William

He had a most comprehensive scheme of the Universe, only that no one could comprehend it.

—*Blake,* 5

It was profitable to steal an epigram from Blake for three reasons—first, that the original phrase was small and would not leave a large gap; second, that it was cosmic and synthetic and could be applied to things in general; third, that it was unintelligible and no one would know it again.

—*Blake,* 46

He was ... a man of slight but genuine poetic feeling, an artist who thoroughly realised the aim of art was to please.

—*Blake,* 49–50

If Blake had always written badly he might be sane. But a man who could write so well and did write so badly must be mad.

—Blake, 93

To sum up Blake's philosophy in any phrase sufficiently simple and popular for our purpose is not at all easy. . . . The plainest way of putting it, I think, is this: this school especially denied the authority of Nature. Some went the extreme length of the mad Manichaeans, and declared the material universe evil in itself. Some, like Blake, and most of the poets considered it as a shadow or illusion, a sort of joke of the Almighty. But whatever else Nature was, Nature was not our mother. . . . if Wordsworth was the Poet of Nature, Blake was specially the Poet of Anti-Nature. Against Nature he set a certain entity which he called Imagination; but the word as commonly used meant very little of what he meant by it. . . . By Imagination, that is, he meant images; the eternal images of things. You might kill all the Lambs of the World and eat them; but you could not kill the Lamb of the Imagination, which was the Lamb of God, that taketh away the sins of the world. Blake's philosophy, in brief, was primarily the assertion that the ideal is more actual than the real: just as in Euclid the good triangle in the mind is more actual (and more practical) than the bad triangle on the blackboard.

—Blake, 156–160

Blasphemy

Blasphemy is an artistic effect, because blasphemy depends upon a philosophical conviction. Blasphemy depends upon belief, and is fading with it. If anyone doubts this, let him sit down seriously and try to think blasphemous thoughts about Thor. I think his family will find him at the end of the day in a state of some exhaustion.

—H, 12–13

Bohemians

It is rather odd to remark, in passing, and rather salutary for professional revolutionists and pioneers, that there is almost always a sort of break, of boredom or disgust, immediately after some very flamboyant figure has defied the convention, and therefore become the fashion. The Bohemian, who is seen everywhere in Society, boldly despising Society, has a high old time while it lasts, and really makes the best of both worlds, the wilderness and the drawing-room, but it does not last very long. Very early in the nineteenth century, it was already old-fashioned to enjoy Byron; as it will never be old-fashioned to enjoy Chaucer or Homer.

—S, 209

Book of Common Prayer

The Book of Common Prayer is the masterpiece of Protestantism. It is more so than the work of Milton. It is one positive possession and attraction; the one magnet and talisman for people even outside the Anglican Church, as are the great Gothic cathedrals for people outside the Catholic Church. I can speak, I think, for many other converts, when I say that the only thing that can produce any sort of nostalgia or romantic regret, any shadow of homesickness in one who has in truth come home, is the rhythm of Cranmer's prose. All the other supposed superiorities of any sort of Protestanism are quite fictitious.

—Well, 45–46

But why has the old Protestant Prayer-Book a power like that of great poetry upon the spirit and the heart? The reason is much deeper than the mere avoidance of journalese. It might be put in a sentence; it has style; it has tradition; it has religion; it was written by apostate Catholics. It is strong, not in so far as it is the first Protestant book, but in so far as it was the last Catholic book.

—Well, 47

Book Worms

Lord Ivywood shared the mental weakness of most men who have fed on books; he ignored not the value but the very existence of other forms of information.

—*Flying*, 52

Books (Old)

You can find all the new ideas in the old books; only there you will find them balanced, kept in their place, and sometimes contradicted and overcome by other and better ideas. The great writers did not neglect a fad because they had not thought of it, but because they had thought of it and of all the answers to it as well.

—*CM*, 23

Bores (in Defense of)

It is a truth of psychology that needs a fuller exposition; for no psychologist has yet written a very necessary book called 'A Defense of Bores.' Perhaps it is the bored rather than the bore that needs defense, but it is true that the bored is the weaker of the two. It is the bore who is joyous and triumphant; the true conqueror of the earth. Or, to put the matter less flippantly, it is true that a living and logical gusto for giving long explanations of everything, though it may be an infliction on the sensitive, is itself an attribute of the strong.

—*C*, 244

Boys

Boys, like dogs, have a sort of romantic ritual which is not always their real selves. And this romantic ritual is generally the ritual of not being romantic; the pretence of being much more masculine and materialistic than they are. Boys in themselves are very sentimental. The most sentimen-

42

tal thing in the world is to hide your feelings; it is making too much of them. Stoicism is the direct product of sentimentalism; and school boys are sentimental individually, but stoical collectively.

—Alarms, 52–53

Brevity and Wit

Somebody once said that brevity is the soul of wit, when he obviously meant to say that wit is the soul of brevity. It is obvious that the brevity is only the body, and the wit the spirit.

—Survey, 155

Brides

Professors find all over the world fragmentary ceremonies in which the bride affects some sort of reluctance, hides from her husband, or runs away from him. The professor then pompously proclaims that this is a survival of Marriage by Capture. I wonder he never says that the veil thrown over the bride is really a net. I gravely doubt whether women ever were married by capture. I think they pretended to be; as they do still.

—WW, 189–190

Broad-mindedness

Nine times out of ten a man's broad-mindedness is necessarily the narrowest thing about him. This is not particularly paradoxical; it is, when we come to think of it, quite inevitable. His vision of his own village may be full of varieties; and even his vision of his own nation may have a rough resemblance to the reality. But his vision of the world is probably smaller than the world. His vision of the universe is certainly much smaller than the universe. Hence he is never so inadequate as when he is universal; he is never so limited as when he generalises.

—Amer, 281

Broadway

When I had looked at the lights of Broadway by night, I made to my American friends an innocent remark that seemed for some reason to amuse them. . . . I said to them, in my simplicity, 'What a glorious garden of wonders this would be, to anyone who was lucky enough to be unable to read.'

—Amer, 33

Browning, Robert

The only difference between the Browningite and the anti-Browningite, is that the second says he was not a poet but a mere philosopher and the first says he was a philosopher and not a mere poet. The admirer disparages poetry in order to exalt Browning; the opponent exalts poetry in order to disparage Browning; and all the time Browning himself exalted poetry above all earthly things, served it with a single-hearted intensity, and stands among the few poets who hardly wrote a line of anything else.

—RB, 17

Buddhism and Christianity

The rough, shorthand way of putting the difference is that the Christian pities men because they are dying, and the Buddhist pities them because they are living. The Christian is sorry for what damages the life of a man; but the Buddhist is sorry for him because he is alive.

—Gen S, 115–116

Burglars

Misers get up early in the morning; and burglars, I am informed, get up the night before.

—TT, 77

Burke, Edmund

Burke is the greatest of political philosophers, because in him only are there distances and perspectives, as there are on the real earth, with its mists of morning and evening, and its blue horizons and broken skies.

—GFW, 20

Burlesque (and Al Capone)

Burlesque and parody are almost impossible in our time, because nothing that happens in fancy can be more fantastic than what happens in fact. We have had no good comic operas of late, because the real world has been more comic than any possible opera. Here is a good example in connexion with this particular matter. Lawyers and law-abiding citizens have been gravely debating, in the United States, whether the chief organizer of murder in America may not perhaps be brought to trial for an error in his income-tax return. . . . There is obviously a delicate and disputable matter of doubt and judgment as to whether a gentleman can be made to pay income tax at all upon the profits of a brewery that is not supposed to exist.

—S, 108–109

Business

Business, especially big business, is now organized like an army. It is, as some would say, a sort of mild militarism without bloodshed; as I should say, a militarism without the military virtues.

— Thing, 34

Businessmen

. . . if there is one type that tends at times to be more utterly godless than another, it is that rather brutal sort of business man. He has no social ideal, let alone religion; he has neither the gentleman's traditions nor the trade unionist's class loyalty. All his boasts about getting good bargains were practically boasts of having cheated people.

—FBO, 682

It is a common error, I think, among the Radical idealists . . . to suggest that financiers and business men are a danger to the empire because they are so sordid or so materialistic. The truth is that financiers and business men are a danger . . . because they can be sentimental about any sentiment, and idealistic about any ideal, any ideal that they find lying about . . . these practical men, unaccustomed to causes, are always inclined to think that if a thing is proved to be an ideal it is proved to be *the* ideal. Many, for example, avowedly followed Cecil Rhodes because he had a vision, they might as well have followed him because he had a nose; a man without some kind of dream of perfection is quite as much of a monstrosity as a noseless man. People say of such a figure. . . . "He knows his own mind," which is exactly like saying. . . . "He blows his own nose."

—H, 299–300

Businessmen (American vs. English)

When two business men in a train are talking about dollars I am not so foolish as to expect them to be talking about the philosophy of St. Thomas Aquinas. But if they were two English business men I should not expect them to be talking about business. Probably it would be about some sport; and most probably some sport in which they themselves never dreamed of indulging. The approximate difference is that the American talks about his work and the Englishman about his holidays. His ideal is not labour but leisure.

—Amer, 105

Byron, Lord

The truth is that Byron was one of a class who may be called the unconscious optimists, who are very often, indeed, the most uncompromising conscious pessimists, because the exuberance of their nature demands for an adversary a dragon as big as the world. But the whole of his essential and unconscious being was spirited and confident, and that unconscious being, long disguised and buried under emotional artifices, suddenly sprang into prominence in the face of a cold, hard, political necessity. In Greece he heard the cry of reality, and at the time that he was dying, he began to live. He heard suddenly the call of that buried and subconscious happiness which is in all of us, and which may emerge suddenly at the sight of the grass of a meadow or the spears of the enemy.

— Types, 38–39

C

Calvinism

Certainly the creed of Calvinism, which all Scottish ministers were forced to teach for two hundred years, was a simple creed. Nothing could be simpler than saying that men go to Hell because God made them on purpose to send them to Hell.

—C, 269

On this view, if a man chooses to damn his soul alive, he is not thwarting God's will but rather fulfilling it.

—STA, 107

Capitalism

The sociology of capitalistic industrialism began with an identification with individualism; but its ultimate organization has corresponded to a complete loss of individuality.

—AIWS, 171

48

With every day that passes there is less importance in the mastery and more importance in the pay.

—C, 61

Too much capitalism does not mean too many capitalists, but too few capitalists; and so aristocracy sins, not in planting a family tree, but in not planting a family forest.

—Div, 47

It is an elementary character of Capitalism that a shipowner need not know the right end of a ship, or a landowner have even seen the landscape, that the owner of a gold mine may be interested in nothing but old pewter, or the owner of a railway travel exclusively in balloons. He may be a more successful capitalist if he has a hobby of his own business; he is often a more successful capitalist if he has the sense to leave it to a manager; but economically he can control the business because he is a capitalist, not because he has any kind of hobby or any kind of sense.

—England, 96–97

The truth is that what we call Capitalism ought to be called Proletarianism. The point of it is not that some people have capital, but that most people only have wages because they do not have capital. . . . For what I complain of, in the current defence of existing capitalism, is that it is a defence of keeping most men in wage dependence; that is, keeping most men without capital.

—Outline, 6–7

And it is really quite pedantic to say that the use of capital must be capitalist. We might as fairly say that anything social must be Socialist; that Socialism can be identified with a social evening or a social glass. Which, I grieve to say, is not the case.

—Outline, 7

Capitalism and Communism

... both Capitalism and Communism rest on the same idea: a centralisation of wealth which destroys private property.

—*EA*, 95

The point about Capitalism and Commercialism, as conducted of late, is that they have really preached the extension of business rather than the preservation of belongings; and have at best tried to disguise the pickpocket with some of the virtues of the pirate. The point about communism is that it only reforms the pickpocket by forbidding pockets.

—*Outline*, 3

Capitalism (Birth of)

We must remember that even to talk of the corruption of the monasteries is a compliment to the monasteries. For we do not talk of the corruption of the corrupt. Nobody pretends that the medieval institutions began in mere greed and pride. But the modern institutions did. Nobody says that St. Benedict drew up his rule of labour in order to make his monks lazy; but only that they became lazy. Nobody says that the first Franciscans practised poverty to obtain wealth; but only that later fraternities did obtain wealth. But it is quite certain that the Cecils and the Russells and the rest did from the first want to obtain wealth. That which was death to Catholicism was actually the birth of Capitalism.

—*Thing*, 125–126

Capitalists and Socialists

The Capitalists praise competition while they create monopoly; the Socialists urge a strike to turn workmen into soldiers and state officials; which is logically a strike against strikes.

—*NJ*, 6

Capitalists (Those Vulgar Exploiters)

For they hold as their chief heresy, in a coarser form, the fundamental falsehood that things are not made to be used but made to be sold. All the collapse of their commercial system in our own time has been due to that fallacy of forcing things on a market where there was no market; of continually increasing the power of supply without increasing the power of demand; or briefly, of always considering the man who sells the potato and never considering the man who eats it.

—AIWS, 137

Carlyle, Thomas

Thus it was with Carlyle: he startled men by attacking not arguments, but assumptions. He simply brushed aside all the matters which the men of the nineteenth century held to be incontrovertible, and appealed directly to the very different class of matters which they knew to be true. He induced men to study less the truth of their reasoning, and more the truth of the assumptions upon which they reasoned. Even where his view was not the highest truth, it was always a refreshing and beneficient heresy.

— Types, 115–116

It is his real glory that he was the first to see clearly and say plainly the great truth of our time; that the wealth of the state is not the prosperity of the people.

—VA, 55

And he never wrote so sternly and justly as when he compared the "divine sorrow" of Dante with the "undivine sorrow" of Utilitarianism, which had already come down to talking about the breeding of the poor and to hinting at infanticide. This is a representative quarrel; for if the Utilitarian spirit reached its highest point in Mill, it certainly reached its lowest point in Malthus.

—VA, 56–57

Carpe Diem as Religion

. . . the *carpe diem* religion is not the religion of happy people, but of very unhappy people. . . . It is true enough, of course, that a pungent happiness comes chiefly in certain passing moments; but it is not true that we should think of them as passing, or enjoy them simply "for those moments' sake." To do this is to rationalize the happiness, and therefore to destroy it. Happiness is a mystery like religion, and should never be rationalized. . . . The lover enjoys the moment, but precisely not for the moment's sake. He enjoys it for the woman's sake, or his own sake. The warrior enjoys the moment, but not for the sake of the moment; he enjoys it for the sake of the flag. . . . the patriot thinks of the flag as eternal; the lover thinks of his love as something that cannot end. These moments are filled with eternity; these moments are joyful because they do not seem momentary.

—H, 102–104

Cart before the Horse

There are a great many other examples of putting the cart before the horse or the means before the end. One very common form of the blunder is to make modern conditions an absolute end and then try to fit human necessities to that end, as if they were only a means. Thus people say, "Home life is not suited to the business life of today." Which is as if they said, "Heads are not suited to the sort of hats now in fashion." Then they might go round cutting off people's heads to meet the shortage or shrinkage of hats; and calling it the Hat Problem.

—Gen S, 40

Catholic Church

The Catholic Church is much too universal to be called international, for she is older than all the nations. She is not some sort of new bridge to be built between these separated islands; she is the very earth and ocean-bed on which they are built.

—GKC, 259

There will be Diocletian persecutions, there will be Dominican crusades, there will be rending of all religious peace and compromise, or even the end of civilization and the world, before the Catholic Church will admit that one single moron, or one single man, "is not worth saving."

— Thing, 18

Catholic Church and Freedom

Tell a Catholic convert that he has lost his liberty, and he will laugh. . . . A Catholic has fifty times more feeling of being free than a man caught in the net of the nervous compromises of Anglicanism. . . . He has the range of two thousand years full of twelve hundred thousand controversies, thrashed out by thinker against thinker, school against school, guild against guild, nation against nation, with no limit except the fundamental logical fact that the things were worth arguing, because they could be ultimately solved and settled.

— Well, 46

Catholic Church and Reason

As for Reason, our monopoly is practically admitted in the modern world. Except for one or two dingy old Atheists in Fleet Street (for whom I have great sympathy), nothing except Rome now defends the reliability of Reason.

— Well, 46

Catholic Practice

It is enough to say that those who know the Catholic practice find it not only right, but always right when everything else is wrong; making the Confessional the very throne of candour where the world outside talks nonsense about it as a sort of conspiracy; upholding humility when everybody is praising pride; charged with sentimental charity when the world is talking a brutal utilitarianism; charged with dogmatic harshness

when the world is loud and loose with vulgar sentimentalism—as it is
today.

—Thing, 71

Catholic Virtues

The human race has always admired the Catholic virtues, however little it
can practise them; and oddly enough it has admired most those of them
that the modern world most sharply disputes.

—BC, 152

Catholicism

A century or two hence Spiritualism may be a tradition and Socialism
may be a tradition and Christian Science may be a tradition. But Catholicism will not be a tradition. It will still be a nuisance and a new and
dangerous thing.

—CCC, 21

The worst things in worldly Catholicism were made worse by Protestantism.
But the best things remained somehow through the era of corruption;
nay, they survived even the era of reform. They survive today in all
Catholic countries . . . in the deepest lessons of practical psychology. And
so completely are they justified . . . that every one of them is now being
copied. . . . Psycho-analysis is the Confessional without the safeguards of
the Confessional; Communism is the Franciscan movement without the
moderating balance of the Church; and American sects, having howled
for three centuries at the Popish theatricality and mere appeal to the
senses, now "brighten" their services by super-theatrical films and rays of
rose-red light falling on the head of the minister.

—Thing, 66

Catholicism (and the English)

You know our controversialists often complain that there is a great deal of ignorance about what our religion is really like. But it is really more curious than that. It is true, and it is not at all unnatural, that England does not know much about the Church of Rome. But England does not know much about the Church of England.

—FBO, 991

Catholics

Catholics know the two or three transcendental truths on which they do agree; and take rather a pleasure in disagreeing on everything else.

— Thing, 167

Cave-man

The cave-man as commonly presented to us is simply a myth or rather a muddle; for a myth has at least an imaginative outline of truth. The whole of the current way of talking is simply a confusion and a misunderstanding, founded on no sort of scientific evidence and valued as an excuse for a very modern mood of anarchy. If any gentleman wants to knock a woman about, he can surely be a cad without taking away the character of the cave-man, about whom we know next to nothing except what we can gather from a few harmless and pleasing pictures on a wall.

—EM, 12

Celebration

There are still festive celebrations of particular dates and events, which people feel as exceptions and enjoy as exceptions. But men cannot even enjoy riot when the riot is the rule. The world of which I speak has come, by this time, to boasting of being lawless; but there is no fun in it, because lawlessness is the law.

—S, 58

Ceremony

All ceremony ... consists in the reversal of the obvious. Thus men, when they wish to be priests or judges, dress up like women.

—NNH, 34

Characters and Real People

There is, of course, no paradox at all in saying that if we find in a good book a wildly impossible character it is very probable indeed that it was copied from a real person. This is one of the commonplaces of good art criticism. For although people talk of the restraints of fact and the freedom of fiction, the case for most artistic purposes is quite the other way. Nature is as free as air: art is forced to look probable. There may be a million things that do happen, and yet only one thing that convinces us as likely to happen. Out of a million possible things there may be only one appropriate thing. I fancy, therefore, that many stiff, unconvincing characters are copied from the wild freak-show of real life.

—CD, 88

Charity

People who lose all their charity generally lose all their logic.

—FBO, 978

Charlatan

The man who really thinks he has an idea will always try to explain that idea. The Charlatan who has no idea will always confine himself to explaining that it is much too subtle to be explained.... The quack lives not by plunging into mystery, but by refusing to come out of it.

—MM, 147

Charles II, King

It is often quoted of poor Charles II that he said that Puritanism was no religion for a gentleman. It is not so often added that he also said that Anglicanism was no religion for a Christian.

—CM, 192

Chesterton, G. K.

The purpose of the Kipling literature is to show how many extraordinary things a man may see if he is active and strides from continent to continent like the giant in my tale. But the object of my school is to show how many extraordinary things even a lazy and ordinary man may see if he can spur himself to the single activity of seeing.

—TT, 5-6

Nearly all the best and most precious things in the universe you can get for a halfpenny.... Also you can get the chance of reading this article for a halfpenny; along, of course, with other and irrelevant matter.

—TT, 297

The return to real thinking is often as abrupt as bumping into a man. Very often (in my case) it is bumping into a man.

—TT, 300

Chesterton, G. K. (and Mockery)

I have received a letter from a gentleman who is very indignant at what he considers my flippancy in disregarding or degrading Spiritualism. I thought I was defending Spiritualism; but I am rather used to being accused of mocking the thing that I set out to justify. My fate in most controversies is rather pathetic. It is an almost invariable rule that the man with whom I don't agree thinks I am making a fool of myself, and the man with whom I do agree thinks I am making a fool of him.

—ATC, 148

Childishness

I confess that there is a real element which might rightly be called childishness, if the term be used in a healthier sense, for something that may or may not have grown up, but has not grown old. There is a quality in Chaucer, and in the whole civilization that produced Chaucer, which men of rather wearier civilizations must make a certain effort to understand. It is something that moderns have mainly praised in childhood; because moderns have not preserved it in manhood. It is gusto; it is zest; it is a certain appetite for things as they actually are, and because they actually are; for a stone because it is a stone, or a story because it is a story. If that is merely simplicity, he was simple. If that is merely stupidity, he was stupid. That is, if we would appreciate him or his age, we must go back to something that stirred in us when we first found that the door of a doll's house would open; or when we first found that the end of a story could be the point of a story, as in the surprise that ends the admirable story of Puss and Boots.

—C, 153

Children

The fascination of children lies in this: that with each of them all things are remade, and the universe is put again upon its trial. As we walk the streets and see below us those delightful bulbous heads, three times too big for the body ... we ought always primarily to remember that within every

58

one of these heads there is new universe, as new as it was on the seventh day of creation. In each of those orbs there is a new system of stars, new grass, new cities, a new sea.

—D, 112–113

The truth is that it is our attitude towards children that is right, and our attitude towards grown-up people that is wrong. Our attitude towards our equals in age consists in a servile solemnity, overlying a considerable degree of indifference or disdain. Our attitude towards children consists in a condenscending indulgence, overlying an unfathomable respect. . . . We make puppets of children, lecture them, pull their hair, and reverence, love, and fear them. When we reverence anything in the mature, it is their virtues or their wisdom, and this is an easy matter. But we reverence the faults and follies of children.

—D, 114–115

Anyone who has ever watched a child for the first five years of its life will know that when the human soul first awakens to the immensities of mere existence, the first thing it does is to begin to act a part.

—HA, 42

Children (and Beauty)

Pleasure in the beautiful is a sacred thing; if a child feels that there is an indescribable witchery in the wedding of two words he feels it alone, as he feels his vanities and his dreams, in places where he cannot be badgered or overlooked or philosophically educated. The act of insisting on his analysing the holy thing, I think, without the smallest doubt or the smallest desire to exaggerate, is as insolent as asking him to dissect his favourite kitten or account for his preference for his mother.

—HA, 84

Children (Influencing)

A young mother remarked to me, "I don't want to teach my child any religion. I don't want to influence him; I want him to choose for himself when he grows up." That is a very ordinary example of a current argument; which is frequently repeated and yet never really applied. Of course the mother was always influencing the child. Of course the mother might just as well have said, "I hope he will choose his own friends when he grows up; so I won't introduce him to any aunts or uncles." The grown up person cannot in any case escape from the responsibility of influencing the child; not even if she accepts the enormous responsibility of not influencing the child. The mother can bring up the child without choosing a religion for him; but not without choosing an environment for him. If she chooses to leave out the religion, she is choosing the environment; and an infernally dismal, unnatural environment too.

—*Gen S*, 10–11

Chivalry

Chivalry is not an obvious idea. It is not as plain as a pike-staff or as a palm-tree. It is a delicate balance between the sexes which gives the rarest and most poetic kind of pleasure to those who can strike it. . . . Wherever there is chivalry there is courtesy; and wherever there is courtesy there is comedy.

—*NJ*, 31–32

Christ

What is the use of a modern man saying that Christ is only a thing like Atys or Mithras, when the next moment he is reproaching Christianity for not following Christ?

—*NJ*, 182

Christendom (the Decline of)

What Mahomet and Calvin and all those thus breaking away from the dying civilization did not realize, is the curious fact that it is a dying civilization that never dies. It does decline, and has done so any number of times; it does decay; it is always at it. But it does not disappear; and, at the end of more or less debased periods, has a way of managing to reappear, when its enemies have in their turn decayed. The moral is, I will venture to think, that it is unwise to desert this perpetually sinking ship, or betray this everlastingly dying creed and culture. It has had another period of final extinction; even since its final extinction at the end of the Middle Ages. It has suffered eclipse in the enlightment of the Age of Reason and Revolution; which in their turn begin to look as if they had seen better days. . . .

The moral is that no man should desert that civilization. It can cure itself; but those who leave it cannot cure it. Not Nestorious nor Mahomet nor Calvin nor Lenin have cured, nor will cure, the real evils of Christendom; for the severed hand does not heal the whole body.

—C, 275–276

Christian Church

When people impute special vices to the Christian Church they seem to entirely forget that the world (which is the only other thing there is) has these vices much more. The Church has been cruel; but the world has been much more cruel. The Church has plotted; but the world has plotted much more. The Church has been superstitious; but it has never been so superstitious as the world is when left to itself.

—ATC, 204

Christian Origins

It is often said by the critics of Christian origins that certain ritual feasts, processions or dances are really of pagan origin. They might as well say that our legs are of pagan origin. Nobody ever disputed that humanity was human before it was Christian; and no Church manufactured the legs with which men walked or danced, either in a pilgrimage or a ballet. . . . Where such a Church has existed it has *preserved* not only the processions but the dances; not only the cathedral but the carnival. One of the chief claims of Christian civilisation is to have preserved things of pagan origin. In short, in the old religious countries men *continue* to dance; while in the new scientific cities they are often content to drudge.

—Div, 87–88

Christianity

If you really want to know what we mean when we say that Christianity has a special power of virtue, I will tell you. The Church is the only thing on earth that can perpetuate a type of virtue and make it something more than a fashion.

—BC, 150

The chief difference between Christianity and the thousand transcendental schools of to-day is substantially the same as the difference nearly two thousand years ago between Christianity and the thousand sacred rites and secret societies of the Pagan Empire. The deepest difference is this: that all the heathen mysteries are so far aristocratic that they are understood by some, and not understood by others. The Christian mysteries are so far democratic that nobody understands them at all.

—Blake, 180–183

Christianity (Founder of)

If we knew nothing else about the Founder of Christianity, for example, beyond the fact that a religious teacher lived in a remote country, and in the course of his peregrinations and proclamations consistently called

Himself "The Son of Man," we should know by that alone that he was a man of almost immeasurable greatness.

—*Types,* 210

Christian-Marxist Dialogue

Of course it is possible to play an endless game with the word "Christian" and perpetually extend its epoch by perpetually diminishing its meaning. By the time that everybody has agreed that being a Christian only means thinking that Christ was a good man, it will indeed be true that few persons outside lunatic asylums can be denied the name of Christian.

—*CM,* 193

Christians

As compared with a Jew, a Moslem, a Buddist, a Deist, or more obvious alternatives, a Christian *means* a man who believes that deity or sanctity has attached to matter or entered the world of the senses.

—*STA,* 41-42

Christmas and Ceremony

... all this secrecy about Christmas is merely sentimental and ceremonial; if you do not like what is sentimental and ceremonial, do not celebrate Christmas at all. . . . I cannot understand why anyone should bother about a ceremonial except ceremonially. If a thing only exists in order to be graceful, do it gracefully or do not do it. . . . I can understand the man who takes off his hat to a lady because it is the customary symbol. . . . I can also understand the man who refuses to take off his hat to a lady, like the old Quakers, because he thinks that a symbol is superstition. But what point would there be in so performing an arbitrary form of respect that it was not a form of respect? We respect the gentleman who takes off his hat to the lady; we respect the fanatic who will not take off his hat to the lady. But what should we think of the man who kept his hands in his pockets and asked the lady to take his hat off for him because he felt tired?

—ATC, 208–209

Christmas Comfort

Comfort, especially this vision of Christmas comfort, is the reverse of a gross or material thing. It is far more poetical, properly speaking, than the Garden of Epicurus. It is far more artistic than the Palace of Art. It is more artistic because it is based upon a contrast, a contrast between the fire and wine within the house and the winter and the roaring rains without. It is far more poetical, because there is in it a note of defense, almost of war; a note of being besieged by the snow and hail; of making merry in the belly of a fort.

—CD, 118–119

Christmas and G. B. Shaw

If a man called Christmas Day a mere hypocritical excuse for drunkenness and gluttony that would be false, but it would have a fact hidden in it somewhere. But when Bernard Shaw says that Christmas Day is only a conspiracy kept up by Poulterers and wine merchants from strictly business motives, then he says something which is not so much false as startlingly and arrestingly foolish. He might as well say that the two sexes were invented by jewellers who wanted to sell wedding rings.

—GBS, 168–169

The Church

When we belong to the Church we belong to something which is outside all of us; which is outside everything you talk about, outside the Cardinals and the Pope. They belong to it, but it does not belong to them. If we all fell dead suddenly, the Church would still somehow exist in God.

—BC, 87

The Church has defended tradition in a time which stupidly denied and despised tradition. But that is simply because the Church is always the only thing defending whatever is at the moment stupidly despised. It is already beginning to appear as the only champion of reason in the twentieth century, as it was the only champion of tradition in the nineteenth.

—*CCC,* 21

The Church will not consent to scorn the soul of a coolie or even a tourist; and the measure of the madness with which men hate her is but their vain attempt to despise.

—*CCC,* 68

If the world grows too worldly, it can be rebuked by the Church; but if the Church grows too worldly, it cannot be adequately rebuked for worldliness by the world.

—*STA,* 24

... it is, in the exact sense of the popular phrase, like nothing on earth.

—*Thing,* 69

In nine cases out of ten the Church simply stood for sanity and social balance against heretics who were sometimes very like lunatics. Yet at each separate moment the pressure of the prevalent error was very strong; the exaggerated error of a whole generation, like the strength of the Manchester School in the 'fifties, or of Fabian Socialism as a fashion in my own youth. A study of the true historical cases commonly shows us the spirit of the age going wrong, and the Catholics at least relatively going right. It is a mind surviving a hundred moods.

—*Thing,* 70

The Church (and the World)

In the long run, which is most mad—the Church or the world? Which is madder, the Spanish priest who permitted tyranny, or the Prussian sophist who admired it? Which is madder, the Russian priest who discourages righteous rebellion, or the Russian novelist who forbids it. That is the final and the blasting test. The world left to itself grows wilder than any creed.

—*BC*, 380

The world takes the trouble to make a big mistake about every little mistake made by the Church.

—*BC*, 381

The Church (Critics of)

It never occurs to the critic to do anything so simple as to compare what is Catholic with what is Non-Catholic. The one thing that never seems to cross his mind, when he argues about what the Church is like, is the simple question of what the world would be like without it.

—*Thing*, 104

Cities

But the great towns have grown intolerable solely because of such suffocating vulgarities and tyrannies. It is not humanity that disgusts us in the huge cities; it is inhumanity. It is not that there are human beings; but that they are not treated as such. We do not, I hope dislike men and women; we only dislike their being made into a sort of jam: crushed together so that they are not merely powerless but shapeless.

—*Alarms*, 138

But the reason we fly from the city is not in reality that it is not poetical; it is that its poetry is too fierce, too fascinating and too practical in its demands.

—L & L, 23

Citizens

The idea of the Citizen is that his individual human nature shall be constantly and creatively active in *altering* the State.

—Crimes, 134

Citizenship (Equal)

In a word, an equal citizenship is quite the reverse of the reality in the modern world; but it is still the ideal in the modern world.

—NJ, 8

Civilisation

Certain modern dreamers say that ants and bees have a society superior to ours. They have, indeed, a civilisation; but that very truth only reminds us that it is an inferior of civilisation. Who ever found an ant-hill decorated with the status of celebrated ants? Who has seen a bee-hive carved with the images of gorgeous queens of old?

—O, 267

Civilisation (and Barbarism)

Civilisation in the best sense merely means the full authority of the human spirit over all externals. Barbarism means the worship of those externals in their crude and unconquered state. Barbarism means the worship of Nature; and in recent poetry, science, and philosophy there has been too much of the worship of Nature.

—ATC, 166

Civilisations

It is a remarkable fact that one civilisation does not satisfy itself by calling another civilisation wicked—it calls it uncivilised. We call the Chinese barbarians, and they call us barbarians.

—RB, 24

Class Distinctions

The true way to overcome the evil in class distinctions is not to denounce them as revolutionists denounce them, but to ignore them as children ignore them.

—CD, 142

Class Sympathies

The class sympathies which, false as they are, are the truest things in so many men. . . .

— Thursday, 41

Classification

It is the very men who say that nothing can be classified, who say that everything must be codified. Thus Mr. Bernard Shaw said that the only golden rule is that there is not golden rule. He prefers an iron rule; as in Russia.

—STA, 174

Cocktails

The Cocktail Habit is to be condemned, not because it is American or alcoholic, not because it is fast or fashionable, but because it is, on a common-sense consideration, a worse way of drinking; more hasty, less healthy, even less desirable to anybody left to the honest expression of his own desires. . . . it is rudimentary human nature that it is more natural to sit still and talk, and even drink, after dinner, than to stand up and gulp before dinner.

—S, 37

Most of my work is, I will not venture to say, literary, but at least sedentary. I never do anything except walk about and throw clubs and javelins in the garden. But I never require anything to give me an appetite for a meal. I never yet needed a tot of rum to help me to go over the top and face the mortal perils of luncheon.

—S, 38

Comfort

Comfort is not always a contemptible thing, when its other name is hospitality.

—RLS, 128

Comic Things

There is an idea that it is humiliating to run after one's hat; and when people say it is humiliating they mean that it is comic. It certainly is comic; but man is a very comic creature, and most of the things he does are comic—eating, for instance. And the most comic of all things are exactly the things that are most worth doing—such as making love. A man running after a hat is not half so ridiculous as a man running after a wife.

—ATC, 26

Commercial Enterprise (Exclusive)

That is, it was a thing which paid not by attracting people, but actually by turning people away. In the heart of plutocracy tradesmen become cunning enough to be more fastidious than their customers. They positively create difficulties so that their wealthy and weary clients may spend money and diplomacy in overcoming them. If there were a fashionable hotel in London which no man could enter who was under six foot, society would meekly make up parties of six-foot men to dine in it. If there were an expensive restaurant which by a mere caprice of its proprietor was only open on Thursday afternoon, it would be crowded on Thursday afternoon.

—FBO, 46–47

Communication (and Content)

The real trouble of the Middle Ages lay in their rudimentary and relatively bad communications for the handing on of their good things; not in the least in their not having the good things to communicate. We are in a position to appreciate the distinction at the present moment; when we have very good communications and nothing to communicate.

—C, 263

Communism

For Communism is the child and heir of Capitalism; and the son would still greatly resemble his father even if he had really killed him. Even if we had what is called the Dictatorship of the Proletariat, there would be the same mechanical monotony in dealing with the mob of Dictators as in dealing with the mob of wage-slaves.

—AIWS, 172

Two Earthly Paradises had collapsed. The first was the natural paradise of Rousseau; the second the economic paradise of Ricardo. Men did not become perfect through being free to live and love; men did not become perfect through being free to buy and sell. It was obviously time for the atheists to find a third inevitable and immediate ideal. They have found it in Communism. And it does not trouble them that it is quite different from their first ideal and quite contrary to their second. All they want is some supposed betterment of humanity which will be a bribe for depriving humanity of divinity.... But they are forced more and more to idealise Bolshevism, simply because it is the only thing left that is still new enough to be offered as a hope, when every one of the revolutionary hopes they have themselves offered has in turn become hopeless.

—*CM*, 75–76

Communism pretends to be oh so modern; but it's not. Throw-back to the superstitions of monks and primitive tribes. A scientific government, with a really ethical responsibility to posterity, would be always looking for the line of promise and progress; not levelling and flattening it all back into the mud again. Socialism is sentimentalism; and more dangerous than a pestilence, for in that at least the fittest would survive.

—*FBO*, 918–919

Communist Habits

When I talked about a Communist habit spreading, I only meant a habit I happen to have noticed about two or three times even today. It is a Communist habit by no means confined to Communists. It is the extraordinary habit of so many men, especially Englishmen, of putting other people's match-boxes in their pockets without remembering to return them.

—*FBO*, 929

Communist Institutions

For the only truly and legitimately Communist institution is the home. 'With all my worldly goods I thee endow' is the only satisfactory Bolshevist proclamation that has ever been made about property. It is, therefore, of course, the one proclamation which Bolshevists would be the first to attack.

— Survey, 44

Compromise

Compromise used to mean that half a loaf was better than no bread. Among modern statesmen it really seems to mean that half a loaf is better than a whole loaf.

— WW, 18

Comradeship

No one has even begun to understand comradeship who does not accept with it a certain hearty eagerness in eating, drinking, or smoking, an uproarious materialism which to many women appears only hoggish. You may call the thing an orgy or a sacrament; it is certainly an essential. . . . In the heart of its rowdiness there is a sort of mad modesty; a desire to melt the separate soul into the mass of unpretentious masculinity. . . . No man must be superior to the things that are common to men. This sort of equality must be bodily and gross and comic. Not only are we all in the same boat, but we are all seasick.

— WW, 115

Comtism (Auguste Comte)

As a philosophy it is unsatisfactory. It is evidently impossible to worship humanity, just as it is impossible to worship the Savile Club; both are excellent institutions to which we may happen to belong. But we perceive clearly that the Savile Club did not make the stars and does not fill the Universe. And it is surely unreasonable to attack the doctrine of the Trinity as a piece of bewildering mysticism, and then to ask men to worship a being who is ninety million per-

72

sons in one God, neither confounding the persons nor dividing the substance.

—*H,* 90

Conceit

If a man must needs be conceited, it is certainly better that he should be conceited about some merits or talents that he does not really possess. For then his vanity remains more or less superficial; it remains a mere mistake of fact. . . . Because the merit is an unreal merit, it does not corrupt or sophisticate his real merits. . . . His truly honourable qualities remain in their primordial innocence; he cannot see them and he cannot spoil them. If a man's mind is erroneously possessed with the idea that he is a great violinist, that need not prevent his being a gentleman and an honest man. But if once his mind is possessed in any strong degree with the knowledge that he is a gentleman, he will soon cease to be one.

—*ATC,* 37

Bad men are almost without exception conceited, but they are commonly conceited of their defects.

—*RB,* 101

Confessing

Nobody, or next to nobody, has ever had to go into so much morbid detail in confessing to a priest as in confessing to a doctor. And the joke of it is that the Protestant great-grandmother, who objected to the gentleman priest, would have been the very first to object to a lady doctor. What matters in the confessional is the moral guilt and not the material details. But the material details are everything in medicine, even for the most respectable and responsible physician, let alone all the anarchical quacks who have been let loose to hear confessions in the name of Psychoanalysis or Hypnotic Cures.

—*Thing,* 176

Conscience

God alone knows what the conscience can survive, or how a man who has lost his honor will still try to save his soul.

—MWKTM, 233

Contemplatives

There is the abstraction of the contemplative, whether he is the true sort of Christian contemplative, who is contemplating Something, or the wrong sort of Oriental contemplative, who is contemplating Nothing.

—STA, 124

The Conventional

The man who has learnt to do all conventional things perfectly has at the same time learnt to do them prosaically.

— Types, 9

Conversationalists

... There are two kinds of men who monopolise conversation. The first are those who like the sound of their own voice; the second are those who do not know what the sound of their own voice is like.

—RB, 113

Converts

Becoming a Catholic broadens the mind. It especially broadens the mind about the reasons for becoming a Catholic. Standing in the centre where all roads meet, a man can look down each of the roads in turn and realise that they come from all points of the heavens.

—CCC, 63

At the last moment of all, the convert often feels as if he were looking through a leper's window. He is looking through a little crack or crooked hole that seems to grow smaller as he stares at it; but it is an opening that looks towards the Altar. Only, when he has entered the Church, he finds that the Church is much larger inside than it is outside.

—*CCC*, 64

To become a Catholic is not to leave off thinking, but to learn how to think.

—*CCC*, 86

I believe in preaching to the converted; for I have generally found that the converted do not understand their own religion.

—*TT*, 44

Copying

...all *copying* has a kind of neatness and precision that is less obvious in creative things.

—*EA*, 181

Copyists

...the two great copyists in human history are the Prussians and the Japanese.

—*EA*, 181–182

The Cosmic and the Comic

When I was a very young journalist I used to be irritated at a peculiar habit of printers, a habit which most persons of a tendency similar to mine have probably noticed also. It goes along with the fixed belief of printers that to be a Rationalist is the same thing as to be a Nationalist. I mean the printer's tendency to turn the word "cosmic" into the word "comic." It annoyed me at the time. But since then I have come to the conclusion that the printers were right. The democracy is always right. What is cosmic is comic.

—ATC, 149–150

Coup d'Etat

To treat the Coup d'etat as unpardonable is to justify riot against despotism, but forbid any riot against aristocracy.

—Crimes, 116

Courage

Courage is almost a contradiction in terms. It means a strong desire to live taking the form of a readiness to die. . . . A soldier surrounded by enemies, if he is to cut his way out, needs to combine a strong desire for living with a strange carelessness about dying. He must not merely cling to life, for then he will be a coward, and will not escape. He must not merely wait for death, for then he will be a suicide, and will not escape. He must seek his life in a spirit of furious indifference to it; he must desire life like water and yet drink death like wine.

—O, 170–171

Creation

Creation was the greatest of all revolutions.

—C, 27

A man looking at a hippopotamus may sometimes be tempted to regard the hippopotamus as an enormous mistake; but he is also bound to confess that a fortunate inferiority prevents him personally from making such mistakes.

—CD, 173

Creed (Progressive)

Materialism says the universe is mindless; and faith says it is ruled by the highest mind. Neither will be satisfied with the new progressive creed, which declares hopefully that the universe is half-witted.

—Diversity, 170

Crime

"A crime," he said slowly, "is like any other work of art. Don't look surprised; crimes are by no means the only works of art that come from an infernal workshop. But every work of art, divine or diabolic, has one indispensable mark—I mean, that the centre of it is simple, however much the fulfilment may be complicated."

—FBO, 63

It is not true, of course, that crime is a disease. It is criminology that is a disease.

—FVF, 55

Criminals

Those criminals with small minds are always quite conventional. They become criminals out of sheer conventionality.

—FBO, 808

We deny the snobbish English assumption that the uneducated are the dangerous criminals. . . . We say that the dangerous criminal is the educated criminal. We say that the most dangerous criminal now is the entirely lawless modern philosopher. Compared to him, burglars and bigamists are essentially moral men; my heart goes out to them. They accept the essential ideal of man; they merely seek it wrongly. Thieves respect property. They merely wish the property to become their property that they may more perfectly respect it. But philosophers dislike property as property; they wish to destroy the very idea of personal possession. Bigamists respect marriage, or they would not go through the highly ceremonial and even ritualistic formality of bigamy. But philosophers despise marriage as marriage. Murderers respect human life; they merely wish to attain a greater fulness of human life in themselves by the sacrifice of what seems to them to be lesser lives. But philosophers hate life itself, their own as much as other people's.

— Thursday, 43

Criminals (the Treatment of)

We hear of the stark sentimentalist, who talks as if there were no problem at all: as if physical kindness would cure everything: as if one need only pat Nero and stroke Ivan the Terrible. This mere belief in bodily humanitarianism is not sentimental; it is simply snobbish. For if comfort gives men virtue, the comfortable classes ought to be virtuous—which is absurd.

— TT, 256

Criticism

All criticism tends too much to become criticism of criticism; and the reason is very evident. It is that criticism of creation is so very staggering a thing. We see this in the difficulty of criticizing any artistic creation. We see it again in the difficulty of criticizing that creation which is spelt with a capital C. The pessimists who attack the Universe are always under this disadvantage. They have an exhilarating consciousness that they could make the sun and moon better; but they also have the depressing consciousness that they could not make the sun and moon at all.

—CD, 173

What embitters the world is not excess of criticism, but absence of self-criticism.

—S, 3

Critics

A good critic should be like God in the great saying of a Scottish mystic. George MacDonald said that God was easy to please and hard to satisfy. That paradox is the poise of all good artistic appreciation.... Good criticism, I repeat, combines the subtle pleasure in a thing being done well with the simple pleasure in it being done at all.

—FVF, 20

Now the mistake of critics is not that they criticise the world; it is that they never criticise themselves. They compare the alien with the ideal; but they do not at the same time compare themselves with the ideal; rather they identify themselves with the ideal.

—NJ, 62

It is sometimes curious to notice how a critic, possessing no little cultivation and fertility, will, in speaking of a work of art, let fall almost accidentally some apparently trivial comment, which reveals to us with an instantaneous and complete mental illumination the fact that he does not, so far as that work of art is concerned, in the smallest degree understand what he is talking about. He may have intended to correct merely some minute detail of the work he is studying, but that single movement is enough to blow him and all his diplomas into the air.

—RB, 162

When the critic calls the present good or bad, he ought to be comparing it with the ideal and not with the rather dismal reality called himself.

—S, 6

After all, what we want is direct and individual impressions of primary objects, whether poets or pine-trees, and not an endless succession of critics learning from critics how to criticize.

—Survey, 8

He is only a very shallow critic who cannot see an eternal rebel in the heart of the Conservative.

—Types, 252

Critics (Modern)

In short . . . the trouble arises from the aged merely praising their own age; just as the rising generation is only praising its own generation.

—S, 5

Critics (Psychological)

. . . psychological critics are rather backward even in psychology. It generally distresses such people more to be behind the times than to be against the truth; and in this case it seems possible that they are both.

—RLS, 143

The Cross

The cross cannot be defeated. . . . For it is Defeat.

—BC, 207

Customs and Aristocracy

The enemies of aristocracy often blame it for clinging to cruel or antiquated customs. Both its enemies and its friends are wrong. Generally speaking the aristocracy does not preserve either good or bad traditions; it does not preserve anything except game. Who would dream of looking among aristocrats anywhere for an old custom? . . . the god of the aristocrats is not tradition, but fashion, which is the opposite of tradition. If you wanted to find an old world Norwegian head dress, would you look for it in the Scandinavian smart set? No; the aristocrats never have customs; at the best they have habits, like the animals. Only the mob has customs.

—WW, 87

Cynicism

Cynicism denotes that condition of mind in which we hold that life is in its nature mean and arid; that no soul contains genuine goodness, and no state of things genuine reliability.

—RB, 124

D

Dark Ages

I take in order the next instance offered: the idea that Christianity belongs to the Dark Ages. . . . in history I found that Christianity, so far from belonging to the Dark Ages, was the one path across the Dark Ages that was not dark. . . . how can we say that the Church wishes to bring us back into the Dark Ages? The Church was the only thing that ever brought us out of them.

—O, 272–274

Darwin, Charles

The general public impression that he had entirely proved his case (whatever it was) was early arrived at, and still remains. It was and is hazily associated with the negation of religion. But (and this is the important point) it was also associated with the negation of democracy. The same Mid-Victorian muddle-headness that made people think that "evolution" meant that we need not admit the supremacy of God, also made them think that "survival" meant that we must admit the supremacy of men.

—VA, 207

Darwinism (Social and Political)

The chief Imperialist journal of Germany, just as war was breaking out, said, "Does the oak ask if it has a right to thrust its way through the thicket?" That is, the aggressor appealed to his Right To Live, just as Japan is supposed to appeal to its Right To Live; which may be more soberly described as its Right To Kill.

—EA, 161–162

Death

The physical fact of death, in a hundred horrid shapes, was more naked and less veiled in times of faith or superstition than in times of science or scepticism. Often it was not merely those who had seen a man die, but those who had seen him rot, who were most certain that he was everlastingly alive.

—FVF, 175

Death, in short, is a positive and defined condition, but it belongs entirely to the dead person.

—L & L, 57

Decadence (Attacking)

In short, it may be complained that I have represented Stevenson as reacting against decadence before it existed. And I answer that this is the only real way in which a fighting man ever does successfully attack a movement; when he attacks later, he attacks too late.

—RLS, 157

Decadents

Decadents talk contemptuously of its conventions and its set tasks; it never occurs to them that conventions and set tasks are the very way to keep that greenness in the grass and that redness in the roses—which they had lost for ever.

—CD, 71

The Byronic young man had an affectation of sincerity; the decadent, going a step deeper into the avenues of the unreal, has positively an affectation of affectation.

— Types, 36

Decorum

Decorum itself is of little social value; sometimes it is a sign of social decay. Decorum is the morality of immoral societies. The people who care most about modesty are often those who care least about chastity; no better examples could be given than oriental Courts or the west-end drawing-rooms.

—L & L, 64

Democracy

Democracy is not philanthropy; it is not even altruism or social reform. Democracy is not founded on pity for the common man; democracy is founded on reverence for the common man, or, if you will, even on fear of him. . . . It does not object so much to the ordinary man being a slave as to his not being a king, for its dream is always the dream of the first Roman republic, a nation of kings.

—H, 270

If there be one thing more than another which is true of genuine democracy, it is that genuine democracy is opposed to the rule of the mob. For genuine democracy is based fundamentally on the existence of the citizen, and the best definition of a mob is a body of a thousand men in which there is no citizen.

—HA, 44

If anybody wants to know what political democracy is, the answer is simple; it is a desperate and partly hopeless attempt to get at the opinion of the best people—that is, of the people who do not trust themselves.

—L & L, 118

Democracy means getting those people to vote who would never have the cheek to govern: and (according to Christian ethics) the precise people who ought to govern are the people who have not the cheek to do it.

—TT, 255–256

On Democracy and Revolution

You can never have a revolution in order to establish a democracy. You must have a democracy in order to have a revolution.

—TT, 94–95

Democracy (English)

. . . our democracy has only one great fault; it is not democratic.

—BC, 74

Democracy (Mob)

Democracy is never quite democratic except when it is quite direct; and it is never quite direct except when it is quite small. So soon as a mob has grown large enough to have delegates it has grown large enough to have despots; indeed the despots are often much the more representative of the two.

—NJ, 133

Democrats and Republicans

It is indeed a quaint paradox to suggest that there could be any meaning in the distinction between the names of two modern political parties. But in the case of Democrats and Republicans there is a difference in the names, even if there is no difference in the parties.

—S, 184

Department Stores

I think the big shop is a bad shop. . . . I think the monster emporium is not only vulgar and insolent, but incompetent and uncomfortable; and I deny that its large organization is efficient. Large organization is loose organization. Nay, it would be almost as true to say that organization is always disorganization. . . . If we collected all the stories from all the housewives and householders about the big shops sending the wrong goods, smashing the right goods, forgetting to send any sort of goods, we should behold a welter of inefficiency. There are far more blunders in a big shop than ever happen in a small shop, where the individual customer can curse the individual shopkeeper. Confronted with modern efficiency, the customer is silent; well aware of that organization's talent for sacking the wrong man. In short, organization is a necessary evil—which in this case is not necessary.

—Outline, 62–63

One of the funniest is the statement that it is convenient to get everything in the same shop. That is to say, it is convenient to walk the length of the street, so long as you walk indoors, or more frequently underground, instead of walking the same distance in the open air from one little shop to another. The truth is that the monopolists' shops are really very convenient— to the monopolist. They have all the advantage of concentrating business as they concentrate wealth, in fewer and fewer of the citizens.

—Outline, 63

Dependence

We're all really dependent in nearly everything, and we all make a fuss about being independent in something.

—MWKTM, 125

Despotism

... despotism can be a development, often a late development and very often indeed the end of societies that have been highly democratic. A despotism may almost be defined as a tired democracy. As fatigue falls on a community, the citizens are less inclined for that eternal vigilance which has truly been called the price of liberty; and they prefer to arm only one single sentinel to watch the city while they sleep.

—EM, 50

The sin and sorrow of despotism is not that it does not love men, but that it loves them too much and trusts them too little. Therefore from age to age in history arise these great despotic dreamers, whether they be Royalists or Imperialists or even Socialists, who have at root this idea, that the world would enter into rest if it went their way and forswore altogether the right of going its own way. When a man begins to think that the grass will not grow at night unless he lies awake to watch it, he generally ends in an asylum or on the throne of an Emperor.

—RB, 31

Despotism and Democracy

But there is a thin difference between good despotism and good democracy; both imply equality, with authority; whether the authority be impersonal or personal. What both detest is oligarchy; even in its more human form of aristocracy, let alone its present repulsive form of plutocracy.

—Bio, 302

Destiny

The normal, or at least the ideal, development of a man's destiny is from the coloured chamber of childhood to an even more romantic garden of the faith and tryst of youth. It is from the child's garden of verses to the man's garden of vows.

—RLS, 53

Detective Stories

A decent detective story is itself a selected bundle of clues, with a few blinds as carefully selected as the clues.

—C, 87

Determinists

The determinist does not believe in appealing to will, but he does believe in changing the environment. He must not say to the sinner, "Go and sin no more," because the sinner cannot help it. But he can put him in boiling oil; for boiling oil is an environment.

—O, 44

The Devil (Renouncing)

"There are two ways of renouncing the devil," he said; "and the difference is perhaps the deepest chasm in modern religion. One is to have a horror of him because he is so far off; and the other to have it because he is so near. And no virtue and vice are so much divided as those two virtues."

—FBO, 809

Dickens' *A Christmas Carol*

The beauty and the real blessing of the story do not lie in the mechanical plot of it, the repentance of Scrooge, probable or improbable; they lie in the great furnace of real happiness that glows through Scrooge and everything round him; that great furnace, the heart of Dickens. Whether the Christmas visions would or would not convert Scrooge, they convert us.

—CD, 123

Dickens, Charles

... it was the whole glory and meaning of Dickens that he confined himself to making jokes that anybody might have made a little better than anybody would have made them.

—ATC, 185

In everybody there is a certain thing that loves babies, that fears death, that likes sunlight: that thing enjoys Dickens.

—CD, 79

He knew very well the essential truth, that the true optimist can only continue an optimist so long as he is discontented. For the full value of this life can only be got by fighting; the violent take it by storm. And if we have accepted everything, we have missed something—

war. This life of ours is a very enjoyable fight, but a very miserable truce.

—CD, 204

...if we ever recover anything like a human quiet in which people can hear themselves think, I have no doubt that they will think it more fun to read Dickens than to read Dreiser. It is said that many have no patience to read Dickens; it would be truer to say that they have no time to read Dickens; their time being occupied with wasting their time on things they do not really want to read.

—S, 249–250

Dickens, Charles (Understanding)

And when I say that everybody understands Dickens I do not mean that he is suited to the untaught intelligence. I mean that he is so plain that even scholars can understand him.

—CD, 79

Digestion

Nobody, strictly speaking, is happier on account of his digestion. He is happy because he is so constituted as to forget all about it.

—RB, 180

Dining

I have already remarked, with all the restraint that I could command, that of all modern phenomena, the most monstrous and ominous, the most manifestly rotting with disease, the most grimly prophetic of destruction, the most clearly and unmistakably inspired by evil spirits, the most instantly and awfully overshadowed by the wrath of heaven, the most near to madness and moral chaos, the most vivid with devilry and despair, is the practice of having to listen to loud music while eating a meal in a restaurant.

Sometimes a guest is actually described as being invited to "a quiet dinner." It is rather a quaint phrase when one considers it; as implying that the dinner itself could be noisy; that the soup would roar like the sea, or the asparagus become talkative, or the mutton-chop shriek aloud like the mandrake. But it does bear witness to the normal conception of comfort; that a quiet dinner means a quiet talk.

—Avowals, 102

A little while ago I happened to be dining in the train; and I am very fond of dining in the train—or, indeed, anywhere else.

—Gen S, 167

Disarmament and Conscription

For both conscription and disarmament are very modern notions. And modern notions of the sort are not only negative but nihilist; they always demand the absolute annihilation or total prohibition of something.

—Well, 123

Discussions (Serious)

I think seriously, on the whole, that the more serious is the discussion the more grotesque should be the terms. For this, as I say, there is an evident reason. For a subject is really solemn and important in so far as it applies to the whole cosmos or to some great spheres and cycles of experience at least. So far as a thing is universal it is serious. And so far as a thing is universal it is full of comic things. . . . If you have, let us say, a theory about man and if you can only prove it by talking about Plato or George Washington, your theory may be a quite frivolous thing. But if you can prove it by talking about the butler or the postman, then it is serious because it is universal.

—ATC, 149

Diseases

It is true that some speak lightly and loosely of insanity as in itself attractive. But a moment's thought will show that if a disease is beautiful, it is generally some one else's disease. . . . In short, oddities only strike ordinary people. Oddities do not strike odd people. This is why ordinary people have a much more exciting time; while odd people are always complaining of the dullness of life.

—O, 26–27

Divorce

. . . it is insisted that a married person must at least find release from the society of a lunatic; but it is also true that the scientific reformers with their fuss about "the feeble-minded," are continually giving larger and looser definitions of lunacy. The process might begin by releasing somebody from a homicidal maniac, and end by dealing in the same way with a rather dull conversationalist.

—Div, 121

The point of divorce reform, it cannot be too often repeated, is that the rascal should not only be regarded as romantic, but regarded as respectable. He is not to sow his wild oats and settle down; he is merely to settle down to sowing his wild oats.

—Div, 128–129

Divorce is a thing which the newspapers now not only advertise, but advocate, almost as if it were a pleasure in itself. It may be, indeed, that all the flowers and festivities will now be transferred from the fashionable wedding to the fashionable divorce. A superb iced and frosted divorce-

92

cake will be provided for the feast, and in military circles will be cut with correspondent's sword. A dazzling display of divorce presents will be laid out for the inspection of the company, watched by a detective dressed as an ordinary divorce guest. Perhaps the old divorce breakfast will be revived; anyhow toasts will be drunk, the guests will assemble on the doorstep to see the husband and wife go off in opposite directions.

—FVF, 145

Some of our liberal friends favour divorce for drunkenness or cruelty. There is a far stronger case for divorcing a woman because her shoes creak, or a man for biting his nails or wearing his hat at an irritating angle. These, Madam, are the things that destroy happiness.

—Judgement, 34

If Americans can be divorced for "incompatibility of the temper" I cannot conceive why they are not all divorced. I have known many happy marriages, but never a compatible one. The whole aim of marriage is to fight through and survive the instant when incompatibility becomes unquestionable. For a man and a woman, as such, are incompatible.

—WW, 67–68

Dogma

A wall is like a rule; and the gates are like the exceptions that prove the rule. The man making it has to decide where his rule will run and where his exceptions shall stand. He cannot have a city that is all gates any more than a house that is all windows; nor is it possible to have a law that consists entirely of liberties.

—NJ, 48

Dogmas

Dogmas are often spoken of as if they were signs of the slowness or endurance of the human mind. As a matter of fact, they are marks of mental promptitude and lucid impatience.... Dogmas are not dark and mysterious; rather a dogma is like a flash of lightning—an instantaneous lucidity that opens across a whole landscape.

—GBS, 19–20

Dogmas (Modern)

For the modern world will accept no dogmas upon any authority; but it will accept any dogmas upon no authority. Say that a thing is so, according to the Pope or the Bible, and it will be dismissed as a superstition without examination. But preface your remark merely with "they say" or "don't you know that?" or try (and fail) to remember the name of some professor mentioned in some newspaper; and the keen rationalism of the modern mind will accept every word you say.

—Div, 73–74

Dogmatists and Egotists

To be dogmatic and to be egotistic are not only not the same thing, they are opposite things. Suppose, for instance, that a vague sceptic eventually joins the Catholic Church. In that act he has at the same moment become less egotistic and become more dogmatic. The dogmatist is by the nature of the case not egotistical, because he believes that there is some solid obvious and objective truth outside him which he has perceived and which he invites all men to perceive. And the egotist is in the majority of cases not dogmatic, because he has no need to isolate one of his notions as being related to truth; all of his notions are equally interesting because they are related to him.

—HA, 151–152

The true egotist is as much interested in his own errors as in his own truth; the dogmatist is interested only in the truth, and only in the truth because it is true. At the most the dogmatist believes that he is in the truth; but the egotist believes that the truth, if there is such a thing, is in him.

—HA, 152

Dogs

The dog has been domesticated—that is, destroyed. Nobody now in London can form the faintest idea of what a dog would look like. You know a Dachshund in the street; you know a St. Bernard in the street. But if you saw a Dog in the street you would run from him screaming.

—Diversity, 69

Doing

If a thing is worth doing, it is worth doing badly.

—WW, 320

Don Quixote

The great truth which lies at the heart of *Don Quixote* is the truth that the conflict of the world is chiefly a conflict between goods. The battle between the idealism of Don Quixote and the realism of the inn-keeper is a battle so hot and ceaseless that we know that they must both be right. A vulgar philosophy laments the wickedness of the world, but when we come to think of it we realise that the confusion of life, the doubt and turmoil and bewildering responsibility of life, largely arise from the enormous amount of good in the world.

There is much to be said for everybody; there are too many points of view; too many truths that contradict each other, too many loves which hate each other. Our earth is not, as Hamlet said, "an unweeded garden", but a garden which is choked and disordered with neglected flowers.

—HA, 25

Drama (Prose and Life)

But there is one thing that no dramatist dare produce upon the stage. That thing is the thing called "Work." There is no playwright who would reproduce upon the stage the first four hours of an ordinary clerk's day.

Nobody would send up the curtain at 8 o'clock on a man adding up figures, and send it down at 10 o'clock on a man still adding up figures. Even an Ibsenite audience would not support the silent symbolism of three scenes all of which were occupied with the same bricklayer laying bricks. We dare not say in artistic form how much there is of prose in men's lives; and precisely because we cannot say how much there is of prose, we cannot say how much there is of poetry.

—HA, 140

Dreams

Our dreams, our aims are always, we insist, quite practical. It is our practice that is dreamy.

—ATC, 201

Dreams, like life, are full of nobility and joy, but of a nobility and joy utterly arbitrary and incalculable. We have gratitude, but never certainty.

—L & L, 31

Dreams and Psychoanalysts

The man who talked about his dreams, who had become rather a bore at breakfast, suddenly found that he had the opportunity of being a broader, brainier, and more universal and philosophical bore in the lecture-room or on the platform of scientific and religious debate. Psychoanalysis resurrected the archaic interpreter of dreams, just as Psychical Research resurrected the ancient necromancer or professional raiser of ghosts.

—Avowals, 127

Dress

Men dress smartly so as not to be noticed; but all women dress to be noticed; gross and vulgar women to be grossly and vulgarly noticed, wise and modest women to be wisely and modestly noticed.

—Glass, 85

Drinking

For in so far as drinking is really a sin it is not because drinking is wild, but because drinking is tame; not in so far as it is anarchy, but in so far as it is slavery. Probably the worst way to drink is to drink medicinally. Certainly the safest way to drink is to drink carelessly; that is, without caring much for anything, and especially not caring for the drink.

—ATC, 172

The sound rule in the matter would appear to be like many other sound rules—a paradox. Drink because you are happy, but never because you are miserable. Never drink when you are wretched without it, or you will be like the grey-faced gin-drinker in the slum; but drink when you would be happy without it, and you will be like the laughing peasant of Italy. Never drink because you need it, for this is rational drinking, and the way to death and hell. But drink because you do not need it, for this is irrational drinking, and the ancient health of the world.

—H, 99

Drunkenness

Doubtless, it is unnatural to be drunk. But then in a real sense it is unnatural to be human. Doubtless, the intemperate workman wastes his tissues in drinking; but no one knows how much the sober workman wastes his tissues by working. No one knows how much the wealthy philanthropist wastes his tissues by talking; or, in much rarer conditions, by thinking.

—ATC, 170–171

The real case against drunkenness is not that it calls up the beast, but that it calls up the Devil. It does not call up the beast, and if it did it would not matter much, as a rule; the beast is a harmless and rather amiable creature, as anybody can see by watching cattle. There is nothing bestial about intoxication; and certainly there is nothing intoxicating or even particularly lively about beasts. Man is always something worse or something better than an animal; and a mere argument from animal perfection never touches him at all. Thus, in sex no animal is either chivalrous or obscene. And thus no animal ever invented anything so bad as drunkenness—or so good as drink.

—ATC, 171

Dullness

. . . dull people always want excitement.

—S, 63

Three quarters of the real luxury or prodigality or profligacy, that is complained of just now, is due to the dullness of people who cannot imagine anything they do not experience. They are so miserably and dismally stupid that they actually have to do things. They are so poor in spirit that they have to have things. They have to have a flying-machine fitted up with every luxury, because they cannot send their souls up while flying a kite. They have to be in a racing car in order to believe that it really races. If this principle of the inner life were understood, we might today restore the sanity of civilisation; and especially the poetry of the home.

—S, 63

E

The Eastern Question

The Moslem had been checked, but he had not been checked enough. The whole story of what was called the Eastern Question, and three-quarters of the wars of the modern world, were due to the fact he was not checked enough.

—NJ, 248

Economists

When, in "A Christmas Carol," Scrooge refers to the surplus population, the Spirit tells him, very justly, not to speak till he knows what the surplus is and where it is. The implication is severe but sound. When a group of superciliously benevolent economists look down into the abyss for the surplus population, assuredly there is only one answer that should be given to them; and that is to say, "If there is a surplus, you are a surplus." And if any one were ever cut off, they would be.

—CD, 126

Education

The whole point of education is that it should give a man abstract and eternal standards, by which he can judge material and fugitive conditions.

—AIG, 22

For my part, I should be inclined to suggest that the chief object of education should be to restore simplicity. If you like to put it so, the chief object of education is not to learn things; nay, the chief object of education is to unlearn things. The chief object of education is to unlearn all the weariness and wickedness of the world and get back into that state of exhilaration we all instinctively celebrate when we write by preference of children....

—ATC, 53

...I learnt the large Greek letters as I learnt the large English letters, at home. I was told about them merely for fun while I was still a child; while the others I learnt during the period of what is commonly called education; that is, the period during which I was being instructed by somebody I did not know, about something I did not want to know.

—Bio, 52

...given the modern philosophy or absence of philosophy, education is turned against itself, destroying that very sense of variety and proportion which it is the object of education to give. No man who worships education has got the best out of education; no man who sacrifices everything to education is even educated.... What is wrong is a neglect of principle; and the principle is that without a gentle contempt for education, no gentleman's education is complete.

—CM, 39–40

The moment men begin to care more for education than for religion they begin to care more for ambition than for education. It is no longer a world in which the souls of all are equal before heaven, but a world in which the mind of each is bent on achieving unequal advantage over the other.

—CM, 40

The truth is that the modern world has committed itself to two totally different and inconsistent conceptions about education. It is always trying to expand the scope of education; and always trying to exclude from it all religion and philosophy. But this is sheer nonsense. You can have an education that teaches atheism because atheism is true, and it can be, from its own point of view, a complete education. But you cannot have an education claiming to teach all truth, and then refusing to discuss whether atheism is true.

—CM, 168–169

The young of the human species, if they are to reach the full possibilities of human culture, so various, so labourious, so elaborate, must be under the protection of responsible persons through very long periods of mental and moral growth. I know there are some who grow merely impatient and irrational at this point; and say they could do just as well without education. But they lie; for they could not even express that opinion, if they had not laboriously learnt one particular language in which to talk nonsense.

—S, 75

Education is initiation; it is in its nature a progression from one thing to another; the arrangement of ideas in a certain order.

—Survey, 163

Education (Business)

He has never been taught to think, but only to count. He lives in a cold temple of abstract calculation, of which the pillars are columns of figures. But he has no basic sense of Comparative Religion . . . by which he may discover whether he is in the right temple, or distinguish one temple from another. . . . Anyhow, that is what is the matter with Business Education; that it narrows the mind; whereas the whole object of education is to broaden the mind; and especially to broaden it so as to enable it to criticize and condemn such narrowness.

—AIG, 23–25

Education (Modern)

It can be stated in half a hundred different ways, but perhaps the simplest way of stating it is to say that a perfectly vigorous and intelligent young American, equipped with all the latest devices of mechanics and chemistry, bursting with all the latest business tips about salesmanship and mass psychology, is not an educated man. He is not educated because he has only been educated in all modern things, and not even in all mortal, let alone all immortal, things. In a word, he has not been made acquainted with human things, and that is what we mean when we say that he has neglected the humanities.

—S, 116

Education (Secular)

. . . I am only pointing out that every education teaches a philosophy; if not by dogma then by suggestion, by implication, by atmosphere. Every part of that education has a connection with every other part. If it does not all combine to convey some general view of life, it is not an education at all.

—CM, 167

Efficiency

. . . All that excellent machinery which is the swiftest thing on earth in saving human labour is also the slowest thing on earth in resisting human interference. It may be easier to get chocolate for nothing out of a shopkeeper than out of an automatic machine. But if you did manage to steal the chocolate, the automatic machine would be much less likely to run after you.

—BC, 333

Ego

The most brilliant exponent of the egoistic school, Nietszche, with deadly and honourable logic, admitted that the philosophy of self-satisfaction led to looking down upon the weak, the cowardly, and the ignorant. Looking down on things may be a delightful experience, only there is nothing, from a mountain to a cabbage, that is really *seen* when it is seen from a balloon. The philosopher of the ego sees everything, no doubt, from a high and rarefied heaven; only he sees everything foreshortened or deformed.

—D, 101

If you consulted your business experience instead of your ugly individualistic philosophy, you would know that believing in himself is one of the commonest signs of a rotter. Actors who can't act believe in themselves; and debtors who won't pay. It would be much truer to say that a man will certainly fail; because he believes in himself. Complete self-confidence is not merely a sin; complete self-confidence is a weakness.

—O, 23

Egoists

The man with the strong magnetic personality is still the man whom those who know him best desire most warmly to kick out of the club. The man in a really acute stage of self-realisation is a no more pleasing object in the club than in the pub. Even the most enlightened and scientific sort of club can see through the superman; and see that he has become a bore.

—CM, 251

The Egoist is not a man; he is a sin.

—HA, 67

Eighteenth-century Society

The life of society was superficial, but it is only very superficial people who object to the superficial. To the man who sees the marvellousness of all things, the surface of life is fully as strange and magical as its interior; clearness and plainness of life is fully as mysterious as its mysteries.

—RB, III

Eliot, T. S.

Mr. T. S. Eliot's wildest verses do, indeed, have rhythm, too much rhythm; really (as the phrase goes) making the head go round, and suggesting a cosy life in the hollow heart of a cyclone or a whirlpool. But there is nothing of this in his essays, which are rather contained and reticent than otherwise. Indeed, when he does make an epigram (and a very good one) he is so ashamed of it that he hides it at the end of a minute footnote, for fear some critic or other should accuse him of brilliancy.

—Survey, 84–85

Eloquence

One of the values we have really lost in recent fiction is the value of eloquence. The modern literary artist is compounded of almost every man except the orator.

—Types, 168

Emancipation (Modern)

Modern emancipation means this: that anybody who can afford it can publish a newspaper. But the Common Man would not want to publish a newspaper, even if he could afford it. He might want, for instance, to go on talking politics in a pothouse or the parlour of an inn. And that is exactly the sort of really popular talk about politics which modern movements have often abolished: the old democracies by forbidding the pothouse, the new dictatorships by forbidding the politics.

—CM, 2

England

... the funniest thing of all is that even if you love it and belong to it, you still can't make head or tail of it.

—FBO, 933

From the standpoint of anyone who can see it from the inside, but see it sanely, the best things in England are poetry and humour; and it so happens that they are both locked up in a language.

—HA, 205

The English

It is nonsense, I regret to say, to claim that they are incapable of boasting. Sometimes they boast most magnificently of their weaknesses and deficiencies. Sometimes they boast of the more striking and outstanding virtues they do not possess. Sometimes (I say it with groans and grovellings before the just wrath of heaven) they sink so low as to boast of not boasting.

—C, 3

But England was saved by a forgotten thing—the English. Simple men with simple motives, the chief one a hate of injustice which grows simpler the longer we stare at it, came out of their dreary tenements and their tidy shops, their fields and their suburbs and their factories and their rookeries, and asked for the arms of men. In a throng that was at last three million men, the islanders went forth from their island, as simply as the mountaineers had gone forth from their mountain with their faces to the dawn.

—*Crimes*, 161

...the English populace has lived on laughter; its substitute for religion, for property, and sometimes even for food.

—*HA*, 49

We all recognize the curse on those who say that charity begins at home; that they so often mean that charity ends at home. But by various historical accidents it is unfortunately true that English charity has had no obvious duty except to begin and end at home, not because England would not have sympathised with Europe, but because England knew hardly anything about anything but England.

—*HA*, 208

It is vital that we should avoid the appearance of offering ourselves as moral models, not because we have not moral advantages, in this or that respect, even as compared with others, but because we have not the intellectual advantages that would enable us to make the comparison or anyhow to make it correctly. In other words, our difficulty in helping them to know us has been, not only that we did not know them, but also that we did not know how much they knew already. There are some features about which some foreigners know much more about us than we do ourselves, but they are not the most genuine or the most general features.

—*HA*, 210

They liked to be called stiff because they thought it meant that they were strong. They liked to be called solemn because they thought it meant that they were responsible. Vanity of this sort is not of course peculiar to them; it is common to the whole human race. But it was simply out of the weakness of vanity that they confessed to the sin of pride.

—HA, 212

English Things

Damn it, I sometimes think the only English thing left in England is cherry brandy.

—FBO, 839

The Englishman

The Englishman has always found it easier to get inspiration from the Italians than from the French; they call to each other across that unconquered castle of reason.

—VA, 188

Englishman (Modern)

Modern England is too prone to present the spectacle of a person who is enormously delighted because he has not got the contrary disadvantages to his own. The Englishman is always saying "My house is not damp" at the moment when his house is on fire.

—ATC, 105

Englishman's House

The man who said that an Englishman's house is his castle said much more than he meant. The Englishman thinks of his house as something fortified, and provisioned, and his very surliness is at root romantic. And this sense would naturally be strongest in wild winter nights, when the lowered port cullis and the lifted drawbridge do not merely bar people out, but bar people in. The Englishman's house is most sacred, not merely when the King cannot enter it, but when the Englishman cannot get out of it.

—*CD,* 119

Ennui

Ennui is, indeed, the great sin, the sin by which the whole universe tends continually to be undervalued and to vanish from the imagination. But it is a quality of the person who feels, not of the person who produces it.

—*L & L,* 56

Equality

There is nothing false in the idea of the equality of man; but there is something utterly false in denying the thing in which men are most obviously equal, which is death.

—*AIWS,* 125

The idea of the equality of men is in substance simply the idea of the importance of man.

—*England,* 203

The truth involved here has many names; that man is the image of God; that he is the microcosm; that he is the measure of all things. He is the microcosm in the sense that he is the mirror, the only crystal we know in which the fantasy and fear in things are, in the double and real sense, things of reflection. In the presence of this mysterious monopoly the differences of men are like dust. That is what the equality of men means to me; and that is the only intelligible thing it ever meant to anybody.

—*FVF,* 144

Ethnology

The Moslem Paradise is a very Earthly Paradise. But with all their fine apprehensions, the Jews suffer from one heavy calamity; that of being a Chosen Race. It is the vice of any patriotism or religion depending on race that the individual is himself the thing to be worshipped; the individual is his own ideal, and even his own idol. This fancy was fatal to the Germans; it is fatal to the Anglo-Saxons, whenever any of them forswear the glorious name of Englishmen and Americans to fall into that forlorn description. This is not so when the nation is felt as a noble abstraction, of which the individual is proud in the abstract.... In short, mere family pride flatters every member of the family; it produced the arrogance of the Germans, and it is capable of producing a much subtler kind of arrogance in the Jews. From this particular sort of self-deception the more savage man of the desert is free. If he is not considering somebody as a Moslem, he will consider him as a man. At the price of something like barbarism, he has at least been saved from ethnology.

−*NJ*, 29–30

Eugenics

The shortest general definition of Eugenics on its practical side is that it does, in a more or less degree, propose to control some families at least as if they were families of pagan slaves.... But it is to be applied at the very least by somebody to somebody, and that on certain calculations about breeding which are affirmed to be demonstrable.

−*Evils*, 13

Now the first principle behind Eugenics becomes plain enough. It is the proposal that somebody or something should criticize men with the same superiority with which men criticize madmen. It might exercise this right with great moderation; but I am not here talking about the exercise, but about the right. Its claim certainly is to bring all human life under Lunacy Laws.

−*Evils*, 48

They do not know what they want, except that they want your soul and body and mind in order to find out. They are quite seriously, as they themselves might say, the first religion to be experimental instead of doctrinal. All other established Churches have been based on somebody having found the truth. This is the first Church that was ever based on not having found it.

—Evils, 102–103

Eugenists

The obvious course for Eugenists is to act towards babies as they act towards kittens. Let all the babies be born; and then let us drown those we do not like. . . . until I see a real pioneer and progressive leader coming out with a good, bold, scientific programme for drowning babies, I will not join the movement.

—Well, 143–144

Europe

Nobody will ever write a History of Europe that will make any sort of sense, until he does justice to the Councils of the Church, those vast and yet subtle collaborations for thrashing out a thousand thoughts to find the true thought of the Church.

—Rome, 62

Evolution

We have heard much of late of something called Emergent Evolution; a phrase which, like many scientific phrases, we may find rather useful so long as we do not use it scientifically. Evolution as explanation, as an ultimate philosophy of the cause of living things, is still faced with the problem of producing rabbits out of an empty hat; a process commonly involving some hint of design.

—C, 172

If evolution destroys anything, it does not destroy religion but rationalism. If evolution simply means that a positive thing called an ape turned very slowly into a positive thing called a man, then it is stingless for the most orthodox; for a personal God might just as well do things slowly as quickly, especially if, like the Christian God, he were outside time. But if it means anything more, it means that there is no such thing as an ape to change, and no such thing as a man for him to change into. . . . At best, there is only one thing, and that is a flux of everything and anything. This is an attack not upon the faith, but upon the mind. . . . You cannot think if you are not separate from the subject of thought. Descartes said, "I think; therefore I am." The philosophic evolutionist reverses and negatives [sic] the epigram. He says, "I am not; therefore I cannot think."

—O, 60–61

Evolution and the Poor

Evolution (the sinister enemy of revolution) does not especially deny the existence of God; what it does deny is the existence of man. And all the despair about the poor, and the cold and repugnant pity for them, has been largely due to the vague sense that they have literally relapsed into the state of the lower animals.

—CD, 197

Evolution (Spiritual)

For a creed is like a ladder, while an evolution is only like a slope. A spiritual and social evolution is generally a pretty slippery slope; a miry slope where it is very easy to slide down again.

—NJ, 50

Evolution (Theory of)

It is not easy for any person who lives in our time, when the dust has settled and the spiritual perspective has been restored, to realize what the entrance of the idea of evolution meant for the men of those days. To us it is the discovery of another link in a chain which, however far we follow it, still stretches back into a divine mystery. To many of the men of that time it would appear from their writings that it was the heartbreaking and desolating discovery of the end and origin of the chain. To them had happened the most black and hopeless catastrophe conceivable to human nature; they had found a logical explanation of all things. To them it seemed that an Ape had suddenly risen to gigantic stature and destroyed the seven heavens.

—HA, 97

But the position of those who regarded the opening of the "Descent of Man" as the opening of one of the seals of the last days, is a great deal sounder than people have generally allowed. It has been constantly supposed that they were angry with Darwinism because it appeared to do something or other to the book of Genesis; but this was a pretext or fancy. They fundamentally rebelled against Darwinism, not because they had a fear that it would affect Scripture, but because they had a fear, not altogether unreasonable or ill-founded, that it would affect morality.

—HA, 97–98

It is difficult, no doubt, for us in somewhat subtler days, to understand how anybody could suppose that the origin of the species had anything to do with the origin of being. To us it appears that to tell a man who asks who made his mind that evolution made it, is like telling a man who asks who rolled a cab-wheel over his leg that revolution rolled it. To state the process is scarcely to state the agent.

—HA, 97–98

Evolutionists

But the moderns, who do not believe in the existence of gods, tend at last not to believe even in the existence of men. Being scientific evolutionists, they cannot tell the difference between a man and a sheep. And being highly civilized townsmen they would probably be very bad judges of the differences between a good sheep and a bad one.

—AIWS, 218

Evolutionists cannot drive us, because of the nameless gradation in Nature, to deny the personality of God, for a personal God might as well work by gradations as in any other way; but they do drive themselves, through those gradations, to deny the existence of a personal Mr. Jones, because he is within the scope of evolution and his edges are rubbed away. The evolutionists uproot the world, but not the flowers. The Titans never scaled heaven, but they laid waste the earth.

—L & L, 192

... it is absurd for the Evolutionist to complain that it is unthinkable for an admittedly unthinkable God to make everything out of nothing, and then pretend that it is *more* thinkable that nothing should turn itself into anything.

—STA, 173

Evolutionists (Creative)

They seem to imagine that they avoid the metaphysical doubt about mere change by assuming (it is not clear why) that the change will always be for the better. . . . What they really mean is that change is not mere change; but is the unfolding of something; and if it is thus unfolded, though the unfolding takes twelve million years, it must be there already. . . . In other words, it is impossible even to say that the change is for the better, unless the best exists somewhere, both before and after the change.

—STA, 174-175

Suppose two entirely new paths open before the progress of Creative Evolution. How is the evolutionist to know which Beyond is the better; unless he accepts from the past and present some standard of the best? By their superficial theory everything can change; everything can improve, even the nature of improvement. But in their submerged common sense, they do not really think that an ideal of kindness could change to an ideal of cruelty. It is typical of them that they will sometimes rather timidly use the word Purpose; but blush at the very mention of the word Person.

—STA, 175–176

Exaggeration

In short, if one is really to exaggerate the truth, one must have some truth to exaggerate. The decadent mystic produces an effect not by exaggerating but by distorting. True exaggeration is a thing both subtle and austere. Caricature is a serious thing; it is almost blasphemously serious.

—Blake, 195

Exile

For exile is the worst kind of bondage. In insisting upon that at least the Zionists have insisted upon a profound truth, with many applications to many other moral issues. It is true that for any one whose heart is set on a particular home or shrine, to be locked out is to be locked in. The narrowest possible prison for him is the whole world.

—NJ, 283

Existence (Inexpressibility of)

And if any of us or all of us are truly optimists, and believe as Browning did, that existence has a value wholly inexpressible, we are most truly compelled to that sentiment, not by any argument or triumphant justification of the cosmos, but by a few of these momentary and immortal sights and sounds, a gesture, an old song, a portrait, a piano, an old door.

—RB, 50–51

Existence (the Wonder of)

There is at the back of all our lives an abyss of light, more blinding and unfathomable than any abyss of darkness; and it is the abyss of actuality, of existence, of the fact that things truly are, and that we ourselves are incredibly and sometimes almost incredulously real. It is the fundamental fact of being, as against not being; it is unthinkable, yet we cannot unthink it, though we may sometimes be unthinking about it; unthinking and especially unthanking. For he who has realized this reality knows that it does outweigh, literally to infinity, all lesser regrets or arguments for negation, and that under all our grumblings there is a subconscious substance of gratitude. That light of the positive is the business of poets, because they see all things in the light of it more than do other men.

—C, 26

Experience

The people who have had misfortunes are generally the people who love to talk about them. Experience is really one of the gaieties of old age, one of its dissipations. Mere memory becomes a kind of debauch. Experience may be disheartening to those who are foolish enough to try to co-ordinate it and to draw deductions from it.

—CD, 84

Experts

People say that specialists are inhuman; but that is unjust. People say an expert is not a man; but that is unkind and untrue. The real difficulty about the specialist or expert is much more singular and fascinating. The trouble with the expert is never that he is not a man; it is always that wherever he is not an expert he is too much of an ordinary man. Wherever he is not exceptionally learned he is quite casually ignorant.

—Blake, 56

This is the great fallacy in the case of what is called the impartiality of men of science. If scientific men had no idea beyond their scientific work it might be all very well—that is to say, all very well for everybody except them. But the truth is that, beyond their scientific ideas, they have not the absence of ideas but the presence of the most vulgar and sentimental ideas that happen to be common to their social clique. If a biologist had no views on art and morals it might be all very well. The truth is that a biologist has all the wrong views of art and morals that happen to be going about in the smart set in his time. . . . in short, the danger of the mere technical artist or expert is that of becoming a snob or average silly man in all things not affecting his peculiar topic of study; wherever he is not an extraordinary man he is a particularly stupid ordinary man.

—Blake, 56–57

People talk about something pedantic in the knowledge of the expert; but what ruins mankind is the ignorance of the expert. . . . in other words, the expert does not escape his age; he only lays himself open to the meanest and most obvious of the influences of his age. The specialist does not avoid having prejudices; he only succeeds in specializing in the most passing and illiterate prejudices.

—Blake, 58–59

Experts are undoubtedly right nine times out of ten, but the tenth time comes, and we find in military matters an Oliver Cromwell who will make every mistake known to strategy and yet win all his battles, and in medical matters a Robert Browning whose views have not a technical leg to stand on and are entirely correct.

—RB, 73

Exploration

The truth is that exploration and enlargement make the world smaller. The telegraph and the steamboat make the world smaller. The telescope makes the world smaller; it is only the microscope that makes it larger. Before long the world will be cloven with a war between telescopists and the microscopists. The first study large things and live in a small world; the second study small things and live in a large world.

—H, 44

Expression

Forms of expression always appear turgid to those who do not share the emotions they represent.

—HA, 43

F

Fable

Fable is, generally speaking, far more accurate than fact, for fable describes a man as he was to his own age, fact describes him as he is to a handful of inconsiderable antiquarians many centuries after.

—Types, 200

Fable is more historical than fact, because fact tells us about one man and fable tells us about a million men.

—Types, 201

Facts

The process called practical, the attempt to rule merely by facts, has in its own nature the essence of all betrayal. We discover that facts, which seem so solid, are of all things the most fluid. As the professors and the prigs say, facts are always evolving; in other words, they are always evading or escaping or running away.

—Thing, 128

Fads

A fad or heresy is the exaltation of something which, even if true, is secondary or temporary in its nature against those things which are essential and eternal, those things which always prove themselves true in the long run. In short it is the setting up of the mood against the mind. For instance: it is a mood, a beautiful and lawful mood, to wonder how oysters really feel. But it is a fad, an ugly and unlawful fad, to starve human beings because you will not let them eat oysters.

—Blake, 167–168

Fairy-tales

Some solemn and superficial people (for nearly all very superficial people are solemn) have declared that the fairy-tales are immoral; they base this on some accidental circumstances or regrettable incidents in the war between giants and boys, some cases in which the latter indulged in unsympathic deceptions or even in practical jokes. The objection, however, is not only false, but very much the reverse of the facts. The fairy-tales are at root not only moral in the sense of being innocent, but moral in the sense of being didactic, moral in the sense of being moralising.

—ATC, 186

If you really read the fairy-tales, you will observe that one idea runs from one end of them to the other—the idea that peace and happiness can only exist on some condition. This idea, which is the core of ethics, is the core of the nursery-tales. The whole happiness of fairyland hangs upon a thread, upon one thread. Cinderella may have a dress woven on supernatural looms and blazing with unearthly brilliance; but she must be back when the clock strikes twelve. . . . A girl may be the bride of the God of Love himself if she never tries to see him; she sees him, and he vanishes away. A girl is given a box on condition she does not open it; she opens it, and all the evils of this world rush out at her. A man and a woman are put in a garden on condition that they do not eat one fruit: they eat it, and lose their joy in all the fruits of the earth.

This great idea, then, is the backbone of all folk-lore—the idea that all happiness hangs on one thin veto; all positive joy depends on one negative.

—ATC, 188–189

Fiction means the common things as seen by the uncommon people. Fairy tales mean the uncommon things as seen by the common people.

—CD, 62

... the things I believe most now, are the things called fairy tales. They seem to me to be the entirely reasonable things. . . . Fairyland is nothing but the sunny country of common sense. . . . There is the great lesson of "Beauty and the Beast"; that a thing must be loved *before* it is loveable. There is the terrible allegory of the "Sleeping Beauty," which tells how the human creature was blessed with all birthday gifts, yet cursed with death; and how death also may perhaps be softened to a sleep.

—O, 87–88

It is far easier to believe in a million fairy tales than to believe in one man who does not like fairy tales.

—TT, 124

... a lady has written me an earnest letter saying that fairy tales ought not to be taught to children even if they are true. She says that it is cruel to tell children fairy tales, because it frightens them. You might just as well say that it is cruel to give girls sentimental novels because it makes them cry.

—TT, 128

Fairy-tales and Ethics

It is surely obvious that all ethics ought to be taught to this fairy-tale tune; that, if one does the thing forbidden, one imperils all the things provided. . . . This is the profound morality of fairy-tales; which so far from being lawless, go to the root of all law. Instead of finding (like common books of ethics) a rationalistic basis for each Commandment, they find the great mystical basis for all Commandments.

— ATC, 189

Fairy-tales (and Moral Imagination)

Fairy tales, then, are not responsible for producing in children fear, or any of the shapes of fear; fairy tales do not give the child the idea of the evil or the ugly; that is in the child already, because it is in the world already. Fairy tales do not give a child his first idea of bogey. What fairy tales give the child is his first clear idea of the possible defeat of bogey. The baby has known the dragon intimately ever since he had an imagination. What the fairy tale provides for him is a St. George to kill the dragon.

— TT, 129–130

Fairy-tales (and Realism)

"Can you not see," I said, "that fairy tales in their essence are quite solid and straightforward; but that this everlasting fiction about modern life is in its nature essentially incredible? Folk-lore means that the soul is sane, but that the universe is wild and full of marvels. Realism means that the world is dull and full of routine, but that the soul is sick and screaming."

— TT, 125

Fairy-tales (on the Banning of)

That is (like a belief in slavery or annexation) one of those intellectual errors which lie very near to ordinary mortal sins. There are some refusals which, though they may be done what is called conscientiously, yet carry so much of their whole horror in the very act of them, that a man must in doing them not only harden but slightly corrupt his heart.

— TT, 121

Faith

The mark of the Faith is not tradition; it is conversion. It is the miracle by which men find truth in spite of tradition and often with the rending of all the roots of humanity.

—CCC, 22

Faith is always at a disadvantage; it is a perpetually defeated thing which survives all its conquerors.

—GFW, 48

Only Shakespeare has been optimistic when he felt pessimistic. This is the definition of a faith. A faith is that which is able to survive a mood.

—L & L, 122

Every faith is a faith which offers everything except faithfulness. It was never so necessary to insist that most of the really vital and valuable ideas in the world, including Christianity, would never have survived at all if they had not survived their own death, even in the sense of dying daily. The ideal was out of date almost from the first day; that is why it is eternal; for whatever is dated is doomed.

—NJ, 73–74

Faith (on the Twilight of)

The desperate modern talk about dark days and reeling altars, and the end of gods and angels, is the oldest talk in the world: lamentations over the growth of agnosticism can be found in the monkish sermons of the dark ages; horror at youthful impiety can be found in the Iliad. This is the thing that never deserts men and yet always, with daring diplomacy, threatens to desert them. It has indeed dwelt among and controlled all the kings and crowds, but only with the air of a pilgrim passing by. It has indeed warmed and lit men from the beginning of Eden with an unending glow, but it was the glow of an eternal sunset.

— GFW, 48

The Fall

The Fall is a view of life. It is not only the only enlightening, but the only encouraging view of life. It holds, as against the only real alternative philosophies, those of the Buddhist or the Pessimist or the Promethean, that we have misused a good world, and not merely been entrapped into a bad one. It refers evil back to the wrong use of the will, and thus declares that it can eventually be righted by the right use of the will. Every other creed except that one is some form of surrender to fate.

— Thing, 226

Family

Of course the family is a good institution because it is uncongenial. It is wholesome precisely because it contains so many divergences and varieties. It is . . . like a little kingdom, and, like most other little kingdoms, is generally in a state of something resembling anarchy. . . . Aunt Elizabeth is unreasonable, like mankind. Papa is excitable, like mankind. Our youngest brother is mischievous, like mankind. Grandpapa is stupid, like the world; he is old, like the world.

— H, 188–189

Family Life (the Attack on)

Much of this business began with the influence of Ibsen, a very powerful dramatist and an exceedingly feeble philosopher.

— Thing, 29

Fascism

Fascism could never be quite satisfactory; for it did not rest on authority but only on power; which is the weakest thing in the world. The Fascists said in effect, "We may not be the majority, but we are the most vigorous and intelligent minority." Which is simply challenging any other intelligent minority to show that it is more vigorous. It may well end in the very anarchy it attempted to avoid.

—Well, 61

Fashion

But fashion, in a feverish sense that exists today, is a totally different thing, a merely destructive thing; indeed, an entirely negative thing. It is as if a man were perpetually carving a statue and smashing it as soon as he carved it. . . . It is as if people began to dig up the foundations of a house before they had finished putting the roof on. . . . It is simply instability and discontent; and one of the marks of it is that it cannot create a custom. It cannot, for instance, create a ceremonial, still less a legend.

—Glass, 35

For a fashion is a custom without a cause. A fashion is a custom to which men cannot get accustomed; simply because it is without a cause.

—Irish, 48

In practice, the pursuit of pleasure is merely the pursuit of fashion. The pursuit of fashion is merely the pursuit of convention; only that it happens to be a new convention.

—Thing, 34

I knew that fashions had an extraordinary way of being first omnipresent and oppressive and then suddenly blank and forgotten.

—Thing, 88

Fat (on being called)

I need not say I do not mind being called fat; for deprived of that jest, I should be almost a serious writer. I do not even mind being supposed to mind being called fat. But being supposed to be contented, and contented with the present institutions of modern society, is a mortal slander I will not take from any man.

—*Diversity,* 160

Fate

Circumstances break men's bones; it has never been shown that they break men's optimism.

—*CD,* 31

Father Christmas (the Death of)

Something made me say, "You look ill Father Christmas."

"I am dying," he said.

I did not speak, and it was he who spoke again.

"All the new people have left my shop. I cannot understand it. They seem to object to me on such curious and inconsistent sort of grounds, these scientific men, and these innovators. They say that I give people superstitions and make them too visionary.... They say my heavenly parts are too heavenly; they say my earthly parts are too earthly; I don't know what they want, I'm sure. How can heavenly things be too heavenly, or earthly things too earthly? How can one be too good or too jolly? I don't understand. But I understand one thing well enough. These modern people are living and I am dead."

"You may be dead," I replied. "You ought to know. But as for what they are doing—do not call it living."

—*TT,* 302–303

Fear (the Origins of)

...fear does not come from fairy tales; the fear comes from the Universe of the soul.

—TT, 129

Feeble-minded Theory

By one of the monstrosities of the feeble-minded theory, a man actually acquitted by judge and jury could then be examined by doctors as to the state of his mind—presumably in order to discover by what diseased eccentricity he had refrained from the crime. In other words, when the police cannot jail a man who is innocent of doing something, they jail him for being too innocent to do anything.

—Evils, 171

Feminine Politics

Many have imagined that feminine politics would be merely pacifist or humanitarian or sentimental. The real danger of feminine politics is too much love of a masculine policy.

—Don Q, 240

Feudalism

All that was good in feudalism is gone; the good humour, the common sports, the apportioned duties, the fraternity that could live without equality. All that is bad in feudalism not only remains but grows, the caprice, the sudden cruelty, the offence to human dignity in the existence of slave and lord.

—GKC, 58

Fiction

The key of this new form of art, which we call fiction, is sympathy. And sympathy does not mean so much feeling with all who feel, but rather suffering with all who suffer.

—VA, 94

Fictitious Stories

That fictitious stories are told about a person is, nine times out of ten, extremely good evidence that there was somebody to tell them about. Indeed some allow that marvelous things were done, and that there may have been a man named Arthur at the time in which they were done; but here, so far as I am concerned, the distinction becomes rather dim. I do not understand the attitude which holds that there was an Ark and a man named Noah, but cannot believe in the existence of Noah's Ark.

—England, 24

Fighting

It is true that there is not, as pacifists and prigs imagine, the least inconsistency between loving men and fighting them, if we fight them fairly and for a good cause.

— St. Francis, 68

Finding the Right Road

For it is often necessary to walk backwards, as a man on the wrong road goes back to a signpost to find the right road. The modern man is more like a traveller who has forgotten the name of his destination, and has to go back whence he came, even to find out where he is going.

—NJ, 1

Finger-prints

The great science of Finger-Prints, discovered by a brilliant French criminologist, has produced its principal or ultimate effect on the world, which is this: that whereas a gentleman was expected to put on gloves to dance with a lady, he may now be expected to put on gloves in order to strangle her. These changes in etiquette, or fine shades of fashion, may or may not correspond with an improvement in dancing or a decrease in strangling.

—Avowals, 171

Focus

What Stevenson had, and what Stevenson's critics often have not and mistake for mere finesse, was a certain sharpness of *focus.* He did not deal merely with pretty figures, whether they were figures of speech or figures of fiction. On the contrary, he dealt oftener with ugly figures, and certainly enjoyed the ugly figures most. But all the figures are figures, and not merely presences or influences.

—Survey, 10

Fools

There is the same difference between a great fool and a small fool as there is between a great poet and a small poet. The great fool is a being who is above wisdom rather than below it.

—CD, 182

A man can be entirely great while he is entirely foolish. We see this in the epic heroes, such as Achilles. Nay, a man can be entirely great because he is entirely foolish. We see this in all the great comic characters of all the great comic writers of whom Dickens was the last.

—CD, 182

Which of us has not known, for instance, a great rustic? — A character so incurably characteristic that he seemed to break through all canons about cleverness or stupidity; we do not know whether he is an enormous idiot or an enormous philosopher; we know only that he is enormous like a hill.

—*CD*, 183

It may be noticed that the great artists always choose great fools rather than great intellectuals to embody humanity. Hamlet does express the aesthetic dreams and the bewilderments of the intellect; but Bottom the Weaver expresses them much better. In the same manner Toots expresses certain permanent dignities in human nature more than any of Dickens' more dignified characters can do it.

—*CD*, 186

There is an apostolic injunction to suffer fools gladly. We always lay the stress on the word suffer, and interpret the passage as one urging resignation. It might be better, perhaps, to lay the stress upon the word gladly, and make our familiarity with fools a delight, and almost a dissipation. Nor is it necessary that our pleasure in fools (or at least in great and godlike fools) should be merely satiric or cruel.

—*CD*, 186

The great fool is he in whom we cannot tell which is the conscious and which the unconscious humour; we laugh with him and laugh at him at the same time. An obvious instance is that of ordinary and happy marriage. A man and a woman cannot live together without having against each other a kind of everlasting joke. Each has discovered the other is a fool, but a great fool. This largeness, this grossness and gorgeousness of folly is the thing which we all find about those with whom we are in intimate contact; and it is the one enduring basis of affection, and even of respect.

—*CD*, 186–187

Fools

The way to be really a fool is to try to be practical about unpractical things.

−NJ, 77

Fools and Failures

"Yes," said Father Brown. "I'm rather fond of people who are fools and failures on their own confession."

"I don't know what you mean," snapped the other.

"Perhaps," said Father Brown wistfully, "it's because so many people are fools and failures without any confession."

−FBO, 905

Ford, Henry

Now Mr. Ford himself is a man of defiant limitations. He is so indifferent to history, for example, that he calmly admitted in the witness box that he had never heard of Benedict Arnold. An American who has never heard of Benedict Arnold is like a Christian who has never heard of Judas Iscariot.

−Outline, 177−178

Forgetting

Beware the man you forget, . . . he is the one man who has you entirely at a disadvantage.

−FBO, 703

Forgiving and Forgetting

It may be a good thing to forget and forgive; but it is altogether too easy a trick to forget and be forgiven.

—Crimes, 77

Fountains

...a fountain is itself a paradox. It is a sort of topsy-turvy prodigy designed to show that water can fall upwards or flow uphill. Water, which was bowed and humbled, for all its brightness, amid the rocks where St. Francis could stroke it like a living thing, is here flung aloft like a flying thing; as if the well could become a volcano. Water also was in a state of rebellion, or at least of resurrection.

—Rome, 11

France

The French Revolution was attacked because it was democratic and defended because it was democratic; and Napoleon was not feared as the last of the iron despots, but as the first of the iron democrats. What France set out to prove France has proved; not that common men are all angels, or all diplomatists, or all gentlemen (for their inane aristocratic illusions were no part of Jacobin theory), but that common men can all be citizens and can all be soldiers; that common men can fight and can rule.

—Crimes, 51

Free Love

They have invented a phrase, a phrase that is a black and white contradiction in two words—'free love'—as if a lover ever had been, or ever could be, free. It is the nature of love to bind itself, and the institution of marriage merely paid the average man the compliment of taking him at his word.

—D, 23

...a man perpetually endeavouring to be a free-lover ... is like endeavouring to be a married bachelor or a white negro.

—D, 24

Thus in love the free-lovers say: 'Let us have the splendour of offering ourselves without the peril of committing ourselves; let us see whether one cannot commit suicide an unlimited number of times.'

—D, 25

Free Speech

It is not natural or obvious to let a man utter follies and abominations which you believe to be bad for mankind anymore than it is natural or obvious to let a man dig up a part of the public road, or infect half a town with typhoid fever. The theory of free speech, that truth is so much larger and stranger and more many-sided than we know of, that it is very much better at all costs to hear every one's account of it, is a theory which has been justified upon the whole by experiment, but which remains a very daring and even a very surprizing theory. It is really one of the great discoveries of the modern time, but once admitted it is a principle that does not merely affect politics, but philosophy, ethics, and finally poetry.

—RB, 174

Free Thought

What is now called free thought is valued, not because it is free thought, but because it is freedom from thought: because it is free thoughtlessness.

—CCC, 86

Freedom

To be everlastingly passing through dangers which we know cannot scathe us, to be taking oaths which we know cannot bind us, to be defying enemies who we know cannot conquer us—this is the grinning tyranny of decadence which is called freedom.

—D, 21–22

The truth is that when people are in exceptionally high spirits, really wild with freedom and invention, they always must, and they always do, create institutions. When men are weary they fall into anarchy; but while they are gay and vigorous they invariably make rules. . . . We are never free until some institution frees us, and liberty cannot exist till it is declared by authority.

—Manalive, 63

We may say that the successful demagogue must denounce demagogy. We may say that the tyrant must despise popularity in order to be popular. The real question is that of the effect on freedom. Now we all agree about freedom. We all agree that we must not take liberty, except from people who take liberties. Unfortunately, it is those systems, which boast of not taking liberty, that do take liberties.

—Rome, 236

Freemasons

The part played by the Freemasons in the politics of every European country was a thing perfectly well known to every man in practical politics anywhere; but it was never discussed in Parliament; certainly it was never discussed by Parliamentarians as a danger to Parliamentarism. We need not discuss here all the various kinds of nonsense, on both sides, on the subject of the Freemasons. They were not Masons; they were certainly not Free; in their most important fields of action they were not even free to say that they were bound.

—Rome, 225

French Revolution

The great dominant idea of the whole of that period, the period before, during, and long after the revolution, is the idea that man would by his nature live in an Eden of dignity, liberty, and love, and that artificial and decrepit systems are keeping him out of that Eden.

—RB, 15

Freud, Sigmund

And the science of Freud would make it essentially impossible to say how far our reason or unreason does go, or where it stops. For if a man is ignorant of his other self, how can he possibly know that the other self is ignorant?

—NJ, 180

Fugitive Slave Law

Any law that sends a man back to his work, when he wants to leave it, is in plain fact a Fugitive Slave Law.

—Bio, 307

Futurists

. . . all the typical Utopias and futuristic world-systems of recent times, it is incessantly and impressively repeated that we must live for the Future, for the Young, for the Rising Generation or the Babe Unborn. The traditional obligations of the past are nothing, and even the temporary contracts and compromises of the present are comparatively little; but we really do have a duty to the future generations. It is apparently the only duty that remains. While we are kicking our grandfather downstairs, we must take care to be very polite to our great-great-grandson, who is not yet present; and if a more enlightened ethic should ever justify us in painlessly poisoning our mother, it will be well to distract the attention by dreaming of some perfect Woman of the Future who may never need to be poisoned.

—*AIG,* 171–172

If you ask me what futurism is, I cannot tell you; even the Futurists themselves seem a little doubtful; perhaps they are waiting for the future to find out.

—*Alarms,* 99

A brave man who wants Atheism in the future calls himself an Atheist; a brave man who wants Socialism, a Socialist; a brave man who wants Catholicism, a Catholic. But a weak-minded man who does not know what he wants in the future calls himself a Futurist.

—*Alarms,* 105

It is a beautiful and even blissful thought that, whatever happens, it will never be what the scientific futurists and fatalists have proved to be inevitable and quite certain to happen. Among many examples there has obviously been a recent Nationalist revival, not to say a Nationalist riot, in various parts of Europe, at the very moment when all prophets of evolutionary ethics have told us that Nationalism was fading from the world and Internationalism fated to take its place.

—*Avowals,* 87

The last Futurist draughtsmanship, for instance, evidently has the aim of drawing a tree as it might be drawn by a child of ten.

—*FVF,* 4

G

Gaelic

I suspect that many names and announcements are printed in Gaelic, not because Irishmen can read them, but because Englishmen can't.

—Irish, 140

Gamblers

Now, the temptation of that type of man is to do a mad thing precisely because the risk will be wonderful in retrospect. He wants to say, 'Nobody but I could have seized that chance or seen that it was then or never. . . . Anybody would say I was made to risk it; but that is how fortunes are made, by the man mad enough to have a little foresight.' In short, it is the vanity of guessing. It is the megalomania of the gambler. The more incongruous the coincidence, the more instantaneous the decision, the more likely he is to snatch the chance.

—FBO, 501–502

Gate-crashing

It means, as everyone knows, I imagine, the habit of certain hilarious parties of the new youth forcing or insinuating themselves into houses or gardens on festive occasions, where they doubtless display every charm and social qualification, except the slight formality of being acquainted with their host or having been invited by anybody.

—S, 42

Genius

I think there is one thing more important than the man of genius—and that is the genius of man.

—L & L, 182

The Gentleman

There is no such thing as being a gentleman at important moments; it is at unimportant moments that a man is a gentleman. At important moments he ought to be something better.

—HA, 130–131

George III

He was a fool who repeatedly relived the monotony of that fact by becoming a lunatic. If anything, he was quieter and less mischievous as a lunatic than he was as a fool.

—Glass, 76

German Re-armament

If a man in a street recently swept by gun-fights puts a cannon on his roof, puts on a new uniform and practices with a pistol in the garden, teaches his two sons to hack each other with sabres and flies a flag with a warlike motto, it is rather worse if he then looks over the wall and explains (like Hitler) that he does not mean to fight. Simple people will answer: "You are either a lunatic or a liar, who does intend to fight. The most respectful view is that you are a liar. The only other is one rather worse than both; that you are a bloody-minded fool who loves to talk and think about fighting, and who dare not fight."

—EA, 62–63

Gibbon, Edward

Gibbon is now a classic; that is, he is quoted instead of being read.

—Glass, 30

God

In short, I had always believed that the world involved magic: now I thought perhaps it involved a magician. And this pointed a profound emotion always present and sub-conscious; that this world of ours has some purpose; and if there is a purpose, there is a person. I had always felt life first as a story: and if there is a story there is a story-teller.

—O, 110

According to most philosophers, God in making the world enslaved it. According to Christianity, in making it, He set it free. God had written not so much a poem, but rather a play; a play he had planned as perfect, but which had necessarily been left to human actors and stagemanagers, who had since made a great mess of it.

—O, 143

The Golden Age

... the golden age only comes to men when they have, if only for a moment, forgotten gold.

—S, 143

Good Friday

All Christian people, whatever their lighter superstitions, have always thought Friday lucky. Otherwise they would have talked about Bad Friday instead of Good Friday.

—Poet, 181

Goodness

The homeless scepticism of our time has reached a sub-conscious feeling that morality is somehow merely a matter of human taste—an accident of psychology. And if goodness only exists in certain human minds, a man wishing to praise goodness will naturally exaggerate the amount of it that there is in human minds or the number of human minds in which it is supreme. Every confession that man is vicious is a confession that virtue is visionary. Every book which admits that evil is real is felt in some vague way to be admitting that good is unreal. The modern instinct is that if the heart of man is evil, there is nothing that remains good. But the older feeling was that if the heart of man was ever so evil, there was something that remained good—goodness remained good.

—ATC, 195–196

Göring, Herman

The world will not forget the weird psychological effect of the Prime Minister of Prussia shouting at a prisoner supposed to be receiving a fair trial, "You wait till I get you outside"; like a very low-class schoolboy threatening what he would do out of school. That sort of thing simply does not happen among civilised people; not even when they are very wicked people. How anybody can see such lunacy dancing in high places, in the broad daylight of political responsibility, and have any further doubt about the sort of danger that threatens the world, is more than I can understand.

—EA, 215–216

Gratitude

I would maintain that thanks are the highest form of thought; and that gratitude is happiness doubled by wonder.

—England, 59

Greed

. . . I do think there is something greedy about trying to enjoy the dinner and the concert at the same time. . . . Eating and drinking and talking have gone together by a tradition as old as the world; but the entrance of this fourth factor only spoils the other three. . . . It seems to me an intolerable insult to a musical artist that people should treat his art as an adjunct to a refined gluttony. It seems yet a more subtle insult to the musician that people should require to be fortified with food and drink at intervals, to strengthen them to endure his music. I say nothing of the deeper and darker insult to that other artist, the cook, in the suggestion that men require to be inspired and rallied with drums and trumpets to attack the dangers of his dinner, as if it were a fortress bustling with engines of death.

—Gen S, 165–166

The Grotesque

. . . there is another reason that makes it almost inevitable that we should defend grotesquely what we believe seriously. It is that all grotesqueness is itself intimately related to seriousness. Unless a thing is dignified, it cannot be undignified. Why is it funny that a man should sit down suddenly in

140

the street? There is only one possible or intelligent reason: that man is the image of God. It is not funny that anything else should fall down; only that a man should fall down. No one sees anything funny in a tree falling down. No one sees a delicate absurdity in a stone falling down. No man stops in the road and roars with laughter at the sight of the snow coming down. The fall of thunderbolts is treated with some gravity. The fall of roofs and high buildings is taken seriously. It is only when a man tumbles down that we laugh. Why do we laugh? Because it is a grave religious matter: it is the Fall of Man. Only man can be absurd: for only man can be dignified.

—ATC, 150

To present a matter in a grotesque manner does certainly tend to touch the nerve of surprise and thus to draw attention to the intrinsically miraculous character of the object itself. It is difficult to give examples of the proper use of grotesqueness without becoming too grotesque. But we should all agree that if St. Paul's Cathedral were suddenly presented to us upside down we should, for the moment, be more surprized at it, and look at it more than we have done all the centuries during which it has rested on its foundations.

—RB, 151

H

Happiness

Happiness is as grave and practical as sorrow, if not more so. We might as well imagine that a man could carve a cardboard chicken or live on imitation loaves of bread, as suppose that any man could get happiness out of things that are merely light or laughable. The really frivolous man, not unknown in fashionable circles, is the man who is too frivolous to enjoy himself.

—HA, 3

Hatred

. . . hatred is beautiful, when it is hatred of the ugliness of the soul.

—Crimes, 119

It never does a man any very great harm to hate a thing that he knows nothing about. It is the hating of a thing when we do know something about it which corrodes the character.

—RB, 114

Head of the House

... even if the man is the head of a house he knows he is the figurehead.

—ATC, 14

Health

The mere pursuit of health always leads to something unhealthy. Physical nature must not be made the direct object of obedience; it must be enjoyed, not worshipped.

—O, 140

Hegel (and No-Hegel)

The Moron refuses to admit that Hegel can both exist and not exist; or that it can be possible to understand Hegel, if there is no Hegel to understand.

—STA, 146–147

Heredity

A man kills because he is blackmailed, or because he is jilted, or because he is a political fanatic, and so on. But how do you inherit a blackmailer, or an unreliable girl, or a political theory? There certainly is inheritance, as of physical type, perhaps of physical temperament, of being indolent or restless and so on. But the number of lazy men who will murder a valet for waking them up is about as large as the number of impatient men who will murder him for keeping them waiting. That is to say, it is very small. The mysterious moral inhibition, or its absence, by which men do or do not murder, is in the individual soul; and I defy anybody to show that it is hereditary.

—AIG, 121

143

Heresy

Heresy always does affect morality, if it's heretical enough. I suppose a man may honestly believe that thieving isn't wrong. But what's the good of saying that he honestly believes in dishonesty?

—FBO, 919

The word "heresy" not only means no longer being wrong; it practically means being clear-headed and courageous. The word "orthodoxy" not only no longer means being right; it practically means being wrong. . . . It means that people care less for whether they are philosophically right. For obviously a man ought to confess himself crazy before he confesses himself heretical.

—H, 4

Heroes (Modern Literary)

When a modern novel is devoted to the bewilderments of a weak young clerk who cannot decide which woman he wants to marry, or which new religion he believes in, we still give this knock-kneed cad the name of "the hero"—the name which is the crown of Achilles.

—CD, 62–63

It is an odd thing that the words hero and heroine have in their constant use in connection with literary fiction entirely lost their meaning. A hero now means merely a young man sufficiently decent and reliable to go through a few adventures without hanging himself or taking to drink.

—HA, 72

Historical Determinism

The man who represents all thought as an accident of environment is simply smashing and discrediting all his own thoughts—including that one.

—TT, 92

Historical Interpretation (Progressive)

It is an amusing fact, by the way, that the quaint old legend, which Protestant prejudice set afloat some sixty years ago, to the effect that the Pope once condemned the study of Chemistry, really referred to this very fact; the fact that medieval religion did attempt to restrain medieval avarice. What the Pope did condemn was the practice of certain quack astrologers and alchemists, who used to go round to houses of poor people and take away all their pots and pans with the promise of turning them all into gold. Against this great step in scientific progress the Pope did indeed set his face with ferocious medieval bigotry. If any modern moral authority were to condemn the somewhat similar students of the Art of Salesmanship, who go round tempting poor people to run into debt for all sorts of furniture and appliances for which they cannot ultimately pay, I for one should welcome such an outburst of Papal persecution. But I have no doubt that the progressive historian would give a simple summary of the incident; by saying that it was made a moral sin to have any chairs and tables.

—C, 63

Historical Materialism

The great human dogma, then, is that the wind moves the trees. The great human heresy is that the trees move the wind. When people begin to say that the material circumstances have alone created the moral circumstances, then they have prevented all possibility of serious change. For if my circumstances have made me wholly stupid, how can I be certain even that I am right in altering those circumstances?

—TT, 92

History

There is no more remarkable psychological element in history than the way in which a period can suddenly become unintelligible.

—GFW, 10

You cannot be just in history. Have enthusiasm, have pity, have quietude and observation, but do not imagine that you will have what you call truth. Applaud, admire, reverence, denounce, execrate. But judge not, that ye be not judged.

—L & L, 49

History is like some deeply planted tree which, though gigantic in girth, tapers away at last into tiny twigs; and we are in the topmost branches.

—MM, 20–21

History does not consist of completed and crumbling ruins, rather it consists of half-built villas abandoned by a bankrupt-builder. This world is more like an unfinished suburb than a deserted cemetery.

—WW, 53

History and Sociology

History and sociology can never be 'scientific' in the sense of subject to exact measurement, because there is always the mystery and doubt inherent in moral evidence affecting one half of the equation, and generally both.

—Survey, 48–49

History (Outline of)

For instance, the general theory implied in a book like the *Outline of History* is that the outline is a continuous and ascending line, a single upward curve with very few breaks in it. I do not mean that the author denies decay and reaction, but that the main moral he would like to draw is that the host of humanity has advanced, with a few halts, along the high road of history. Above all, he implies a human unity, and the idea that the host that has halted is the same as the host that has advanced. I think myself that he greatly exaggerates this continuity; leans too heavily on the alleged links, and especially misses the missing links. He makes the amoeba and the anthropoid much nearer to us than they really are. At the same time, he makes the ancient Greek or the medieval Christian much more inferior to us than they really are.

—Survey, 49

History (Teaching of)

It is very unlucky that for some time our teaching of history has been rather the unteaching of history, because it has been the unteaching of tradition.

—Diversity, 61

Hobbes as Hitlerite

Hobbes was a Rationalist hating every trace and tradition of the old religious sentiment. But Hobbes was a Royalist, in the sense that his despotic theory of the State involved the implication of a royal despot. Indeed, Hobbes was a Hitlerite, and his whole theory of the Totalitarian State turns on a pivot of personal government.

—AIWS, 15ʳ

Holidays

A bank holiday means presumably a day which bankers regard as holy. A half-holiday means, I suppose, a day on which a schoolboy is only partially holy.

—H, 93

Homeric Unity

What is called Homeric unity may be a fact or not. The Iliad may have been written by one man. It may have been written by a hundred men. But let us remember that there was more unity in those times in a hundred men than there is unity now in one man. Then a city was like one man. Now one man is like a city in civil war.

—GKC, 36

Hope

It is currently said that hope goes with youth, and lends to youth its wings of a butterfly; but I fancy that hope is the last gift given to man, and the only gift not given to youth. Youth is pre-eminently the period in which a man can be lyric, fanatical, poetic; but youth is the period in which a man can be hopeless. The end of every episode is the end of the world. But the power of hoping through everything, the knowledge that the soul survives its adventures, that great inspiration comes to the middle-aged; God has kept that good wine until now. It is from the backs of the elderly gentlemen that the wings of the butterfly should burst.

—CD, 26–27

Call it faith, call it vitality, call it the will to live, call it the religion of tomorrow morning, call it the immortality of man, call it self-love and vanity; it is the thing that explains why man survives all things and why there is no such thing as a pessimist. It cannot be found in any dictionary or rewarded in any commonwealth: there is only one way in which it can even be noticed and recognized. If there be anywhere a man who has really lost it, his face out of a whole crowd of men will strike us like a blow. He may hang himself or become Prime Minister; it matters nothing. The man is dead.

—GFW, 49

Hope and Allegory

It represents a certain definite thing, the word "hope." But what does the word "hope" represent? It represents only a broken instantaneous glimpse of something that is immeasurably older and wilder than language, that is immeasurably older and wilder than man; a mystery to saints and a reality to wolves. To suppose that such a thing is dealt with by the word "hope," any more than America is represented by a distant view of Cape Horn would indeed be ridiculous. It is not merely true that the word itself is, like any other word, arbitrary; that it might as well be "pig" or "parasol"; but it is true that the philosophical meaning of the word, in the conscious mind of man, is merely part of something immensely larger in the unconscious mind, that the gusty light of language only falls for a moment on a fragment, and that obviously a semi-detached, unfinished fragment of a certain definite pattern on the dark tapestries of reality. It is vain and worse than vain to declaim against the allegoric, for the very word "hope" is an allegory, and the very word "allegory" is an allegory.

—GFW, 46–47

House of Lords

There is one really good defense of the House of Lords, though admirers of the peerage are strangely coy about using it; and that is, that the House of Lords, in its full and proper strength, consists of stupid men. It really would be a plausible defense of that otherwise indefensible body to point out that the clever men in the Commons, who owed their power to cleverness, ought in the last resort to be checked by the average men in the Lords, who owed their power to accident.

—H, 272–273

Human Body

The Catholic argument can be put shortly by saying that there is nothing the matter with the human body; what is the matter is with the human soul.

—Thing, 186

Human Condition

It is the misfortune of the non-religious ages that they tend to cultivate a sense of individuality, not only at the expense of religion, but at the expense of humanity itself.

—GFW, 69

Human Nature

Can you alter human nature? In strict logic and philosophy, if you could actually alter the nature of human beings they would cease to be human beings. So you could not really point to them as human beings whose nature had been altered.

—AIWS, 145

Human Race

The human race, according to religion, fell once, and in falling gained the knowledge of good and evil. Now we have fallen a second time, and only the knowledge of evil remains to us.

—H, 24

Humanists

But I do most heartily agree with them in one thing, and it seems to me very much the most important thing. It is substantially this. The Humanist says to the Humanitarian: 'You are always telling me to forget divine things and think of human things. And then you talk to me eagerly and earnestly about the pathetic helplessness of human beings, their faulty environment, their fatal heredity, their obvious animal origins, their uncontrollable animal instincts, ending with the old fatalist cry that we must forgive everything because there is nothing to forgive. But these things are not the *human things*. These are specially and specifically the subhuman things; the things we share with nature and the animals. The specially and outstandingly human things are exactly the things that you dismiss as merely divine things. The human things are free will and responsibility and authority and self-denial, because they exist only in humanity.'

—Survey, 74–75

Humanitarians

Humanitarians of a material and dogmatic type, the philanthropists and the professional reformers go to look for humanity in remote places and in huge statistics. Humanitarians of a more vivid type, the Bohemian artists, go to look for humanity in thieves' kitchens and the studios of the Quartier Latin. But Humanitarians of the highest type, the great poets and philosophers, do not go to look for humanity at all. For them alone among all men the nearest drawing-room is full of humanity, and even their own families are human.

—RB, 111

Humanity (Divine Origin of)

The great conception at the back of the oldest religions in the world is, of course, the conception that man is of divine origin, a sacred and splendid heir, the eldest son of the universe. But humanity could not in practice carry out this conception that everyone was divine. The practical imagina-

151

tion recoils from the idea of two gods swindling each other over a pound of cheese. The mind refuses to accept the idea of sixty bodies, each filled with blazing divinity, elbowing each other to get into an omnibus.

—HA, 72–73

Humility

A god can be humble, a devil can only be humbled.

—BC, 279

The new philosophy of self-esteem and self-assertion declares that humility is a vice. If it be so, it is quite clear that it is one of those vices which are an integral part of original sin. . . . Humility, again, is said . . . to be the peculiar growth of Christianity. . . . But the essence of Christianity was in a literal sense the New Testament—a convenant with God which opened to men a clear deliverance. They thought themselves secure;. . . . they believed themselves rich with an irrevocable benediction which set them above the stars; and immediately they discovered humility. It was only another example of the same immutable paradox. It is always the secure who are humble.

—D, 99

Upon one point and one point only, was there really a moral revolution that broke the back of human history. And that was upon the point of Humility. There was this definite thing about the best Pagan; that in him dignity did mean pride. It was a change that stood alone; and was worthy to stand alone. For it was the greatest psychological discovery that man has made, since man has sought to know himself.

—EA, 218

Humility is the mother of giants. One sees great things from the valley; only small things from the peak.

—FBO, 173

Humility is so practical a virtue that men think it must be a vice. Humility is so successful that it is mistaken for pride. It is mistaken for it all the more easily because it generally goes with a certain simple love of splendour which amounts to vanity. . . . In a word, the failure of this virtue actually lies in its success; it is too successful as an investment to be believed in as a virtue. Humility is not merely too good for this world; it is too practical for this world; I had almost said it is too worldly for this world.

—H, 64–65

No great works will seem great, and no wonders of the world will seem wonderful, unless the angle from which they are seen is that of historical humility.

—NJ, 78

. . . the old humility made a man doubtful about his efforts, which might make him work harder. But the new humility makes a man doubtful about his aims, which will make him stop working altogether.

—O, 56

Humour (Modern)

By the wholesome tradition of mankind, a joke was a thing meant to amuse men; a joke which did not amuse them was a failure, just as a fire which did not warm them was a failure. . . . If a joke falls flat, a small school of aesthetes only ask us to notice the wild grace of its falling and its perfect flatness after its fall. The old idea that the joke was not good enough for the company has been superseded by the new aristocratic idea that the company was not worthy of the joke. They have introduced an almost insane individualism into that one form of intercourse which is specially and uproariously communal. They have made even levities into secrets. They have made laughter lonelier than tears.

—ATC, 175

The old jester was disappointed that men did not see the joke. The new jester is delighted that they do not see the joke. Their blank faces are a proof of his own exquisite and individualised talent; the joke is too good to be seen. Laughter has been from the beginning the one indestructable brotherhood, the one undeniably social thing. But these moderns have made even laughter a lonely thing. They are always hunting for a humour that shall be completely original. But if a thing were completely original it would be completely unintelligible.

—HA, 31

Humorists

All men are mad, but the humourist, who cares for nothing and possesses everything.

—NNH, 65

Hypocrites

For the worst and most dangerous hypocrite is not he who affects unpopular virtue, but he who affects popular vice. The jolly fellow of the saloon bar and the race course is the real deceiver of mankind; he has misled more than any false prophet, and his victims cry to him out of hell.

—CD, 134

A man driven absolutely into a corner might humiliate himself, and gain a certain sensation almost of luxury in that humiliation, in pouring out all his imprisoned thoughts and obscure victories. For let it never be forgotten that a hypocrite is a very unhappy man; he is a man who has devoted himself to a most delicate and arduous intellectual art in which he may achieve masterpieces which he must keep secret, fight thrilling battles, and win hair's-breadth victories for which he cannot have a whisper of praise. A really accomplished imposter is the most wretched of geniuses; he is a Napoleon on a desert island.

—RB, 197–198

Hypothesis

The form it took here was the repeated suggestion that a Modern person cannot believe in anything except as a hypothesis. In other words, that he cannot believe in anything at all. For you cannot believe in a hypothesis; you can only give it a fair chance to prove itself a thesis that can be believed.

—AIWS, 142

I

Ibsen, Henrik

Ibsen himself was in spirit and essence always the enemy of the people; far more the enemy of the people than poor Nietzsche. To this day those few of the real people who have heard his name hate it.

In all this he was sincere beyond the point of sublimity. He had the largest kind of courage and what commonly goes with courage—simplicity. I cannot understand those who regard him as a mere artist. He seems to me to be as fierce as Mr. Bernard Shaw upon his own dogma. Only, as in the case of Mr. Bernard Shaw, his dogma is that there is no dogma.

—HA, 138

Idealistic Movements (Modern)

I have often been haunted with a fancy that the creeds of men might be paralleled and represented in their beverages. Wine might stand for genuine Catholicism and ale for genuine Protestantism; for these at least are real religions with comfort and strength in them. Clean cold Agnosticism would be clean cold water, an excellent thing, if you can get it. Most modern ethical and idealistic movements might be well represented by soda-water—which is a fuss about nothing.

—Blake, 98–99

Ideals (Modern)

Every one of the popular modern phases and ideals is a dodge in order to shirk the problem of what is good. We are fond of talking about "liberty"; that, as we talk of it, is a dodge to avoid discussing what is good. We are fond of talking about "progress"; that is a dodge to avoid discussing what is good. . . . The modern man says, "Let us leave all these arbitrary standards and embrace liberty." This is, logically rendered, "Let us not decide what is good, but let it be considered good not to decide it." He says, "Away with your old moral formulae; I am for progress." This, logically stated, means, "Let us not settle what is good; but let us settle whether we are getting more of it."

—H, 25–26

Ideas

It was enough for our youth to show that our ideas were suggestive; it is the task of our senility and second childhood to show that they are conclusive.

—Come, XIII

General ideas used to dominate literature. They have been driven out by the cry of "art for art's sake." General ideas used to dominate politics. They have been driven out by the cry of "efficiency," which may roughly be translated as "politics for politics' sake". . . . General theories of the relation of things have thus been extruded from both; and we are in a position to ask, "What have we gained or lost by this extrusion? Is literature better, is politics better, for having discarded the moralist and the philosopher?

—H, 9

Ideas are dangerous, but the man to whom they are least dangerous is the man of ideas. He is acquainted with ideas, and moves among them like a lion-tamer. Ideas are dangerous but the man to whom they are most dangerous is the man of no ideas. The man of no ideas will find the first idea fly to his head like wine to the head of a teetotaller.

—H, 299

Ideas (Modern)

There exists a misunderstanding rather than a quarrel about medieval and modern ideas; because the two do not meet on the same plane. The medieval world, with all its crimes and crudities, was intensely concerned with ideas as ideas; and not in the least concerned with them as medieval ideas. But the moderns, and especially the modernists, are intensely concerned with the fact the modern ideas are modern. They are sometimes so much excited about it that they neglect to make them anything like ideas.

—C, 58

Ideas (Original)

A man who is vague in his ideas does not speak obscurely, because his own dazed and drifting condition leads him to clutch at phrases like ropes and use the formulae that everyone understands. . . . But if a young man really has ideas of his own, he must be obscure at first, because he lives in a world of his own in which there are symbols and correspondences and categories unknown to the rest of the world.

—RB, 38

Images (Graven)

They speak more truly than they know who say that the sign and scandal of the Catholic Church is the Graven Image. The Church forbids us to worship it save as a symbol; but as a symbol it is most solidly symbolic. For it stands for this strange mania of Certitude, without which Rome will remain a riddle; it stands for the intolerant and intolerable notion that something is really true; true in every aspect and from every angle; true from the four quarters of the sky; true by the three dimensions of the Trinity. We turn from it and it does not vanish; we analyze it and it does not dissolve; at last, after long and laborious experiments in scepticism, we are forced to believe our eyes.

—Rome, 74–75

Imagination

The prime function of imagination is to see our whole orderly system of life as a pile of stratified revolutions. In spite of all revolutionaries it must be said that the function of imagination is not to make strange things settled, so much as to make settled things strange; not so much to make wonders facts as to make facts wonders. To the imaginative the truisms are all paradoxes, since they were paradoxes in the Stone Age; to them the ordinary copy-book blazes with blasphemy.

—D, 60

No man has less right to be lawless than a man of imagination. For he has spiritual adventures, and can take his holidays when he likes.

—MWKTM, 336

The most essential educational product is Imagination.

—S, 62

Imitating Oneself

This tendency is, of course, the result of self-consciousness and theatricality of modern life in which each of us is forced to conceive ourselves as part of a *dramatis personae* and act perpetually in character.

—RB, 142

Imitation

... almost all original poets, particularly poets who have invented an artistic style, are subject to one most disastrous habit—the habit of writing imitations of themselves. Every now and then in the works of the noblest classical poets you will come upon passages which read like extracts from an American book of parodies.

—RB, 142

Every young writer, however original, does begin by imitating other people, consciously or unconsciously, and nearly every old writer would be quite as willing to admit it.

—RLS, 96

Immoral Attitudes

In the fifteenth Century men cross-examined and tormented a man because he preached some immoral attitude; in the nineteenth Century we fêted and flattered Oscar Wilde because he preached such an attitude, and then broke his heart in penal servitude because he carried it out. It may be a question which of the two methods was the more cruel; there can be no kind of question which was the more ludicrous. The Age of the Inquisition has not at least the disgrace of having produced a society which made an idol of the very same man for preaching the very same things which it made him a convict for practicing.

—H, 8

Impartiality

There is something that is higher than impartiality, and Macaulay possessed it; poetical justice; the living impartiality of the imagination rather than the dead impartiality of the reason.

—HA, 108

Impressionism

Impressionism is scepticism. It means believing one's immediate impressions at the expense of one's more permanent and positive generalisations. It puts what one notices above what one knows. It means the monstrous heresy that seeing is believing.

—*Blake,* 137–138

Improvement

Nobody seems to have any notion of improving anything except by pouring it into something else; as if a man were to pour the tea into the coffee or the sherry into the port. The one idea in all human things, from friendship to finance, is to pool everything. It is a very stagnant pool.

—*S,* 18

Incomprehensible Things

Agnosticism (which has, I am sorry to say, almost entirely disappeared from the modern world) is always an admirable thing, so long as it admits that the thing which it does not understand may be much superior to the mind which does not understand it. Thus if you say that the cosmos is incomprehensible, and really mean (as most moderns do) that it is not worth comprehending; then it would be much better for your Greek agnosticism if it were called by its Latin name of ignorance. But there is one thing that any man can fairly consider incomprehensible, and yet in some ways superior. There is one thing that any man may worry about, and still respect; I mean any woman.

—*HA,* 163

The Indefinable

The thing that cannot be defined is the first thing; the primary fact. It is our arms and legs, our pots and pans, that are indefinable. The indefinable is the indisputable. The man next door is indefinable, because he is too actual to be defined. And there are some to whom spiritual things have the same fierce and practical proximity; some to whom God is too actual to be defined.

$-CD,$ 3

Independent Intellect

Putting aside the strict sense of a Catholic courage, the world ought to be told something about Catholic intellectual independence. It is, of course, the one quality which the world supposes that Catholics have lost. It is also, at this moment, the one quality which Catholics perceive that all the world has lost. The modern world has many marks, good as well as bad; but by far the most modern thing in it is the abandonment of individual reason, in favour of press stunts and suggestion and mass psychology and mass production. The Catholic Faith, which always preserves the unfashionable virtue, is at this moment alone sustaining the independent intellect of man.

$-Thing,$ 163–164

The Individual (Sanctity of)

All men matter. You matter. I matter. It's the hardest thing in theology to believe.

$-FBO,$ 846

Information (Political)

It is enough to note, as one aspect of the rudeness and delay of medieval communications, that revolutions could occur in one part of the country without the most powerful persons, in another part of the country, having even the power to parley with them. And if, on the other hand, something happened about which any parley was undesirable, there was then no really efficient machinery for keeping the public misinformed on the matter.

—C, 265

Ingratitude

Ingratitude is surely the chief of the intellectual sins of man. He takes his political benefits for granted, just as he takes the skies and the seasons for granted. He considers the calm of a city street a thing as inevitable as the calm of a forest clearing, whereas it is only kept in peace by a sustained stretch and effort similar to that which keeps up a battle or a fencing match. Just as we forget where we stand in relation to natural phenomena, so we forget it in relation to social phenomena. We forget that the earth is a star, and we forget that free speech is a paradox.

—RB, 173–174

Inn (English)

You can find good English inns left by accident everywhere, like fossils. . . .

— Thursday, 88

Inspiration

A good man might possibly be prompted by a bad spirit; and in any case a man is himself also a spirit. And it seems to me nearer to the true Christian tradition to hold that man creates in his capacity of the image of God; and he is in nothing so much the image of God as in creating images. On the other hand, it is by no means impossible that such direct and all but divine creation might be deflected and confused, if he merely listened to all the loose elemental forces that might be wandering about in the universe. It seems to me that this did, in fact, very often happen, in the actual history of literature.

—HA, 78

Very great men have certainly talked of being inspired, but I doubt if it was when they were most great.

To take a famous case, William Blake certainly did claim that his works were sometimes dictated by more exalted spirits. But what works did the exalted spirits dictate? With the most polite apologies to them, and with the warmest and even wildest admiration for Blake, I think that any impartial person, reading steadily through some of his most specially inspired Prophetical Books, will form a rather low opinion of the lucidity and capacity for connected narrative shown by the presiding angels.

—HA, 78–79

Intellect

I think there would be a case for maintaining this: that the world has improved in everything *except* intellect. . . . I think that most modern people are much stupider than those in the age of my father, and probably very much stupider than those in the age of my grandfather. I have reasons for my belief, but it illustrates my point that the modern reader would hardly listen to a long process of reasoning. I believe I could even prove it, if people now were patient enough to listen to proof.

—AIG, 26–27

When a thing of the intellect is settled it is not dead: rather it is immortal.

—ATC, 61

My friend said that he opened his intellect as the sun opens the fans of a palm tree, opening for opening's sake, opening infinitely for ever. But I said that I opened my intellect as I opened my mouth, in order to shut it again on something solid.

— TT, 34–35

Intellectual Vanity

A man who is intellectually vain does not make himself incomprehensible, because he is so enormously impressed with the difference between his readers' intelligence and his own that he talks down to them with elaborate repetition and lucidity. What poet was ever vainer than Byron? What poet was ever so magnificently lucid? But a young man of genius who has a genuine humility in his heart does not elaborately explain his discoveries, because he does not think that they are discoveries.

—RB, 37–38

Intellectual World

What we call the intellectual world is divided into two types of people — those who worship the intellect and those who use it. There are exceptions; but, broadly speaking, they are never the same people. Those who use the intellect never worship it; they know too much about it. Those who worship the intellect never use it; as you can see by the things they say about it.

— Thing, 47

Intellectualism

Detached intellectualism is (in the exact sense of a popular phrase) all moonshine; for it is light without heat, and it is secondary light, reflected from a dead world.

—O, 50

Intellectuals

It did not seem to occur to such controversialists that if Cardinal Newman was really a man of intellect, the fact that he adhered to dogmatic religion proved exactly as much as the fact that Professor Huxley, another man of intellect, found that he could not adhere to dogmatic religion; that is to say (as I cheerfully admit), it proved precious little either way. If there is one class of men whom history has proved especially and supremely capable of going quite wrong in all directions, it is the class of highly intellectual men.

—ATC, 155–156

. . . you don't need any intellect to be an intellectual. . . .

—FBO, 830

Intelligence

Modern intelligence won't accept anything on authority. But it will accept anything without authority.

—MWKTM, 180

Intelligence does exist even in the Intelligentsia. It does sometimes happen that a man of real talent has a weakness for flattery, even the flattery of fools. He would rather say something that silly people think clever than something which only clever people could perceive to be true.

— Thing, 48

Internationalism

But internationalism is not a religion; it is an "ism"; and an "ism" is never a religion. It is an abstraction without being an absolute. Now, a nation is a thing; it may be a bad thing or a deplorable thing, but it is a thing and not a theory.

—Avowals, 88–89

In one sense what is Catholic must be international; but it is never quite normal if it is not also national. When people try to thrust mere internationalism down the throat of Catholic nations, there is always a violent national reaction. . . . For Catholics know in their bones that men are citizens of a city, and not merely of a cosmos; and that the hearth is sacred as well as the altar.

—Rome, 210

Interruptions

. . . he who has the impatience to interrupt the words of another seldom has the patience rationally to select his own.

—Judgement, 24

The Irish

The Irish believe far too much in spirits to believe in spiritualism.

—MWKTM, 53

Irony (Human)

For it is another example of the human irony that it seems easier to die in battle than to tell the truth in politics.

—Bio, 264

Irony (Infernal)

Sometimes it is a joy in the very heart of hell to tell the truth. And, above all, to tell it so that everybody misunderstands it.

—FBO, 763

Isolation and Comraderie

... there are no words to express the abyss between isolation and having one ally. It may be conceded to the mathematicians that four is twice two. But two is not twice one; two is two thousand times one. That is why, in spite of a hundred disadvantages, the world will always return to monogamy.

— *Thursday,* 89

J

Jazz

For one thing, the nightmare of noise, recalling the horns of hell rather than the horns of elfland, is generally accompanied by that undercurrent of battering monotony which I believe is supposed to be one of the charms of jazz. And without professing to know much about music, I have formed a very strong impression about jazz. It does express something; and what it expresses is slavery. That is why the same sort of thrill can be obtained by the throb of savage tom-toms, in music or drama connected with the great slaveland of Africa.

—Avowals, 102–103

Jazz is the very reverse of an expression of liberty, or even an excessive expression of liberty, or even an expression of license. It is the expression of the pessimist idea that nature never gets beyond nature, that life never rises above life, that man always finds himself back where he was at the beginning, that there is no revolt, no redemption, no escape for the slaves of the earth and of the desires of the earth. There is any amount of pessimistic poetry on that theme that is thrilling enough in its own way; and doubtless the music on that theme can be thrilling also. But it cannot be liberating, or even loosening; it does not escape as a common or vulgar melody can escape. It is the Song of the Treadmill.

—Avowals, 103

Jazz and Cocktails

I do not demand a high place in English letters, or a prominent position in the Golden Treasury, for the chorus of my youth which ran "Beer, beer, glorious beer, fill yourself right up to here." But I do say that nobody, after consuming any number of cocktails, has yet been inspired to cry aloud anything so spirited and spontaneous and direct. The poetry inspired by cocktails is timid and torturous and self conscious and indirect. I do not say that the song beginning "Daisy, Daisy," is one of the supreme achievements of the English muse, but I do say that it is a song that can be sung. And in the age of jazz and cocktails, men either write songs that could not possibly be sung, or leave off writing songs and write fragments of a demented diary instead.

—Avowals, 104–105

Jerusalem

Jerusalem is a small town of big things; and the average modern city is a big town full of small things. All the most important and interesting powers in history are here gathered within the area of a quiet village; and if they are not always friends, at least they are necessarily neighbors.

—NJ, 113

A voice not of my reason but rather sounding heavily in my heart, seemed to be repeating sentences like pessimistic proverbs. There is no place for the Temple of Solomon but on the ruins of the Mosque of Omar. There is no place for the nation of the Jews but in the country of the Arabs. And these whispers came to me first not as intellectual conclusions upon the conditions of the case, of which I should have much more to say and to hope, but rather as hints of something immediate and menacing and yet mysterious. I felt almost a momentary impulse to flee from the place, like one who has received an omen. For two voices had met in my ears; and within the same narrow space and in the same dark hour, electric and yet eclipsed with cloud, I had heard Islam crying from the turret and Israel wailing at the wall.

—NJ, 127

Jesus Christ

Joy, which was the small publicity of the pagan, is the gigantic secret of the Christian. . . . The tremendous figure which fills the Gospels towers in this respect, as in every other, above all the thinkers who ever thought themselves tall. His pathos was natural, almost casual. The Stoics, ancient and modern, were proud of concealing their tears. He never concealed His tears; He showed them plainly on His open face at any daily sight, such as the far sight of His native city. Yet He concealed something. Solemn supermen and imperial diplomatists are proud of restraining their anger. He never restrained His anger. He flung furniture down the front steps of the Temple. . . . Yet He restrained something. I say it with reverence; there was in that shattering personality a thread that must be called shyness. There was something that He hid from all men when He went up a mountain to pray. There was something that He covered constantly by abrupt silence or impetuous isolation. There was some one thing that was too great for God to show us when He walked upon our earth; and I have sometimes fancied that it was His mirth.

—*O*, 298–299

To begin with, we must protest against a habit of quoting and paraphrasing at the same time. When a man is discussing what Jesus meant, let him state first of all what He said, not what the man thinks He would have said if he had expressed Himself more clearly.

—*Types*, 141

Jews

I lived to have later on the name of an Anti-Semite; whereas from my first days at school I very largely had the name of a Pro-Semite. I made many friends among the Jews, and some of these I have retained as life long friends; nor have our relations ever been disturbed by differences upon the political or social problems. I am glad that I began at this end; but I have not really ended any differently from the way in which I began. I held by instinct then, and I hold by knowledge now, that the right way is to be interested in Jews as Jews: and then to bring into greater prominence the very much neglected Jewish virtues, which are the complement and sometimes even the cause of what the world feels to be the Jewish faults.

—Bio, 70

When the Jew in France or in England says he is a good patriot he only means that he is a good citizen, and he would put it more truly if he said he was a good exile.

—NJ, 285

Joan of Arc

I have seen long and learned German arguments, showing that Joan of Arc was a German; because she was brave and true and pious and lived in Lorraine. A young woman lives and dies to crown the French King in the French shrine, fights under the French oriflamme to clear the French soil of foreigners; and the German professors say she was a German.

—EA, 74

We *know* that she was not afraid of an army, while Nietzsche, for all we know, was afraid of a cow. Tolstoy only praised the peasant; she was the peasant. Nietzsche only praised the warrior; she was the warrior. She beat them both at their own antagonistic ideals; she was more gentle than the one, more violent than the other. Yet she was a perfectly practical person who did something, while they are wild speculators who do nothing.

—O, 78–79

Jokes

Nothing has been worse than the modern notion that a clever man can make a joke without taking part in it; without sharing in the general absurdity that such a situation creates. It is unpardonable conceit not to laugh at your own jokes. Joking is undignified; that is why it is so good for one's soul. Do not fancy you can be a detached wit and avoid being a buffoon; you cannot. If you are the Court Jester you must be the Court Fool.

—Alarms, 201

Journalism

It is the one great weakness of journalism as a picture of our modern existence, that it must be a picture made up entirely of exceptions. We announce on flaring posters that a man has fallen off a scaffolding. We do not announce on flaring posters that a man has not fallen off a scaffolding. Yet this latter fact is fundamentally more exciting, as indicating that that moving tower of terror and mystery, a man, is still abroad upon the earth. That the man has not fallen off a scaffolding is really more sensational; and it is also some thousand times more common. But journalism cannot reasonably be expected thus to insist upon the permanent miracles. Busy editors cannot be expected to put on their posters, "Mr. Wilkinson still safe," or "Mr. Jones, of Worthing, not dead yet."

—BC, 68–69

Writing badly is the definition of journalism.

—HA, 202

...no man of the world believes all he sees in the newspaper; and no journalist believes a quarter of it.

—Tyranny, 34

Journalism and Politics

Of course, politics and journalism are, as it happens, very vulgar. But their vulgarity is not the worst thing about them. Things are so bad with both that by this time their vulgarity is the best thing about them.

—ATC, 33

Journalism (Anonymous)

Anonymous journalism is dangerous, and is poisonous in our existing life simply because it is so rapidly becoming an anonymous life. That is the horrible thing about our contemporary atmosphere. Society is becoming a secret society. The modern tyrant is evil because of his elusiveness. He is more nameless than his slave.... We are suffering from the shyness of tyrants; from the shrinking modesty of tyrants. Therefore we must not encourage leader-writers to be shy; we must not inflame their already exaggerated modesty. Rather we must attempt to lure them to be vain and ostentatious; so that through ostentation they may at last find their way to honesty.

—ATC, 7–8

Journalism (New)

The chief characteristic of the "New Journalism" is simply that it is bad journalism. It is beyond all comparison the most shapeless, careless, and colorless work done in our day.

—H, 117

Journalism (School for)

I say it with no particular hostility or bitterness, but it is a fact that the school of commerce or the school of journalism might almost as well be called a school of impudence or a school of swagger or a school of grab and greed.

—S, 89

Journalists

... there exists in the modern world, perhaps for the first time in history, a class of people whose interest is not that things should happen well or happen badly, should happen successfully or happen unsuccessfully, should happen to the advantage of this party or the advantage of that party, but whose interest simply is that things should happen.

—*BC,* 68

They cannot announce the happiness of mankind at all. They cannot describe all the forks that are not stolen, or all the marriages that are not judiciously dissolved. Hence the complete picture they give of life is of necessity fallacious; they can only represent what is unusual.

—*BC,* 69

It is already becoming crudely obvious that our journalism juggles with the news. Even in the most respectable papers, great blocks of information will appear in one sheet and be utterly absent from the other; and next day be absent from both.

—*EA,* 216

... they will complain that a sermon cannot be interrupted, and call a pulpit a coward's castle; though they do not call an editor's office a coward's castle.... the clergyman appears in person and could easily be kicked as he came out of church; the journalist conceals even his name so nobody can kick him.

—*EM,* xii

"Well, you know everybody knows whatever he knows," said Father Brown smiling, "when he thinks it convenient to print it."

—*FBO,* 790

Journalists and Public Opinion

Journalists do control public opinion; but it is not controlled by the arguments they publish—it is controlled by the arguments between the editor and sub-editor, which they do not publish.

—ATC, 105

Journalists (Opinions)

My correspondent . . . is very angry with me indeed. . . . First, he asks me what right I have to talk about Spiritualism at all, as I admit I have never been to a *séance.* This is all very well, but there are a good many things to which I have never been, but I have not the smallest intention of leaving off talking about them. I refuse (for instance) to leave off talking about the Siege of Troy. I decline to be mute in the matter of the French Revolution. . . . If nobody has any right to judge of Spiritualism except a man who has been to a *séance,* the results, logically speaking, are rather serious: it would almost seem as if nobody had any right to judge of Christianity who had not been to the first meeting at Pentecost. Which would be dreadful. I conceive myself capable of forming my opinion of Spiritualism without seeing spirits, just as I form my opinion of . . . American millionaires without (thank God) seeing an American millionaire. Blessed are they who have not seen and yet have believed: a passage which some have considered as a prophecy of modern journalism.

—ATC, 150–151

Joyce, James

The new Ulysses is the opposite of the old Ulysses, for the latter moved amid ogres and witches with a level-headed and almost prosaic common sense, while the former moves among common lamp-posts and public-houses with a fixed attitude of mind more fantastic than all the fairy-tales. I am not here either adequately praising or adequately criticizing this much controverted work; I am merely using it as an illustration of the isolation of one mind, or even of one mood.

Rabelais sometimes seems confusing, because he is like twenty men talking at once; but Joyce is rather inaudible, because he is talking to himself.

—S, 217

Judgement Day

"I mean that we here are on the wrong side of the tapestry," answered Father Brown. "The things that happen here do not seem to mean anything; they mean something somewhere else. Somewhere else retribution will come on the real offender. Here it often seems to fall on the wrong person."

—FBO, 146

... very few people in this world would care to listen to the real defense of their own characters. The real defense, the defense which belongs to the Day of Judgment, would make such damaging admissions, would clear away so many artificial virtues, would tell such tragedies of weakness and failure, that a man would sooner be misunderstood and censured by the world than exposed to that awful and merciless eulogy.

—RB, 188

Jurors (Impartial)

What people call impartiality may simply mean indifference, and what people call partiality may simply mean mental activity. It is sometimes made an objection ... to a juror that he has formed some *primâ-facie* opinion upon a case: if he can be forced under sharp questioning to admit that he has formed such an opinion, he is regarded as manifestly unfit to conduct the inquiry. Surely this is unsound. If his bias is one of interest, of class, or creed, or notorious propaganda, then that fact certainly proves that he is not an impartial arbiter. But the mere fact that he did form some temporary impression from the first facts as far as he knew them—this does not prove that he is not an impartial arbiter—it only proves that he is not a cold-blooded fool.

—ATC, 153-154

If we walk down the street taking all the jurymen who have not formed opinions and leaving all the jurymen who have formed opinions, it seems highly probable that we shall only succeed in taking all the stupid jurymen and leaving all the thoughtful ones. Provided that the opinion formed . . . has no suggestion of settled motive or prejudice, we might well regard it not merely as a promise of capacity, but literally as a promise of justice. The man who took the trouble to deduce from the police reports would probably be the man who would take the trouble to deduce further and different things from the evidence. The man who had the sense to form an opinion would be the man who would have the sense to alter it.

—ATC, 154

But whatever be the truth about exceptional intelligence and the masses, it is manifestly most unreasonable that intelligent men should be divided upon the absurd modern principle of regarding every clever man who cannot make up his mind as an impartial judge, and regarding every clever man who can make up his mind as a servile fanatic. As it is, we seem to regard it as a positive objection to a reasoner that he has taken one side or the other. We regard it (in other words) as a positive objection to a reasoner that he has contrived to reach the object of his reasoning.

—ATC, 156

K

Kitchen Gardens

I was walking the other day in a kitchen garden, which I find has somehow got attached to my premises, and I was wondering why I liked it. After a prolonged spiritual self-analysis I came to the conclusion that I like a kitchen garden because it contains things to eat. . . . a kitchen garden is as beautiful as an orchard; but why is it that the word "orchard" sounds as beautiful as the word "flower-garden," and yet also sounds more satisfactory? I suggest again my extraordinary dark and delicate discovery: that it contains things to eat.

—Alarms, 43

Knives

A knife is never bad except on such rare occasions as that in which it is neatly and scientifically planted in the middle of one's back.

—D, 5

L

Ladies (English)

One of the crimes of the English Lady is an unconscious class-consciousness.

—*FFF*, 170

Language

When we are pressed and taunted upon our obstinacy in saying the Mass in a dead language, we are tempted to reply to our questioners by telling them that they are apparently not fit to be trusted with a living language. When we consider what they have done with the noble English language, as compared with the English of the Anglican Prayer-Book, let alone the Latin of the Mass, we feel that their development may well be called degenerate.

—*Thing*, 161

Language (on the Infallibility of)

Every religion and every philosophy must, of course, be based on the assumption of the authority or the accuracy of something. But it may well be questioned whether it is not saner and more satisfactory to ground our faith on the infallibility of the Pope, or the infallibility of the Book of

Mormon, than on the astounding modern dogma of the infallibility of human speech.

—GFW, 43

Every time one man says to another, "Tell us plainly what you mean?" he is assuming the infallibility of language: that is to say, he is assuming that there is a perfect scheme of verbal expression for all the internal moods and meanings of men. Whenever a man says to another, "Prove your case; defend your faith," he is assuming the infallibility of language: that is to say, he is assuming that a man has a word for every reality in earth, or heaven, or hell. He knows that there are in the soul tints more bewildering, more numberless and more nameless than the colours of an autumn forest; he knows that there are abroad in the world and doing strange and terrible service in it crimes that have never been condemned and virtues that have never been christened. Yet he seriously believes that these things can every one of them, in all their tones and semi-tones, in all their blends and unions, be accurately represented by an arbitrary system of grunts and squeals.

—GFW, 43-44

. . . whenever a man says that he cannot explain what he means, and that he hates argument, that his enemy is misrepresenting him, but he cannot explain how; that man is a true sage, and has seen into the heart of the real nature of language. Whenever a man refuses to be caught by some dilemma about reason and passion, or about reason and faith, or about fate and free-will, he has seen the truth. Whenever a man declines to be cornered as an egotist, or an altruist, or any such modern monster, he has seen the truth. For the truth is that language is not a scientific thing at all, but wholly an artistic thing, a thing invented by hunters, and killers, and such artists long before science was dreamed of. The truth is simply that—that the tongue is not a reliable instrument, like a theodolite or a camera. The tongue is most truly an unruly member, as the wise saint has called it, a thing poetic and dangerous like music or fire.

—GFW, 44-45

Language (Scientific)

We have turned scientific language into a sort of slang; the sort of slang that is used to save trouble. Anybody can talk about problems and nobody need bother about solutions; anybody is free to talk about a complex so long as he can ignore its complexity; anybody can borrow a word from the studios or the workshops; so long as he does not pay it back by making any study or doing any work.

—AIWS, 85

Latins

Latins are logical and have a reason for going mad.

—FBO, 721

Laughter

...the tendency of recent culture has been to tolerate the smile but discourage the laugh. There are three differences involved here. First, that the smile can unobtrusively turn into the sneer; second, that the smile is always individual and even secretive (especially if it is a little mad), while the laugh can be social and gregarious, and is perhaps the one genuine surviving form of the General Will; and third, that laughing lays itself open to criticism, is innocent and unguarded, has the sort of humanity which has always something of humility.... Therefore, in this modern conflict between the Smile and the Laugh, I am all in favor of Laughing. Laughter has something in it in common with the ancient winds of faith and inspiration; it unfreezes pride and unwinds secrecy; it makes men forget themselves in the presence of something greater than themselves; something (as the common phrase goes about a joke) that they cannot resist.

—CM, 157–158

There is no necessary connexion between wit and mirth. A man's wit over-powers his enemies; but his mirth overpowers him. As long as a man is merely witty he can be quite dignified; in other words, as long as he is witty he can be entirely solemn. But if he is mirthful he at once abandons dignity, which is another name for solemnity, which is another name for spiritual pride. A mere humourist is merely admirable; but a man laughing is laughable. He spreads the exquisite and desirable disease by which he is himself convulsed. But our recent comedians have distrusted laughter for exactly the same reason that they have distrusted religion or romantic love. A laugh is like a love affair in that it carries a man completely off his feet; a laugh is like a creed or a church in that it asks that a man should trust himself to it.

—HA, 28–29

A man must sacrifice himself to the God of Laughter, who has stricken him with a sacred madness. As a woman can make a fool of a man, so a joke makes a fool of a man. And a man must love a joke more than himself, or he will not surrender his pride for it. A man must take what is called a leap in the dark, as he does when he is married or when he dies, or when he is born, or when he does almost anything else that is important.

—HA, 29

It is no small thing to be laughed at by something at once lower and stronger than oneself.

— Thursday, 172

Laughter and Respect (Antagonism of)

The equal and eternal human being will alter that antagonism, for the human being sees no real antagonism between laughter and respect, the human being, the common man, whom mere geniuses like you and me can only worship like a god. When dark and dreary days come, you and I are necessary, the pure fanatic, the pure satirist. We have between us remedied a great wrong. . . . But in healthy people there is no war between us. We are but the two lobes of the brain of a ploughman. Laughter and

183

love are everywhere. The cathedrals, built in the ages that loved God, are full of blasphemous grotesques. The mother laughs continually at the child, the lover laughs continually at the lover, the wife at the husband, the friend at the friend. You have a halberd and I a sword, let us start our wanderings over the world. For we are its two essentials.

—NNH, 197

Law

Any one of the strange laws we suffer is a compromise between a fad and a vested interest.

—FVF, 181

Learning

The mind conquers a new province like an emperor; but only because the mind has answered the bell like a servant. The mind has opened the doors and windows, because it is the natural activity of what is inside the house to find out what is outside the house. If the mind is sufficient to itself, it is insufficient for itself.

—STA, 183

Legends

A legend is something that grows slowly and naturally and generally does symbolise some sort of relative truth about history.

—EA, 65

It is quite easy to see why a legend is treated, and ought to be treated, more respectfully than a book of history. The legend is generally made by the majority of people in the village, who are sane. The book is generally written by the one man in the village who is mad.

—O, 84–85

Leisure

And as for the third form of leisure, the most precious, the most consoling, the most pure and holy, the noble habit of doing nothing at all—that is being neglected in a degree which seems to me to threaten the degeneration of the whole race. It is because artists do not practise, patrons do not patronize, crowds do not assemble to reverently worship the great work of Doing Nothing, that the world has lost its philosophy and even failed to invent a new religion.

—Gen S, 131

... to hurry through one's leisure is the most unbusiness-like of actions.

—TT, 287

Liars

A real liar does not tell wanton and unnecessary lies. He tells nice and necessary lies.

—Mr. Pond, 149

Liberals

A liberal may be defined approximately as a man who, if he could, by waving his hand in a dark room, stop the mouths of all the deceivers of mankind for ever, would not wave his hand.

—RB, 86–87

Liberty (Religious)

Religious liberty might be supposed to mean that everybody is free to discuss religion. In practice it means that hardly anybody is allowed to mention it.

—Bio, 244

Lie Detectors

"I reckon you'll be shocked," replied Greywood Usher, "as I know you don't cotton to the march of science in these matters. . . . Now, in my opinion that machine can't lie."

"No machine can lie," said Father Brown, "nor can it tell the truth. . . . You always forget . . . that the reliable machine always has to be worked by an unreliable machine."

"Why, what do you mean?" asked the detective.

"I mean Man," said Father Brown, "the most unreliable machine I know of."

—FBO, 307

Lies

It is a deadly error (an error at the back of much of the false placidity of our politics) to suppose that lies are told with excess and luxuriance, and truths told with modesty and restraint. Some of the most frantic lies on the face of life are told with modesty and restraint; for the simple reason that only modesty and restraint will save them.

—CD, 134

Life

At any innocent tea-table we may easily hear a man say, "Life is not worth living." We regard it as we regard the statement that it is a fine day. . . . And yet if that utterance were really believed, the world would stand on its head. Murderers would be given medals for saving men from life; firemen would be denounced for keeping men from death; poisons would be used as medicines; doctors would be called in when people were well; the Humane Society would be rooted out like a horde of assassins.

—H, 6

The general inference from *Vanity Fair* is that life largely deceives and disappoints *all* people, bad and good; but that there is a difference, and that is (though the stupid optimist could not see it) rather on the side of the good.

—*HA,* 60

It is quite as certain as it ever was that life is a gift of God immensely valuable and immensely valued; and anybody can prove it by putting a pistol to the head of a pessimist.

—*Thing,* 55

Life (Burdens of)

We need not deny that the grasshopper on a man's shoulder is a burden; but we need not pay much respect to a gentleman who is always calling out that he would rather have an elephant when he knows there are no elephants in the country.

—*TT,* 50

Life (Daily)

It is in our own daily life that we are to look for the portents and the prodigies. . . . Compared with this life, all public life, all fame, all wisdom, is by its nature cramped and cold and small. For on that defined and lighted public stage men are of necessity forced to profess one set of accomplishments, to rise to one rigid standard. It is the utterly unknown people, who can grow in all directions like an exuberant tree.

—*CD,* 187

Life (Modern)

It is very puzzling to look at the real society around us at this moment, and consider whether it has a purpose.

—C, 169

It has continually struck us that there is no element in modern life that is more lamentable than the fact that the modern man has to seek all artistic existence in a sedentary state. If he wishes to float into fairyland, he reads a book; if he wishes to dash into the thick of battle, he reads a book; if he wishes to soar into heaven, he reads a book; if he wishes to slide down the banisters, he reads a book.

—Queer, 46

Life (Mystery of)

The mystic does not bring doubts or riddles: the doubts and riddles exist already. We all feel the riddle of the earth without anyone to point it out. The mystery of life is the plainest part of it. The clouds and curtains of darkness, the confounding vapours, these are the daily weather of this world. Whatever else we have grown accustomed to, we have grown accustomed to the unaccountable. Every stone or flower is a hieroglyphic of which we have lost the key; with every step of our lives we enter into the middle of some story which we are certain to misunderstand.

—Blake, 131

Life (Perplexity of)

...the perplexity of life arises from there being too many interesting things in it for us to be interested properly in any of them; what we call its triviality is really the tag-ends of numberless tales; ordinary and unmeaning existence is like ten thousand thrilling detective stories mixed up with a spoon.

—TT, 17

Literary Artists (Modern)

Half the outcry against them arose, rightly or wrongly, because they insisted that their books must be repulsive in order to be realistic or sordid in order to be true. They insisted on a free hand in describing sex; and seemed to assume, in their own apologia, that to describe sex is to describe sin—and sorrow. They insisted that anything pretty must be a pretense; and never saw how sharply they were reflecting on the end of that very dance of pretty nymphs and cupids, which had brought them the license that they liked best. In short, they seemed to make two claims; first to be free to find the perfect happiness of passion; and second, to be free to describe how exceedingly unhappy it is.

—RLS, 161–162

Literary Criticism

It is entirely useless to attempt to discuss the philosophy of Robert Browning apart from his poetry. The project is quite as ridiculous as the project of explaining the inspirations of Turner to a blind man, or of making the peculiar gospel of Wagner or Chopin clear to a deaf one. There is something in Turner beyond paint and turpentine, there is something in Wagner which could not be expressed by any instrument. But to describe the message of Turner without ever mentioning chrome yellow or flake white, to convey the importance of Wagner's work without any reference to the musical laws by which he worked, would be entirely ridiculous. It is nevertheless assumed that in literature the message can be detached from the words, a thing unknown in any other art.

—HA, 91

As it is we approach a masterpiece like *Hamlet* through the haze of an atmosphere which the masterpiece has itself created. We know that the thing is great before we begin to ask if it is good. There is something absurd in the very attempt to discuss how the thing should have been done; just as there is something absurd in the modern philosophical attempts to point out how the cosmos or the creation should have been conducted. How can we discuss how we should have written Shakespeare? Shakespeare has written us. And you and I (I am sure you agree) are two of his best characters.

—*HA*, 201

The usual way of criticizing an author, particularly an author who had added something to the literary forms of the world, is to complain that his work does not contain something which is obviously the specialty of somebody else.

—*RB*, 138–139

In the case of Stevenson, criticism has always tended to be hypercriticism. It is as if the critic were strung up to be as strict with the artist as the artist was with himself. But they are not very consistent or considerate in the matter. They blame him for being fastidious; and so become more fastidious themselves. They condemn him for wasting time in trying to find the right words; and then waste more time in not very successful attempts to prove it was the wrong word.

—*RLS*, 97

Literary Style

I am one of those humble characters for whom the main matter of style is concerned with making a statement; and generally, in the case of Stevenson, with telling a story. Style takes its own most loving and therefore most fitting form from within; as the narrative quickens and leaps, or the statement becomes warm or weighty, by being either authoritative or argumentative. The sentence takes its shape from motion; as it takes its motion from motive. And the motive (for us outcasts) is what the man has to say.

—*RLS*, 95

Literature

Literature, classic and enduring literature, does its best work in reminding us perpetually of the whole round of truth and balancing other and older ideas against the ideas to which we might for a moment be prone.

—*CM*, 22

... literature should know all men and judge none. It is the dead who are judged, and the creatures of literature should never die.

—*HA*, 26

Books without morality in them are books that send one to sleep standing up.

—*HA*, 67

Literature and Translation

... it is strictly true that we can translate anything in reason. We cannot translate anything that is beyond reason; like the way in which mere sound and spelling can be a spell.

—*C*, 205

Literature (Modern)

Perhaps the change I describe, from the revolt of the nineteenth century to the realism of the twentieth, could not be better measured than by the distance between two dates; the day on which Mr. H. G. Wells, laying the foundations of the first of his Utopias, declared that its first principle should be that Original Sin is a lie—to the day when Mr. Aldous Huxley, heir of the great scientific house in its next generation, wrote that the mediaeval mind was far wiser than the nineteenth-century minds, because it recognised Original Sin.

—*S*, 220

Modern literature takes insanity as its centre.

— TT, 126

Logic

Logic is a machine of the mind, and if it is used honestly it ought to bring out an honest conclusion.

— Types, 113

Logicians

The fault of the great mass of logicians is not that they bring out a false result, or, in other words, are not logicians at all. Their fault is that by an inevitable psychological habit they tend to forget that there are two parts of a logical process, the first the choosing of an assumption, and the second the arguing upon it, and humanity, if it devotes itself too persistently to the study of sound reasoning, has a certain tendency to lose the faculty of sound assumption.

— Types, 114

Love

Passion makes every detail important; there is no realism like the insatiable realism of love.

— HA, 94

The way to love anything is to realise that it might be lost.

— TT, 56

To love anything is to love its boundaries; thus children will always play on the edge of anything. They build castles on the edge of the sea, and can only be restrained by public proclamation and private violence from walking on the edge of the grass. For when we have come to the end of a thing we have come to the beginning of it.

— TT, 222

The fact that it is an animal necessity only comes to the naturalistic philosopher after looking abroad, studying its origins and results, constructing an explanation of its existence, more or less natural and conclusive. The fact that it is a spiritual triumph comes to the first errand boy who happens to feel it. If a lad of seventeen falls in love and is struck dead by a hansom cab an hour afterwards, he has known the thing as it is, a spiritual ecstasy; he has never come to trouble about the thing as it may be, a physical destiny. If anyone says that falling in love is an animal thing, the answer is very simple. The only way of testing the matter is to ask those who are experiencing it, and none of those would admit for a moment that it was an animal thing.

— Types, 213

Love and Youth

But most men know that there is a difference between the intense momentary emotion called up by memory of the loves of youth, and the yet more instantaneous but more perfect pleasure of the memory of childhood. The former is always narrow and individual, piercing the heart like a rapier; but the latter is like a flash of lightning, for one split second revealing a whole varied landscape; it is not the memory of a particular pleasure any more than of a particular pain, but of a whole world that shone with wonder. The first is only a lover remembering love; the second is like a dead man remembering life.

—RLS, 163

Love of Humanity

The phrase has unfortunately a false and pedantic sound. The love of humanity is a thing supposed to be professed only by vulgar and officious philanthropists, or by saints of a superhuman detachment and universality. As a matter of fact, love of humanity is the commonest and most natural of the feelings of a fresh nature, and almost every one has felt it alight capriciously upon him when looking at a crowded park or a room full of dancers. The love of those whom we do not know is quite as eternal a sentiment as the love of those whom we do know. In our friends the richness of life is proved to us by what we have gained; in the faces in the street the richness of life is proved to us by the hint of what we have lost.

—RB, 43

Those thinkers who cannot believe in any gods often assert that the love of humanity would be in itself sufficient for them; and so, perhaps, it would, if they had it. There is a very real thing which may be called the love of humanity; in our time it exists almost entirely among what are called uneducated people; and it does not exist at all among the people who talk about it.

— TT, 168

Love of Low Company

A shabby, larky, good-natured clerk would, as a matter of fact, spend hours in the society of a little servant girl if he found her about the house. It would arise partly from a dim kindliness, and partly from that mysterious instinct which is sometimes called, mistakenly, a love of low company— that mysterious instinct which makes so many men of pleasure find something soothing in the society of uneducated people, particularly uneducated women. It is the instinct which accounts for the otherwise unaccountable popularity of barmaids.

—CD, 90

Lovers

Lovers may be lunatics; lovers may be children; lovers may be unfit for citizenship and outside human argument; you can take up that position if you will. But lovers do not only desire love; they desire marriage. The root of legal monogamy does not lie ... in the fact that the man is a mere tyrant and the woman a mere slave. It lies in the fact that if their love for each other is the noblest and freest love conceivable, it can only find its heroic expression in both becoming slaves.

—GBS, 187

Lunacy

The madman is not the man who has lost his reason. The madman is the man who has lost everything except his reason.

—O, 32

A lunatic is not startling to himself, because he is quite serious; that is what makes him a lunatic.

—TT, 126

Lunacy and Determinism

... that able writer Mr. R. B. Suthers said that free will was lunacy, because it meant causeless actions, and the actions of a lunatic would be causeless.... Obviously if any actions, even a lunatic's, can be causeless, determinism is done for.... The last thing that can be said of a lunatic is that his actions are causeless. If any human acts may loosely be called causeless, they are the minor acts of a healthy man; whistling as he walks; slashing the grass with a stick.... It is the happy man who does the useless things; the sick man is not strong enough to be idle. It is exactly such careless and causeless actions that the madman could never understand; for the madman (like the determinist) generally sees too much cause in everything. He would think that the loping of the grass was an attack on private property. He would think that the kicking of the heels was a signal to an accomplice. If the madman could for an instant become careless, he would become sane.

—O, 30-31

Lunatics

The difference between us and the maniac is not about how things look or how things ought to look, but about what they self-evidently are. . . . The lunatic does not say he is as wise as Shakespeare; Bernard Shaw might say that. The lunatic says he is Shakespeare.

—Evils, 42

The lunatic is he who loses his way and cannot return.

—Poet, 63

Luther, Martin

When he quoted a Scripture text, inserting a word that is not in Scripture, he was content to shout back at all hecklers: "Tell them that Dr. Martin Luther will have it so!" That is what we now call Personality. A little later it was called Psychology. After that it was called Advertisement or Salesmanship.

—STA, 195

Lutheranism

It had one theory that was the destruction of all theories; in fact it had its own theology which was itself the death of theology. Man could say nothing to God, nothing from God, nothing about God, except an almost inarticulate cry for mercy and for the supernatural help of Christ, in a world where all natural things were useless. Reason was useless. Will was useless. Man could not move himself an inch any more than a stone. Man

196

could not trust what was in his head any more than a turnip. Nothing remained in earth or heaven, but the name of Christ lifted in that lonely imprecation; awful as the cry of a beast in pain.

—STA, 193

Lying

It is a good thing to tell a half-truth so long as one thinks that it is the whole truth.

—HA, 155

Lying in Bed

I am sure that it was only because Michael Angelo was engaged in the ancient and honourable occupation of lying in bed that he ever realised how the roof of the Sistine Chapel might be made into an awful imitation of a divine drama that could only be acted in the heavens.

—TT, 75

For those who study the great art of lying in bed there is one emphatic caution to be added. Even for those who can do their work in bed (like journalists), still more for those whose work cannot be done in bed (as, for example, the professional harpooner of whales), it is obvious that the indulgence must be very occasional. But that is not the caution I mean. The caution is this: if you do lie in bed, be sure you do it without reason or justification at all.

—TT, 78

. . . if a healthy man lies in bed, let him do it without a rag of excuse; then he will get up a healthy man. If he does it for some secondary hygienic reason, if he has some scientific explanation, he may get up a hypochondriac.

—TT, 79

M

Madmen

Madmen are always serious; they go mad from lack of humour.

—NNH, 37

Madness

Of course there is no absolute definition of madness except the definition which we should each of us endorse that madness is the eccentric behaviour of somebody else.

—L & L, 10

Make-believe

This seems to imply that the mind makes itself believe something. . . . I do not think there is even this slight crack of falsity in the crystal clearness and directness of the child's vision of a fairy-palace. . . . In one sense the child believes much less, and in another much more than that. I do not think the child is deceived; or that he attempts for a moment to deceive himself. I think he instantly asserts his direct and divine right to enjoy beauty; that he steps straight into his own lawful kingdom of imagination, without quibbles or questions such as arise afterwards out of false moralities and philosophies, touching the nature of falsehood and truth.

—CM, 56–57

Man

Man is an exception, whatever else he is. If he is not the image of God, then he is a disease of the dust. If it is not true that a divine being fell, then we can only say that one of the animals went entirely off its head.

—ATC, 170

He cannot sleep in his own skin, he cannot trust his own instincts. He is at once a creator moving miraculous hands and fingers and a kind of cripple. He is wrapped in artificial bandages called clothes; he is propped on artificial crutches called furniture. His mind has the same doubtful liberties and the same wild limitations. Alone among the animals he is shaken with the beautiful madness called laughter. . . . Alone among the animals he feels the need of averting his thoughts from the root realities of his own bodily being; of hiding them as in the presence of some higher possibility which creates the mystery of shame.

—EM, 19

Men in a state of decadence employ professionals to fight for them, professionals to dance for them, and a professional to rule them.

—Five Types, 69

Man can hardly be defined, after the fashion of Carlyle, as an animal who makes tools; ants and beavers . . . make tools, in the sense that they make an apparatus. Man can be defined as an animal that makes dogmas. . . . When he drops one doctrine after another in a refined scepticism . . . when he says that he disbelieves in finality, when, in his own imagination, he sits as God, holding no form of creed but contemplating all, then he is by that very process sinking slowly backwards into the vagueness of the vagrant animals and the unconsciousness of the grass. Trees have no dogmas. Turnips are singularly broadminded.

—H, 288

In one way Man was to be haughtier than he had ever been before; in another way he was to be humbler than he had ever been before. Insofar as I am Man I am the chief of creatures. Insofar as I am *a* man I am the chief of sinners.

—O, 173

Man (as Man)

We Catholics are all agnostics. We Catholics have only in that sense got as far as realizing that a man is a man. But your Ibsens and your Zolas and your Shaws and your Tolstoys have not even got so far.

—BC, 142

Man (Civilised)

The civilised man, like the religious man, is one who recognizes the strange and irritating fact that something exists besides himself. What Jefferson called, with his fine restraint, "A decent respect for the opinion of mankind"; what medieval people called Christendom or the judgment of all Christian princes; what any Christian will call the conscience of man as a witness to the justice of God; that, in one form or another, does everywhere affect civilised people. An Agnostic may hesitate about giving it the name of God. An American may very reasonably hesitate about giving it the name of the League of Nations. But in one way or another, that is the test; that the man does not think his dignity lowered by admitting a general law, though it may go against him.

—EA, 18–19

Man (Common)

The vast mass of humanity, with their vast mass of idle books and idle words, have never doubted and never will doubt that courage is splendid, that fidelity is noble, that distressed ladies should be rescued, and vanquished enemies spared. There are a large number of cultivated persons who doubt these maxims of daily life. . . .

—*D*, 16

Man (Good)

A good man, as Thackery said with such thorough and searching truth, grows simpler as he grows older.

—*CD*, 69

Man (Great)

That is the mark of the truly great man: that he sees the common man afar off, and worships him. The great man tries to be ordinary, and becomes extra-ordinary in the process. But the small man tries to be mysterious, and becomes lucid in an awful sense—for we can all see through him.

—*Diversity*, 33

A great man in any age must be a common man, and also an uncommon man. Those that are only uncommon men are perverts and sowers of pestilence.

—*VA*, 156

Man (Honest)

The error of Diogenes lay in the fact that he omitted to notice that every man is both an honest man and a dishonest man. Diogenes looked for his honest man inside every crypt and cavern; but he never thought of looking inside the thief. And there is where the Founder of Christianity found the honest man; he found him on a gibbet and promised him Paradise.

—CD, 11

Man (Literary)

...the idea that a great literary man who has said something novel and important to mankind can vanish suddenly and finally is ridiculous. The pessimists who believe it are people who could believe that the sun is destroyed for ever every time it sinks in the west. Nothing is lost in the magnificent economy of existence; the sun returns, the flowers return, the literary fashions return. If life is a continual parting it is also a continual heaven of reconciliation. The old legends were right when they said that Arthur would come back. All things return; the world uses all its forces, the return of the stars, the return of the seasons, the return of the heroes.

—HA, 6

Man (Love for)

Christ commanded us to have love for all men, but even if we had equal love for all men, to speak of having the same love for all men is merely bewildering nonsense. If we love a man at all, the impression he produces on us must be vitally different to the impression produced by another man whom we love. To speak of having the same kind of regard for both is about as sensible as asking a man whether he prefers chrysanthemums or billiards. Christ did not love humanity; He never said He loved humanity; He loved men. Neither He nor anyone else can love humanity; it is like loving a gigantic centipede.

— Types, 143

Man (Mediaeval)

But the citizens of the mediaeval republic were certainly under the limitation of only being asked to die for the things with which they had always lived, the houses they inhabited, the shrines they venerated and the rulers and representations they knew; and had not the larger vision calling them to die for the latest rumours about remote colonies as reported in anonymous newspapers.

— St. Francis, 64

Man (Misunderstood)

The man who is misunderstood has always this advantage over his enemies, that they do not know his weak point or his plan of campaign. They go out against a bird with nets and against a fish with arrows.

—H, 47

Man (Modern)

If the modern man is indeed the heir of all the ages, he is often the kind of heir who tells the family solicitor to sell the whole damned estate, lock, stock, and barrel, and give him a little ready money to throw away at the races or the night-clubs. He is certainly not the kind of heir who ever visits his estate: and, if he really owns all the historic lands of ancient and modern history, he is a very absentee landlord.

—Avowals, 81

... half the trouble about the modern man is that he is educated to understand foreign languages and misunderstand foreigners.

—Bio, 322

Don't you understand how shallow all these moderns are, when they tell you there is no such thing as Atonement or Expiation; when that is the one thing for which the whole heart is sick, in sight of the sins of the world?

—FFF, 221

We know we are brilliant and distinguished, but we do not know we are right. We swagger in fantastic artistic costumes; we praise ourselves; we fling epigrams right and left; we have the courage to play the egoist and the courage to play the fool, but we have not the courage to preach.

—GFW, 14

. . . the one thing modern people really do believe in is damnation.

—TT, 133

They all wore tall shiny hats as if they could not lose an instant even to hang them on a peg, and they all had one eye a little off, hypnotised by the huge eye of the clock. In short, they were the slaves of the modern bondage, you could hear their fetters clanking. Each was, in fact, bound by a chain; the heaviest chain ever tied to a man—it is called a watch-chain.

—TT, 287

Man (Modern European)

Every man of us to-day is three men. There is in every modern European three powers so distinct as to be almost personal, the trinity of our earthly destiny. The three may be rudely summarised thus. First and nearest to us is the Christian, the man of the historic church, of the creed that must have coloured our minds incurably whether we regard it (as I do) as the crown and combination of the other two, or whether we regard it as an accidental superstition which has remained for two thousand years. First, then, comes the Christian; behind him comes the Roman, the citizen of that great cosmopolitan realm of reason and order in the level and equality of which Christianity arose. . . . He is the republican who is so much prouder than kings. He it is that makes straight roads and clear laws, and for whom good sense is good enough. And the third man—he is harder to speak of. He has no name, and all true tales of him are blotted out; yet he walks behind us in every forest path and wakes within us when the wind wakes at night. He is the origins—he is the man in the forest.

—*Blake,* 106–107

Man (of the Future)

The man of the future must not be taught; he must be bred. This notion of producing superior human beings by the methods of the stud farm had often been urged, though its difficulties had never been cleared up. . . . The first and most obvious objection to it of course is this: that if you are to breed men as pigs, you require some overseer who is as much more subtle than a man as a man is more subtle than a pig. Such an individual is not easy to find.

—*GBS,* 211

Man (Plain)

Perhaps every plain man's life holds the real mystery, the secret of sins avoided.

—*MWKTM,* 337

Man (Practical)

For some strange reason, it is the custom to say of this sort of practical man that "he knows his own mind." Of courage this is exactly what he does not know. He may in a few fortunate cases know what he wants, as does a dog or a baby of two years old; but even then he does not know why he wants it. And it is the why and the how that have to be considered when we are tracing out the way in which some culture or tradition has got into a tangle. What we need, as the ancients understood, is not a politician who is a business man, but a king who is a philosopher.

—*CM,* 175

Man (Proud)

But this generalization is almost always safe: that a man who talks like a torrent for hours on end is a humble man. Dr. Johnson was dogmatic and humble; Mr. Bernard Shaw was dogmatic and humble. The proud man will scarcely ever lay down the law. The proud man will scarcely ever talk too much. He will lie in wait and drop in the epigram where it is exactly needed. He will feast upon speechless superiority, while the modest and unconscious man goes on like Niagara explaining the principles of socialism or the humours of his eldest son. The humble man will be always talkative; for he is interested in his subject and knows that it is best shown in talk. But the proud man will be generally silent; for he is not interested in his subject but in himself. And he knows that he looks best when he is not talking.

—HA, 152

Man (Sane)

He is a man who can have tragedy in his heart and comedy in his head.

—TT, 257

Man (Superiority of)

But here again the difficulty always is that the things near us seem larger than they are, and so seem to be a permanent part of mankind, when they may really be only one of its parting modes of expression. Few people, for instance, realize that a time may easily come when we shall see the great outburst of Science in the nineteenth century as something quite splendid, brief, unique, and ultimately abandoned, as the outburst of Art at the Renascence.

—CD, 207

Man (Worldly)

The worldly man, who really lives only for this world and believes in no other, whose worldly success and pleasure are all he can ever snatch out of nothingness—that is the man who will really do anything, when he is in danger of losing the whole world and saving nothing. It is not the revolutionary man but the respectable man who would commit any crime—to save his respectability.

—FBO, 806

Mankind (Unity of)

It is when you really perceive the unity of mankind that you really perceive its variety. It is not a flippancy, it is very sacred truth, to say that when men really understand that they are brothers they instantly begin to fight.

—UU, 104

Man's Life

A man's life is held to mean what he did, the whole external pantomime of his existence. But this is in fact the most lifeless part of him, being the furthest removed from the centre of his life. . . . The only biography that is really possible is autobiography. To recount the actions of another man is not biography, it is zoology, the noting down of the habits of a new and outlandish animal. It is most valuable and interesting, but it does not deal with the spring and spirit of a man's existence. It may fill ten volumes with anecdotes without once touching upon his life. It was drawed [sic] a man, but it has not drawed [sic] his soul.

—HA, 1

Man's Merits

. . . when we are seeking for the real merits of a man it is unwise to go to his enemies, and much more foolish to go to himself.

—*H*, 37

Mariolatry

I am very proud of what people call Mariolatry; because it introduced into religion in the darkest ages that element of chivalry which is now being belatedly and badly understood in the form of feminism.

—*Bio*, 76

Marriage

A man imagines a happy marriage as a marriage of love; even if he makes fun of marriages that are without love, or feels sorry for lovers who are without marriage.

—*C*, 121

"Really and truly," he said, "it's as serious—as serious as the halfpenny bun. It is expensive, like the bun; one pays for it. It is indigestable, like the bun. It hurts."

—*FBO*, 83

In the majority of sane human lives there is no problem of sex at all; there is no problem of marriage at all; there is no problem of temperament at all; for all these problems are dwarfed and rendered ridiculous by the standing problem of being a moderately honest man and paying the butcher.

—*HA*, 139

Marriage (and the Modern Absence of Mind)

If anybody thinks I exaggerate the mindlessness of the modern comment on this matter, I am content to refer him to the inscription under a large photograph of a languishing lady, in the newspaper now before me. It states that the lady has covered herself with glory as the inventor of "Companionate Divorce." It goes on to state, in her own words, that she will marry her husband again if he asks her again; and that she has been living with him ever since she was divorced from him. If mortal muddle-headedness can go deeper than that, in this vale of tears, I should like to see it.

—S, 72

Martyrs

A martyr is a man who cares so much for something outside him, that he forgets his own personal life. A suicide is a man who cares so little for anything outside him, that he wants to see the last of everything.

—O, 133

Martyrs (Modern)

The incident of the Suffragettes who chained themselves with iron chains to the railings of Downing Street is a good ironical allegory of most modern martyrdom. It generally consists of a man chaining himself up and then complaining that he is not free.

—ATC, 81

The modern notion of impressing the public by a mere demonstration of unpopularity, by being thrown out of meetings or thrown into jail, is largely a mistake. It rests on a fallacy touching the true popular value of martyrdom. People look at human history and see that it has often happened that persecutions have not only advertised but even advanced a persecuted creed, and given to its validity the public and dreadful witness of dying men. . . . modern people think that anyone who makes

209

himself slightly uncomfortable in public will immediately be uproariously popular. . . . The assumption is that if you show your ordinary sincerity (or even your political ambition) by being a nuisance to yourself as well as to other people, you will have the strength of the great saints who passed through the fire.

—ATC, 81–82

Modern martyrdoms fail even as demonstrations, because they do not prove even that the martyrs are completely serious. . . . modern martyrs are generally serious, perhaps a trifle too serious. But their martyrdom does not prove it; and the public does not always believe it. . . . A person might be chucked out of meetings just as young men are chucked out of music-halls—for fun. But no man has himself eaten by a lion as a personal advertisement.

—ATC, 85

The mere grammatical meaning of the word 'martyr' breaks into pieces at a blow the whole notion of the privacy of goodness. The Christian martyrdoms were more than demonstrations: they were advertisements. In our day the new theory of spiritual delicacy would desire to alter all this. It would permit Christ to be crucified if it was necessary to His Divine nature, but it would ask in the name of good taste why He could not be crucified in a private room. It would declare that the act of a martyr in being torn in pieces by lions was vulgar and sensational, though, of course, it would have no objection to being torn in pieces by a lion in one's own parlour before a circle of really intimate friends.

—D, 40

Masterpieces

By a curious confusion, many modern critics have passed from the proposition that a masterpiece may be unpopular to the other proposition that unless it is unpopular it cannot be a masterpiece.

—Gen S, 2

Materialism

Materialism is really our established Church; for the government will really help it to persecute its heretics. Vaccination, in its hundred years of experiment, has been disputed almost as much as baptism in its approximate two thousand. But it seems quite natural to our politicians to enforce vaccination; and it would seem to them madness to enforce baptism.

—Evils, 98

... there is materialism or the very muddiest sort of atheism. It has the obscure assumption that everything begins with the digestion, and not with the divine reason. . . . In their hapless topsy-turvy philosophy, digestion is the creator and divinity the creature. They have at the back of their minds, in short, the idea that there is really nothing at the back of their minds except the brute thing called the body. To them, therefore, there is nothing comic or incongruous about saying that a violin solo should be a servant of the body or of the brute; for there is no other god for it to serve.

—Gen S, 106

All the towering materialism which dominates the modern mind rests ultimately upon one assumption; a false assumption. It is supposed that if a thing goes on repeating itself it is probably dead; a piece of clockwork. . . . The repetition in Nature may not be a mere recurrence; it may be a theatrical *encore.* Heaven may *encore* the bird who laid an egg. If the human being conceives and brings forth a human child instead of bringing forth a fish, or a bat, or a griffin, the reason may not be that we are fixed in an animal fate without life or purpose. It may be that our little

211

tragedy has touched the gods, that they admire it from their starry galleries, and that at the end of every human drama man is called again and again before the curtain.

—O, 107–109

I might convince a man that matter as the origin of the Mind is quite meaningless, if he and I were very fond of each other and fought each other every night for forty years.

—STA, 38

Materialism (Economic)

It is putting it too feebly to say that the history of man is not only economic. Man would not have any history if he were only economic. The need for food is certainly universal, so universal that it is not even human. Cows have an economic motive, and apparently . . . only an economic motive. The cow eats grass anywhere and never eats anything else. In short, the cow does fulfill the materialist theory of history: that is why the cow has no history. "A History of Cows" would be one of the simplest and briefest of standard works. But . . . if the cow with the crumpled horn were worshipped by some cows and gored to death by others; if cows began to have obvious moral preferences over and above a desire for grass, then cows would begin to have a history. They would also begin to have a highly unpleasant time, which is perhaps the same thing.

—MM, 61

Materialism (Modern)

Modern hygienic materialism is very like cocoa; it would be impossible to express one's contempt for it in stronger terms than that.

—Blake, 99

Materialist Theory of History

The materialist theory of history, that all politics and ethics are the expression of economics, is a very simple fallacy indeed. It consists simply of confusing the necessary conditions of life with the normal preoccupations of life, that are quite a different thing. It is like saying that because a man can only walk about on two legs, therefore he never walks about except to buy shoes and stockings. . . . Cows may be purely economic, in the sense that we cannot see that they do much beyond grazing and seeking better grazing grounds; and that is why a history of cows in twelve volumes would not be very lively reading. . . . It will be hard to maintain that the Crusaders went from their homes into a howling wilderness because cows go from a wilderness to a more comfortable grazing-ground.

—EM, 158–159

Materialists

Materialists as a race are rather innocent and simple-minded.

—FBO, 857

It is obvious that a materialist is always a mystic. It is equally true that he is often a mystagogue. He is a mystic because he deals entirely in mysteries, in things that our reason cannot picture; such as mindless order or objective matter merely becoming subjective mind. . . . He pontificates; he is pompous, he tries to bully or to hypnotize, by the incantation of long and learned words, or by very simple things said in a very solemn fashion. This is the character of much popular science; at the best it is mysterious, and at the worst meaningless.

—Gen S, 14

Oh, the doubts of a materialist are not worth a dump.

—Thursday, 174

Medical Technology (Progress of)

The professor was, of course, bursting with hope and progressive optimism. He thinks that everything is going very well indeed, and the world improving with wonderful rapidity. As an example of this, he says that men are losing their eyes, teeth, hair, and sense of hearing with a rapidity that raises the happiest anticipations in a humane lover of his kind. He explained that when we have got rid of all these rude and extinct organs, we should have mechanical scientific substitutes. . . . He did not explain how soon it will be possible to manufacture that minor part of the machinery which has hitherto escaped so many inquiring mechanics; I mean the little thing that actually sees, hears, smells, speaks, and thinks. For, strange and exasperating as it seems without that one little thing (which nobody can find anywhere) it will generally be found that telescopes cannot see by themselves, telephones cannot hear by themselves, books cannot write themselves or read themselves; and a man cannot even talk entirely without thinking. Though he sometimes comes pretty near it.

—Come, 137

Men

. . . you never know the best about men till you know the worst about them.

—MWKTM, 232

Men and Cowards

Brave men are all vertebrates; they have their softness on the surface and their toughness in the middle. But these modern cowards are all crustaceans; their hardness is all on the cover, and their softness is inside.

— TT, 267

Men (Great)

There is a great man who makes every man feel small. But the real great man is the man who makes every man feel great.

—*CD*, 8

And almost without exception all the great men have come out of this atmosphere of equality. Great men may make despotisms; but democracies make great men.

—*CD*, 9

... "Why have we no great men?" We have no great men chiefly because we are always looking for them. We are connoisseurs of greatness, and connoisseurs can never be great; we are fastidious, that is, we are small.

—*CD*, 11

... a great man knows he is not God, and the greater he is the better he knows it. That is the paradox; everything that is merely approaching to that point is merely receding from it. Socrates, the wisest man, knows that he knows nothing. A lunatic may think he is omniscience and a fool may talk as if he were omniscient. But Christ is in another sense omniscient if he not only knows, but knows that he knows.

—*EM*, 249

Men trust an ordinary man because they trust themselves. But men trust a great man because they do not trust themselves. And hence the worship of great men always appears in times of weakness and cowardice; we never hear of great men until the time when all other men are small.

—*H*, 271

Men with Convictions

A man with a definite belief always appears bizarre, because he does not change with the world; he has climbed into a fixed star and the earth whizzes below him like a zoetrope. Millions of mild black coated men call themselves sane and sensible merely because they always catch the fashionable insanity, because they are hurried into madness after madness by the maelstrom of the world.

—H, 32

Metaphor

So far from it being irreverent to use silly metaphors on serious questions, it is one's duty to use silly metaphors on serious questions. It is a test of one's seriousness. It is the test of a responsible religion or theory whether it can take examples from pots and pans and boots and butter-tubs. It is the test of a good philosophy whether you can defend it grotesquely. It is the test of a good religion whether you can joke about it.

—ATC, 149

The Metaphysician

He tries to convey the substance of a passage by stripping away the ornaments and the verbiage, and he finds he has nothing left but the shadow. The process resembles a sort of conjuring trick in which a man should tear off the hat and coat of a man and fling them out the window, and then discover that they remained in his hands, and it was the man that he had thrown away.

—HA, 105

Metaphysics

...metaphysics is the only thoroughly emotional thing.

—TT, 34

Militarism

The evil of militarism is that it shows most men to be tame and timid and excessively peaceable. The professional soldier gains more and more power as the general courage of a community declines.... The military man gains the civil power in proportion as the civilian loses the military virtues.

—H, 37

Millionaires

Millionaires I can understand ... they are nearly all mad.

— Thursday, 132

Milton, John

No man, perhaps, has ever had such power over his art since the arts of humanity were made.

—HA, 77

The Mind

The world is now occupied with the study of the mind rather than the use of the mind. This is what is meant by calling it the Age of Psychology. It is also what is meant by calling it, in a somewhat sinister sense, the Age of Physical Jerks.

—AIG, 89

Mind (Gifts of)

All things are from God; and above all reason and imagination and the great gifts of the mind. They are good in themselves; and we must not altogether forget their origin even in their perversion.

—FBO, 578

Mind (the Common)

Commonness and the common mind are now generally spoken of as meaning in some manner inferiority and the inferior mind; the mind of the mere mob. But the common mind means the mind of all the artists and heroes; or else it would not be common. Plato had the common mind; Dante had the common mind; or that mind was not common. Commonness means the quality common to the saint and the sinner, to the philosopher and the fool; and it was this that Dickens grasped and developed.

—CD, 79

Miracles

The most incredible thing about miracles is that they happen.

—FBO, 6

The modern mind always mixes up two different ideas: mystery in the sense of what is marvelous, and mystery in the sense of what is complicated. That is half its difficulty about miracles. A miracle is startling; but it is simple. It is simple because it *is* a miracle. It is power coming directly from God (or the devil) instead of indirectly through nature or human wills.

—FBO, 131

Nobody can get behind that fundamental difference about the reason of things; and it is as rational for a theist to believe in miracles as for an atheist to disbelieve in them. In other words there is only one intelligent reason

218

why a man does not believe in miracles and that is that he does believe in materialism.

— St. Francis, 204

Only witches and wicked sorcerers make men captives by their enchantments; imprison them in beast or birds or turn them to stone statues. God's miracles always free men from captivity and give them back their bodies.

— Surprise, 15

Miser

The miser is the man who starves himself, and everybody else, in order to worship wealth in its dead form, as distinct from its living form.

—AIWS, 161

Moderation

Moderation is *not* a compromise; moderation is a passion; the passion of great judges.

— Types, 255

The Modern Age

The modern world has immeasurably surpassed the medieval world in organization and the application of such ideas as it has; so that the general improvement in certain kinds of humanity, certain kinds of instruction, and certain kinds of arbitration and order, is not merely an idea, but a material fact. But that does not alter the moral fact; that when we compare medieval ideas with modern ideas, we often find that the modern ideas are comparatively hasty, superficial or unbalanced; or else that the ideas, as ideas, really do not exist at all.

—C, 58

As usual, the wisest men of the age are not dominated by the spirit of the age. But perhaps the best summary in the matter of our own age would be this; that the stupid people are sneering at the last generation and the intelligent people are sneering at their own generation. But I think it must be admitted that most of them are sneering.

—S, 215–216

Modernism

The real objection to modernism is simply that it is a form of snobbishness. It is an attempt to crush a rational opponent not by reason, but by some mystery of superiority, by hinting that one is specially up to date or particularly "in the know." To flaunt the fact that we have had all the last books from Germany is simply vulgar. . . . To introduce into philosophical discussions a sneer at a creed's antiquity is like introducing a sneer at a lady's age. It is caddish because it is irrelevant. The pure modernist is merely a snob; he cannot bear to be a month behind the fashion.

—ATC, 5

A man who seriously describes his creed as Modernism might just as well invent a creed called Mondayism, meaning that he puts special faith in the fancies that occurred to him on Monday; or a creed called Morningism, meaning that he believes in the thoughts that occurred to him in the morning but not in the afternoon.

—CM, 165

The Modernist

The Modernist, or man who boasts of being modern, is generally rather like a man who overeats himself so much on Christmas Eve that he has no appetite on Christmas Day. It is called being In Advance of the Times; and is incumbent upon all who are progressive, prophetic, futuristic and generally looking towards what Mr. Belloc calls the Great Rosy Dawn: a dawn which generally looks a good deal rosier the night before than it does the morning after.

— *Thing*, 131

Modernity (Battle of)

The question is so enormous and so important, that it is difficult to state even by reason of its reality. For in this world of ours we do not so much go on and discover small things; rather we go on and discover big things. It is the details that we see first; it is the design we only see very slowly; and some men die never having seen it at all. We all wake up on a battle-field. . . . But it often takes us a long time to realise what the fight is about or even who is fighting whom. . . . How shall we manage to state in an obvious and alphabetical manner the ultimate query, the primordial pivot on which the whole modern problem turns? It cannot be done in long rationalistic words; they convey by their very sound the suggestion of something subtle. One must try to think of something in the way of a plain street metaphor or an obvious analogy. For the thing is not too hard for human speech; it is actually too obvious for human speech.

— *Blake*, 196–198

Moderns

Grave moderns told us that we must not even say "poor fellow," of a man who had blown his brains out, since he was an enviable person, and had only blown them out because of their exceptional excellence.

— *O*, 131

Moderns (and Contradiction)

No sceptics work sceptically; no fatalists work fatalistically; all without exception work on the principle that it is possible to assume what it is not possible to believe. No materialist who thinks his mind was made up for him, by mud and blood and heredity, has any hesitation in making up his

221

mind. No sceptic who believes that truth is subjective has any hesitation
about treating it as objective.

—STA, 185

Moderns vs. Traditionalists

There have been many intelligent and distinguished moderns, who have
thought quite gravely that certain great changes in habit or manners, in
diet or discipline of life, would make practically all men good and happy.
There is only one person who is immune from that illusion. And that is
the man who happens to know that nearly every one of these diets and
disciplines has already existed somewhere; where it did not prevent people
from being as naughty or silly as they chose.

—Avowals, 110–111

Modesty

Modesty is too fierce and elemental a thing for the modern pedants to
understand. . . .

—Blake, 177

Monarchy

Monarchy in its healthiest days had the same basis as democracy: the belief
in human nature when entrusted with power. A king was only the first
citizen who received the franchise.

—Types, 232

Monogamy (Modern Attack on)

The philosophical upshot of most problem plays is practically this, that if
two married people moon about in large rooms all day long, it is highly
probable that they will get on each other's nerves. On this basis (a purely

plutocratic basis) a large number of modern people have erected an attack upon monogamy; saying that it is not good for two people to be always together. The only weakness in the argument is that in actual human monogamy the two people are not always together. . . . We read poems and legends of parted lovers. Why, half the affectionate married couples of the world are perpetually parted lovers. An omnibus conductor and his wife see almost as little of each other as Romeo and Juliet. . . . Hence follows the fact that none of our intellectuals can understand; that the actual emotions of the democracy are much simpler and younger and more straightforward than those of a more fortunate class. A very hard-working man cannot get tired of his family. A very hard-working man can hardly get used to them.

—HA, 139–140

Monopoly

It is certainly not private enterprise. The American Trust is not private enterprise. It would be truer to call the Spanish Inquisition private judgment. Monopoly is neither private nor enterprising. It exists to prevent private enterprise. And that system of trust or monopoly, that complete destruction of property, would still be the present goal of all our progress, if there were not a Bolshevist in the world.

—Outline, 4

Monuments

There is the French monumental style, which consists in erecting very pompous statues, very well done. There is the German monumental style, which consists in erecting very pompous statues, badly done. And there is the English monumental method, the great English way with statues, which consists in not erecting them at all.

—ATC, 63

The Moral Imagination

The popular preference for a story with "A happy ending" is not, or at least was not a mere sweet-stuff optimism; it is the remains of the old idea of the triumph of the dragon-slayer, the ultimate apotheosis of the man beloved of heaven.

—CD, 63

Moralists (Modern)

I do not, as some do, denounce all these modern moralists as immoral. I only say that the most modern moralists are now at one with the most antiquated moralists. Like their Puritan great-grandfathers, they have nothing but negative morality.

—Survey, 68

Morality (as Teacher)

It is said that art cannot teach a lesson. This is true, and the only proper addition is the statement that neither, for the matter of that, can morality teach a lesson. For a thing to be didactic, in the strict and narrow and scholastic sense, it must be something about facts or the physical sciences: you can only teach a lesson about such a thing as Euclid or the making of paper boats. The thing is quite inapplicable to the great needs of man, whether moral or aesthetic. Nobody ever held a class in philanthropy with fifteen millionaires in a row writing cheques. Nobody ever held evening continuation classes in martyrdom, or drilled boys in a play-ground to die for their country.

—GFW, 56

Morality (New)

... your new morality means that it shall be always the faithful who suffers, and only the faithful who suffers. Your new morality provides that the faithless shall always be happy, that he or she only needs to be faithless in order to be happy. Suffer me to retain my prejudice in favor of a more primitive philosophy. I am not yet converted to a creed which systematically rewards people for breaking their word, and punishes them for keeping it.

—Judgement, 82

Music (Militant)

I remember a debate in which I had praised militant music in ritual, and someone asked me if I could imagine Christ walking down the street before a brass band. I said I could imagine it with the greatest of ease; for Christ definitely approved a natural noisiness at a great moment.

— TT, 138

Mystery Stories

... the author of a mystery story reveals. He is enjoyed not because he creates mystery, but because he destroys mystery. Nobody would have the courage to publish a detective-story which left the problem exactly where it found it. That would rouse even the London public to revolution. No one dare publish a detective-story that did not detect.

—ATC, 87–88

Mysticism

Mysticism keeps men sane. As long as you have mystery you have health; when you destroy mystery you create morbidity. The ordinary man has always been sane because the ordinary man has always been a mystic. He has permitted the twilight. He has always had one foot in earth and the other in fairyland. . . . He has always cared more for truth than for consistency. If he saw two truths that seemed to contradict each other, he would take the two truths and the contradiction along with them.

—O, 48

Mysticism and Common Sense

Carlyle was, as we have suggested, a mystic, and mysticism was with him, as with all its genuine professors, only a transcendent form of common sense. Mysticism and common sense alike consist in a sense of the dominance of certain truths and tendencies which cannot be formally demonstrated or even formally named. Mysticism and common sense are alike appeals to realities that we all know to be real, but which have no place in argument except as postulates.

—Types, 116–117

Mystics

The mystic is not the man who makes mysteries but the man who destroys them.

—Blake, 131

The perfect mystic would be always socially alert. The perfect mystic would be always correctly dressed. To such heights of transcendentalism some of us may find it difficult to soar; and such honest and unselfconscious failure, though it is certainly a weakness, is not an unpardonable or inhuman one.

—HA, 173

N

Narrative Process (Understanding the)

Most modern people cannot really do this; they have read too many novels. They have forgotten the very verbal meaning, by which novels once meant news. They have lost the positive pleasure in a double fashion; partly because they have been bewildered by too many plots; partly because they have been even more bewildered by the newer sort of novels, which have not got any plots.

—C, 153

Nationalism and Arrogance

Before we congratulate ourselves upon the absence of certain faults from our nation or society, we ought to ask ourselves why it is that these faults are absent. Are we without the fault because we have the opposite virtue? Or are we without the fault because we have the opposite fault? It is a good thing assuredly, to be innocent of any excess; but let us be sure that we are not innocent of excess merely by being guilty of defect.

—ATC, 39

Nationalism (Nazi)

Many of the things the new Germans are saying are quite true. But they do not say that the truths are true; they only say they are German. Many of the things they do are right. But they do not say they are right; they say they are German. That is, they do not refer to, or recognise, any standard outside themselves. When they say they worship the German God, they really mean that they would not be judged, even on the Day of Judgement, by any god who was not a German. But the Founder of Christianity and Christendom neglected to make Himself a German.

—EA, 20–21

The essence of Nazi Nationalism is to preserve the purity of a race in a continent where all races are impure. You can make frontiers and keep them like articles of faith; but if you merely follow race wanderings, you will follow one tribe through a complexity of tribes, which you will always be trying to simplify by tales of extermination, colonisation or conquest.

—EA, 113–114

Nations

A nation that has nothing but its amusements will not be amused for very long.

—C, 169

... there are three stages in the life of a strong people. First, it is a small power, and fights small powers. Then it is a great power, and fights great powers. Then it is a great power, and fights small powers, but pretends that they are great powers, in order to rekindle the ashes of its ancient emotion and vanity.

—H, 267

Nations and Empire

Being a nation means standing up to your equals, whereas being an empire only means kicking your inferiors.

—*TT*, 230

Nazis

Unfortunately it is a hysteria of self-praise, which is fed by its own virtues as much as its own vices. For that is the vital or rather mortal weakness of Pride. It says: "I did a fine thing kicking out a Jew usurer"; but it also says: "Bashing a Catholic boy scout was a fine thing, because I did it." It is in no partisan spirit that any Christian will smell evil in this vast explosion of gas and wind.

—*EA*, 219–220

Herr Hitler and his group have done many things of which I cannot approve. They murdered a number of people without trial during a sort of week-end trip. They murdered a man merely for being an influential Catholic; and, what is even worse, explained that they had murdered him by mistake. They beat and bully poor Jews in concentration camps. They talk about preserving the purity of their blood. They commit every crime.

—*EA*, 192

Nazis and Bolsheviks

The Prussian and the Russian will agree about everything, especially about Poland. They may differ in many things, but in hatred of the Christian civilisation they are truly international.

—*EA*, 169

Prussia has proved her Paganism once again in the Nazi movement; as for that matter in the Nudist movement or half a hundred heathen fads. But above all, in this vital or very deadly fact; that the *Nazi is ready to dally with the Communists.* That is the flash of fact and reality that blasts all sorts of labels and conventions. The Nazi may be Nationalist and the Bolshie may be Internationalist. . . . But they both feel they are of the same stuff; a stuff which they would call the new forces and I should call the old barbarism.

—*EA*, 169

Nazis and Race

Even the Lutheran remembers that there was somebody before Luther; for whom Luther himself expressed some regard. And the ethnological proofs that Jesus Christ was a pure Nordic Teuton are not so satisfactory as was hoped. But the German sceptic can be completely sceptical about anyone who was not a German; and can put Luther as high above Christ as he likes. It is of the very nature of this new religion of Race that it flourishes better in a world of irreligion, than of anything that we used to call religion.

—*EA*, 206

Nazis (and Treaties)

. . . Prime Minister Goering, who seems to have said, "They say we do not observe our treaties; look at our treaty with Poland." This treaty has actually been running for more than a year; and the suggestion is that Göring has searched the whole history of Prussia for any other example of a treaty that was not broken.

—*EA*, 105

The Nazi's Hysteria

Now it always seems to me that what is wrong with the Germans is hysteria. People may even think this a paradox; because Germans are generally heavy and stodgy, while Italians shout and yell and throw plates. But Italians are not in the least hysterical; they are only angry. Any doctor will tell you that hysteria is deepest when it is secret and silent. . . . It is a curious sort of sensitiveness and brooding, which breaks out intermittently as bragging. But the brooding and the bragging have both that sort of egoism and self-pity which are almost a medical disease.

—EA, 56–57

New York

New York is a cosmopolitan city, but it is not a city of cosmopolitans. Most of the masses in New York have a nation whether or no it be the nation to which New York belongs. . . . They are exiles or they are citizens; there is no moment when they are cosmopolitans. But very often the exiles bring with them not only rooted traditions, but rooted truths.

—Amer, 35

One of the first questions I was asked was how I should be disposed to explain the wave of crime in New York. Naturally I replied that it might possibly be due to the number of English lecturers who had recently landed.

—Amer, 54

Newman, John Henry

Whatever else is right, the theory that Newman went over to Rome to find peace and an end of argument, is quite unquestionably wrong. He had far more quarrels after he had gone over to Rome. But though he had far more quarrels, he had far fewer compromises: and he was of that temper which is tortured more by compromise than by quarrel. He was a case at once of abnormal energy and abnormal sensibility: nobody without that combination could have written the *Apologia.*

—VA, 46–47

But always his triumphs are the triumphs of a highly sensitive man: a man must feel insults before he can so insultingly and splendidly avenge them. He is a naked man, who carries a naked sword. The quality of his literary style is so successful that it succeeds in escaping definition. The quality of his logic is that of a long but passionate patience, which waits until he has fixed all corners of an iron trap. But the quality of his moral comment on the age remains what I have said: a protest of the rationality of religion as against the increasing irrationality of mere Victorian comfort and compromise.

—VA, 47–48

Newspaper Editors

... the modern editor regards himself far too much as a kind of original artist, who can select and supress facts with the arbitrary ease of a poet or a caricaturist. He "makes up" the paper as man "makes up" a fairy tale, he considers his newspapers solely as a work of art, meant to give pleasure, not to give news.

—ATC, 124

Newspaper Headlines

The few really untrue and unscrupulous things I have seen in American 'stories' have always been in the headlines. And the headlines are written by somebody else; some solitary and savage cynic locked up in the office, hating all mankind and raging and revenging himself at random, while the neat, polite, and rational pressman can safely be let loose to wander about the town.

—Amer, 58

Newspapers

Everything in a newspaper that is not the old human love of altar or fatherland is the old human love of gossip.

—TT, 264

Newspapers (and Rearmament)

...a man does not give up his umbrella at the exact moment when a thundercloud is threatening to crash over his head; a man does not give up his sword at the exact moment when his next-door neighbour, who has obviously gone mad, is waving sabres and battle-axes over the wall.... But to expect people to go on talking about nothing except the price of umbrellas during the steady increase of the deluge, or to talk about nothing but the price of armaments under the instant threat of an appeal to arms, is simply not within the limits of human sanity. Yet it is the only topic recognised as really respectable in our national newspapers. It is horribly typical of such organs of opinion that they are always quite content with the continuity of a discussion, quite apart from whether there is ever any decision, or whether it is the wrong decision.

—EA, 214

Newspapers (Modern)

As modern newspapers are conducted, the most honest and most important news is the police news. If it be true that in the twentieth century more space was given to murder than to politics, it was for the excellent reason that murder was a more serious subject.

—FBO, 290

Nietzsche, Friedrich Wilhelm

Nietzsche ... preached a doctrine which he and his followers regard apparently as very revolutionary; he held that ordinary altruistic morality had been the invention of a slave class to prevent the emergence of superior types to fight and rule them. Now, modern people, whether they agree with this or not, always talk of it as a new and unheard-of idea. It is calmly and persistently supposed that the great writers of the past, say Shakespeare for instance, did not hold this view, because they had never imagined it; because it had never come into their heads. Turn up the last act of Shakespeare's *Richard III* and you will find not only all that

233

Nietzsche had to say put into two lines, but you will find it put in the very words of Nietzsche. Richard Crookback says to his nobles:

> "Conscience is but a word that cowards use,
> Devised at first to keep the strong in awe."

—CM, 24

And when Nietzsche says, "A new commandment I give to you, 'Be hard,' " he is really saying, "A new commandment I give to you, 'Be dead.' " Sensibility is the definition of life.

—H, 83

Nietzsche will stand very well as the type of the whole of this failure of abstract violence. The softening of the brain which ultimately overtook him was not a physical accident. If Nietzsche had not ended in imbecility, Nietzscheism would end in imbecility. Thinking in isolation and with pride ends in being an idiot. Every man who will not have softening of the heart must at least have softening of the brain.

—O, 75

Nietzsche (Disciples of)

The disciple of Nietzsche, indeed, embraces immorality like an austere and difficult faith. He urges himself to lust and cruelty with the same tremulous enthusiasm with which a Christian urges himself to purity and patience; he struggles as a monk struggles with bestial visions and temptations with the ancient necessities of honour and justice and compassion.

—Types, 122

Nihilism

There is nothing to be done with Nothing.

—RLS, 64

Nihilists and Athiests

... there is a difference between worshipping Nothing and not worshipping anything.

—RLS, 64

Nineteen Thirty-three (the Stupidest Thing of)

Having been asked the question "What in your opinion were the most stupid things of 1933?" I can answer it very simply if I may be permitted to answer it sincerely. By far the stupidest thing done, not only in the last year, but in the last two or three centuries, was the acceptance by the Germans of the Dictatorship of Hitler—to say nothing of Goering.

—EA, 61

Nineteenth-century Mind

The man of that aggressive nineteenth century had many wild thoughts, but there was one thought that never even for an instant strayed across his burning brain. He never once thought, "Why should I understand the cat, anymore than the cat understands me?" He never thought, "Why should I be just to the merits of a Chinaman, anymore than a pig studies the mystic virtues of a camel?" He affronted heaven and the angels, but there was one hard arrogant dogma that he never doubted even when he doubted Godhead: he never doubted that he himself was as central and responsible as God.

—GFW, 36

Nominalism

I remember when Mr. H. G. Wells had an alarming fit of Nominalist philosophy; and poured forth book after book to argue that everything is unique and untypical; as that a man is so much an individual that he is not even a man.

—STA, 174

Novels

People wonder why the novel is the most popular form of literature; people wonder why it is read more than books of science or books of metaphysics. The reason is very simple; it is merely that the novel is more true than they are. Life may sometimes legitimately appear as a book of science. . . . But life is always a novel. Our existence may cease to be a song; it may cease even to be a beautiful lament. Our existence may not be an intelligible justice, or even a recognizable wrong. But our existence is still a story.

—H, 192

I merely say, therefore, that where I say "novel," I mean a fictitious narrative (almost invariably, but not necessarily, in prose) of which the essential is that the story is not told for the sake of its naked pointedness as an anecdote, or for the sake of the irrelevant landscapes and visions that can be caught up in it, but for the sake of some study of the difference between human beings.

—VA, 90

Novels (Historical)

Before systematic historical criticism came into existence, all-armed like Pallas from the brain of Jove, it was hardly possible to draw a distinction between history proper and the historical novel. Pliny declared that all the world's historians down to his own time were but "narrators of fables," and his opinion still finds supporters, who unkindly refuse to acquiesce in his own exception of himself.

—HA, 199

Novels (Modern)

... in the modern psychological novel the hero is abnormal; the centre is not central. Hence the fiercest adventures fail to affect him adequately, and the book is monotonous. You can make a story out of a hero among dragons; but not out of a dragon among dragons. The fairy tale discusses what a sane man will do in a mad world. The sober realistic novel of to-day discusses what an essential lunatic will do in a dull world.

—O, 26–27

The problem of the fairy tale is—what will a healthy man do with a fantastic world? The problem of the modern novel is—what will a madman do with a dull world? In the fairy tales the cosmos goes mad; but their hero does not go mad. In the modern novels the hero is mad before the book begins, and suffers from the harsh steadiness and cruel sanity of the cosmos.

—TT, 125

The Novelist

If for the artist his art is a fizzle, his life is often far more of a fizzle: it is even far more of a fiction.

—RLS, 19

Nudists

The cult of nakedness, which used to be called the Adamite Heresy, does, in fact, reveal its falsity at the beginning, even in the merely material aspect.... Nakedness is not even practical, except on selected occasions that are entirely artificial.... It is not native to man to go without clothes, unless it is native to man to die of double pneumonia in about a month.

—AIG, 14–15

237

O

Oligarchy

A man can rise to any rank in an oligarchy. But an oligarchy is simply a prize for impudence. An oligarchy says that the victor may be any kind of man, so long as he is not a humble man.

—L & L, 118

The Omniscient

The omniscient are often ignorant. They are often especially ignorant of ignorance.

—FFF, 24

One Thing at a Time

Friends ask each other to dinner for a quiet little chat, in restaurants where they have to howl at each other through the noise of a brass band; and cannot utter the slightest jest or the most delicate compliment without making certain that it is louder than the big drum. They will not listen to the music and they cannot listen to the conversation. If these people are pleasure-seekers they are certainly the prize idiots of all human history in their manner of seeking it. For an idiot surely deserves a prize for idiocy

238

when he manages to destroy two pleasures by one action; and kill two singing-birds with one stone.

—S, 59–60

Opinions

To put my meaning broadly, the opinions which nobody can agree with are mostly in the books that nobody can read.

—Blake, 97

Opinions and Personal Philosophies

The modern habit of saying, 'This is my opinion, but I may be wrong,' is entirely irrational. If I say that it may be wrong I say that it is not my opinion. The modern habit of saying, 'Every man has a different philosophy; this is my philosophy and it suits me:' the habit of saying this is a mere weak-mindedness. A cosmic philosophy is not constructed to fit a man; a cosmic philosophy is constructed to fit a cosmos. A man can no more possess a private religion than he can posses a private sun and moon.

—GKC, 41–42

Opinions (Silly)

A little while ago the family of a young lady attempted to shut her up in an asylum because she believed in Free Love. This atrocious injustice was stopped; but many people wrote to the papers to say that marriage was a very fine thing—as indeed it is. Of course the answer was simple: that if everyone with silly opinions were locked up in an asylum, the asylums of the twentieth century would have to be somewhat unduly enlarged.

—Blake, 78

Optimism

There is a great deal of difference between the optimism which says that things are perfect and the optimism which merely says (with a more primeval modesty) that they are very good. One optimism says that a one-legged man has two legs because it would be so dreadful if he had not. The other optimism says that the fact that the one-legged was born of a woman, has a soul, has been in love, and has stood alive under the stars, is a fact so enormous and thrilling that, in comparison, it does not matter whether he has one leg or five. One optimism says that this is the best of all possible worlds. The other says that it is certainly not the best of all possible worlds, but it is the best of all possible things that a world should be possible.

—GFW, 66–67

It is surely obvious that no one can be argued into optimism since no one can be argued into happiness.

—RB, 179

The reaction from the idea that what is good is always unsuccessful is the idea that what is good is always victorious. And from that many slide into the worse delusion; that what is victorious is always good.

—RLS, 88

Optimists

These higher optimists, of whom Dickens was one, do not approve of the Universe; they do not even admire the Universe; they fall in love with it. They embrace life too closely to criticize or even to see it. Existence to such men has the wild beauty of a woman, and those love her with most intensity who love her with least cause.

—CD, 31–32

If optimism means a general approval, it is certainly true that the more a man becomes an optimist the more he becomes a melancholy man. If he manages to praise everything, his praise will develop an alarming resemblance to a polite boredom. He will say that the marsh is as good as the garden; he will mean that the garden is as dull as the marsh.

$-CD$, 203

The person who is really in revolt is the optimist, who generally lives and dies in a desperate and suicidal effort to persuade all the other people how good they are. . . . Every one of the great revolutionists, from Isaiah to Shelley, have been optimists. They have been indignant, not about the badness of existence, but about the slowness of men in realizing its goodness.

$-D$, 4

Orators

Those who are quick in talking are not always quick in listening. Sometimes even their brilliancy produces a sort of stupidity.

$-FBO$, 481

It is the whole difference between the aim of the orator and the aim of any other artist, such as the poet or the sculptor. The aim of the sculptor is to convince us that he is a sculptor; the aim of the orator is to convince us that he is not an orator.

$-H$, 48

Oratory

I do feel a certain contempt for those who call every phrase affected that happens to be effective; or who charge a man with talking for effect, as if there were anything else to talk for.

—RLS, 88

Oratory (Political)

The conversational persuasion at elections is perfectly human and rational; it is the silent persuasions that are utterly damnable.

—ATC, 33

The speeches in our time are more careful and elaborate, because they are meant to be read, and not to be heard. And exactly because they are more careful and elaborate, they are not so likely to be worthy of a careful and elaborate report. They are not interesting enough. So the moral coward-ice of modern politicians has, after all, some punishment attached to it by the silent anger of heaven. Precisely because our political speeches are meant to be reported, they are not worth reporting. Precisely because they are carefully designed to be read, nobody reads them.

—ATC, 129–130

Original Sin

Carlyle said that men were mostly fools. Christianity, with a surer and more reverent realism, says that they are all fools. This doctrine is some-times called the doctrine of original sin. It may also be described as the doctrine of the equality of men.

—H, 165–166

Orthodoxy

People have fallen into a foolish habit of speaking of orthodoxy as something heavy, humdrum, and safe. There never was anything so perilous or so exciting as orthodoxy. It was sanity: and to be sane is more dramatic than to be mad. . . . It is easy to be a madman: it is easy to be a heretic. It is always easy to let the age have its head; the difficult thing is to keep one's own. It is always easy to be a modernist; as it is easy to be a snob. . . . It is always simple to fall; there are an infinity of angles at which one falls, only one at which one stands. To have fallen into any one of the fads from Gnosticism to Christian Science would indeed have been obvious and tame. But to have avoided them all has been one whirling adventure; and in my vision the heavenly chariot flies thundering through the ages, the dull heresies sprawling and prostrate, the wild truth reeling but erect.

—*O,* 187

Overwork

Remember always that there is one thing that cannot be endured by anybody or anything. That one unendurable thing is to be overworked and also neglected. For instance, you can overwork women—everybody does. But you can't neglect women—I defy you to.

—*TT,* 294

Oxford

If the sensitive man on the *Outlook* does not like the phrase, "Playground of the rich," I can suggest a phrase that describes such a place as Oxford perhaps with more precision. It is a place for humanising those who might otherwise be tyrants, or even experts.

—*ATC,* 71

P

Pacifists and Prussianists

A Pacifist is something which it is wise to be in the presence of a Prussianist. A Prussianist is something which it is safe to be in the presence of a Pacifist.

—*EA,* 210

Paganism

The worst temptation of the most pagan youth is not so much to denounce monks for breaking their vow as to wonder at them for keeping it.

—*CCC,* 28–29

Paganism is better than pantheism, for paganism is free to imagine divinities, while pantheism is forced to pretend, in a priggish way, that all things are equally divine.

—*CCC,* 89

It is not Pagan to revile the gods nor is it Pagan to exalt a streetwalker into a symbol of all possible pleasure. The Pagan felt that there was a sort of easy and equable force pressing upon us from Nature; that this force was

244

breezy and beneficent, though not specially just or loving; in other words, that there was, as the strength in wine or trees or the ocean, the energy of kindly but careless gods.

—HA, 68

Nothing distinguishes paganism from Christianity so clearly as the fact that the individual thing called philosophy had little or nothing to do with the social thing called religion.

—St. Francis, 44

A Pagan is a person who can do what hardly any person for the last two thousand years could do: a person who can take Nature naturally.

—VA, 139

Pain

Pain, it is said, is the dominant element of life; but this is true only in a very special sense. If pain were for one single instant literally the dominant element in life, every man would be found hanging dead from his own bed-post by the morning. . . . The literature of joy is infinitely more difficult, more rare and more triumphant than the black and white literature of pain.

—D, 93

Palestine

The sorrow of all Palestine is that its divisions in culture, politics and theology are like its divisions in geology. The dividing line is horizontal instead of vertical. The frontier does not run between states but between stratified layers. The Jew did not appear beside the Canaanite but on top of the Canaanite; the Greek not beside the Jew but on top of the Jew; the Moslem not beside the Christian but on top of the Christian. It

245

is not merely a house divided against itself, but one divided across itself.

—NJ, 107–108

Pantheism

There is no real possibility of getting out of pantheism any special impulse to moral action. For pantheism implies in its nature that one thing is as good as another; whereas action implies in its nature that one thing is greatly preferable to another.

—O, 247

Parental Authority

I have read hundreds and thousands of times, in all the novels and newspapers of our epoch, certain phases about the just right of the young to liberty, about the unjust claim of the elders to control, about the conception that all souls must be free or all citizens equal, about the absurdity of authority or the degradation of obedience. . . . what strikes me as astounding, in a logical sense, is that not one of these myriad novelists and newspaper-men ever seem to think of asking the next and most obvious question. It never seems to occur to them to inquire what becomes of the opposite obligation. The child is free from the first to disregard the parent, why is not the parent free from the first to disregard the child?

—Thing, 30

Particulars

All unsophisticated human beings instinctively accept the sacramental principle that the particular thing is closest to the general, the tangible thing closest to the spiritual; the child with the doll, the priest with a relic, the girl with an engagement ring, the soldier with a medal, the modern agnostic with his little scarab for luck. One can recall the soul of boyhood better by smelling peppermint then by reading about adolescence. . . .

—*HA*, 69

Party Politics and Democracy

The real danger of the two parties with their two policies is that they unduly limit the outlook of the ordinary citizen. They make him barren instead of creative, because he is never allowed to do anything except prefer one existing policy to another. We have not got real democracy when the decision depends upon the people. We shall have real democracy when the problem depends upon the people. The ordinary man will decide not only how he will vote, but what he is going to vote about.

—*MM*, 37–38

The Past

Finally, a truth is to be remembered which scarcely ever is remembered in estimating the past. It is the paradox that the past is always present: Yet it is not what was, but whatever seems to have been; for all the past is a part of faith.

—*England*, 25

Past vs. Present and Future

We talk of people living in the past; and it is commonly applied to old people or old-fashioned people. But, in fact, we all live in the past, because there is nothing else to live in. To live in the present is like proposing to sit on a pin. It is too minute, it is too slight a support, it is too uncomfortable a posture, and it is of necessity followed immediately by totally different experiences, analogous to those of jumping up with a yell. To live in the future is a contradiction in terms. The future is dead; in the perfectly definite sense that it is not alive. It has no nature, no form, no feature. . . . The past can move and excite us, the past can be loved and hated, the past consists largely of lives that can be considered in their completion; that is, literally in the fullness of life.

—Avowals, 198

Patriotism

'My country, right or wrong,' is a thing that no patriot would think of saying except in a desperate case. It is like saying, 'My mother, drunk or sober.' No doubt if a decent man's mother took to drink he would share her troubles to the last; but to talk as if he would be in a state of gay indifference as to whether his mother took to drink or not is certainly not the language of men who know the great mystery.

—D, 125

Patriotism is not the first virtue. Patriotism rots into Prussianism when you pretend it is the first virtue. But patriotism is sometimes the last virtue. A man will swindle or seduce who will not sell his country.

—MWKTM, 238

People

People are often very misleading when they talk about themselves; even when they are perfectly honest, and even modest, in talking about themselves. But people tell a great deal so long as they talk about everything except themselves.

—Don Q, 232

People (Enlightened)

"That," answered Eden, "is because educated and enlightened people never think. Your enlightened man is always taking away the number he first thought of. It seems to be a sign of education first to take a thing for granted and then to forget to see if it is still there. Weapons are a very good

248

working example. The man says he won't go on wearing a sword because it is no longer any good against a gun. Then he throws away all the guns as relics of barbarism; and then he is surprised when a barbarian sticks him through with a sword."

— Don Q, 249

People (Kinds of)

Roughly speaking, there are three kinds of people in the world. The first kind of people are People; they are the largest and probably the most valuable class. We owe to this class the chairs we sit down on, the clothes we wear, the houses we live in; and, indeed (when we come to think of it), we probably belong to this class ourselves. The second class may be called for convenience the Poets; they are often a nuisance to their families, but, generally speaking, a blessing to mankind. The third class is that of the Professors or Intellectuals; sometimes described as the thoughtful people; and these are a blight and a desolation both to their families and also to mankind.

— Alarms, 147

People (Modern)

. . . the chief charm of medieval people was that they never thought about being medieval. It is the chief inferiority of modern people that they do think about being modern.

— HA, 136

People (Stupid)

When a man says that democracy is false because most people are stupid, there are several courses which the philosopher may pursue. The most obvious is to hit him smartly and with precision on the exact tip of the nose. But if you have scruples (moral or physical) about this course, you may proceed to employ Reason, which in this case has all the savage solidity of a blow with the fist. It is stupid to say that "most people" are stupid. It is like saying "most people are tall," when it is obvious that "tall" can only mean taller than most people. It is absurd to denounce the majority of mankind as below the average of mankind.

—Alarm, 63

People (Who Complain)

People who complain are just jolly human Christian nuisances; I don't mind them. But people who complain that they never complain are the devil.

—FBO, 722

The gentleman may permit himself to curse the dinner and tell himself that he would behave much better if it were a mere matter of starvation.

—TT, 50

Pessimism

Pessimism is not always inane and drifting, like the kind described by Tennyson; pessimism is sometimes courageous; strange as it may seem, it is sometimes cheerful. The good done by sceptical philosophers, indeed, has almost always resolved itself into the fact that while they were pessimists about everything else they were optimists about their own opinions: they might be living in the worst of all possible worlds, but they were the best of all possible judges of it.

—HA, 104

Sorrow and pessimism are by their natures opposite: sorrow rests upon the value of something; pessimism on the value of nothing.

—HA, 106

What is the matter with the pessimist? I think it can be stated by saying that he is the cosmic anti-patriot. And what is the matter with the anti-patriot? I think it can be stated, without undue bitterness, by saying that he is the candid friend. . . .

I venture to say that what is bad in the candid friend is simply that he is not candid. He is keeping something back—his own gloomy pleasure in saying unpleasant things. He has a secret desire to hurt, not merely to help. This is certainly, I think, what makes a certain sort of anti-patriot irritating to healthy citizens.

—O, 124

All pessimism has a secret optimism for its object.

—TT, 55

Philanthropy

It is not always certain whether philanthropy means a love of men, or of man, or of mankind. There is a difference.

—Mr. Pond, 81

The trouble with the philanthropist is not that he does not love all men moderately, but rather that he generally loves one man too well.

—S, 4

Philistines

A Philistine is only a man who is right without knowing why.

—FBO, 690

Philosophers

Like a true philosopher, Flambeau had no aim in his holiday; but, like a true philosopher, he had an excuse.

—FBO, 137

A philosopher cannot talk about any single thing, down to a pumpkin without showing whether he is wise or foolish; but he can easily talk about everything with anyone having any views about him beyond gloomy suspicions.

—GFW, 54

There is of course a certain tendency among all interesting and novel critical philosophers to talk as if they had discovered things which it is perfectly impossible that any human being could ever have denied; to shout that the birds fly, and declare that in spite of persecution they will still assert that cows have four legs. In this way some raw pseudo-scientists talk about heredity or the physical basis of life as if it were not a thing embedded in every creed and legend, and even the very languages of men.

—GFW, 55

Now it is the supreme function of the philosopher of the grotesque to make the world stand on its head that people may look at it. If we say "a man is a man" we awaken no sense of the fantastic, however much we ought to, but if we say, in the language of the old satirist, "that man is a two-legged bird, without feathers," the phrase does, for a moment, make us look at man from the outside and give us a thrill in his presence.

—RB, 151

The true philosopher does not think of coming just in time for his train except as a bet or a joke.

—TT, 260

Philosophers and Mystics

In short, both the mystic and the mere philosopher agree that the spiritual is more important than the material considered in itself. The philosopher thinks that the spiritual lies very far beyond the material, like a remote landmark behind a plain. The mystic thinks that the spiritual is very close behind the material, like a brigand hiding behind a bush. Science is always saying that the other world, if it exists, is too distant to be seen. Religion is always saying it is too close to be seen.

—HA, 70

Philosophers and Poets

The system of Kant; the system of Hegel; the system of Schopenhauer and Nietzsche and Marx and all the rest. In each of these examples a man sprang up and pretended to have a thought that nobody had ever had. But the great poet only professes to express the thought that everybody has always had.

—C, 19

Philosophers (Sham)

Many men can make an epic who could not make an epigram. What is true of the comic anecdote is true also of that extended anecdote, the sensational story with a point to it. All real philosophy is apocalyptic, and if a man can give us revelations of heaven it is certainly better than giving us horrible revelations of high life. But I would rather have the man who devotes a short story to saying that he can solve the problem of a murder in Margate than the man who devotes a whole book to saying that he cannot solve the problem of things in general.

—HA, 171

Philosophies (New)

The new philosophies and new social systems cannot draw up their own plans for emancipating mankind without still further enslaving mankind. They cannot carry out even what they regard as the most ordinary reforms without instantly imposing the most extraordinary restrictions. We are to live under a sort of martial law lest we should hear of anything martial. . . . Everybody is to be drilled with an antimilitarist discipline which is quite as stiff and strict as a militarist discipline.

—Avowals, 38–39

Philosophy

The best reason for a revival of philosophy is that unless a man has a philosophy certain horrible things will happen to him. He will be practical; he will be progressive; he will cultivate efficiency; he will trust in evolution. . . . he will devote himself to deeds, not words. Thus struck down by blow after blow of blind stupidity and random fate, he will stagger on to a miserable death with no comfort but a series of catchwords. . . .

—CM, 173

An imbecile habit has arisen in modern controversy of saying that such and such a creed can be held in one age but cannot be held in another. Some dogma, we are told, was credible in the twelfth century, but is not credible in the twentieth. You might as well say that a certain philosopher can be believed on Mondays but cannot be believed on Tuesdays. You might as well say of a view of the cosmos that it was suitable to half-past three, but not suitable to half-past four. What a man can believe depends upon his philosophy, not upon the clock of the century. . . . the point is not whether it was given in our time, but whether it was given in answer to our question.

—O, 135–137

A philosophy begins with Being; with the end and value of a living thing; and it is manifest that a materialism that only considers economic ethics, cannot cover the question at all. If the problem of happiness were so solved by economic comfort, the classes who are now comfortable would be happy, which is absurd.

—Well, 128

Philosophy (Ancient)

... atheist philosophy was founded, not on the fact that Nature is kind but on the fact that Nature is cruel; not that fields are free and beautiful, but that scientific men and industrialists are so energetic, that they will soon cover all the fields with factories and warehouses. Now there was a new substitute for God. ... It was now positively stated that economic liberty, the freedom to buy and sell and hire and exploit, would make people so blissfully happy that they would forget all their dreams of the fields of heaven. ... And somehow that also has been a little disappointing.

—CM, 75

Philosophy (Modern)

... modern philosophies are [considered] modern in the sense that the great men of the past did not think of them. They thought of them; only they did not think much of them.

—CM, 24

Most modern philosophics are not philosophy but philosophic doubt; that is, doubt about whether there can be any philosophy.

—STA, 185

Philosophy (Thomistic)

It is the return of the Thomistic Philosophy; which is the philosophy of commonsense, as compared with the paradoxes of Kant and Hegel and the Pragmatists. The Roman religion will be, in the exact sense, the only Rationalistic religion. The other religions will not be Rationalist but Relativist; declaring that the reason is itself relative and unreliable; declaring that Being is only Becoming or that all time is only a time of transition. . . . Instead of the materialist who said that the soul did not exist, we shall have the new mystic who says that the body does not exist. Amid all these things the return of the Scholastic will simply be the return of the sane man.

—Well, 193–194

Phonetic Spelling

The people who want phonetic spelling generally depress the world with tireless and tasteless explanations of how much easier it would be for children or foreign bagmen if "height" were spelt "hite." Now children would curse spelling whatever it was, and we are not going to permit foreign bagmen to improve Shakespeare.

—GBS, 66

Photography vs. Painting

To begin with, it is unfair to talk about "photographic art" as an equivalent to representative or realistic art. A camera does not copy the details of every weed and nettle with the pious patience of a Pre-Raphaelite; because a camera is not pious or even patient. A camera does not work out thoroughly the whole scheme of a piece of still life, with the craftsmanship and technical honesty of a Dutch painter; because a camera is not a craftsman; and a camera can no more be honest than dishonest.

—HA, 185–186

Piety

Piety produces intellectual greatness precisely because piety in itself is quite indifferent to intellectual greatness.

—CD, 9

Pigs and Man

We breed pigs to turn them into pork, not to exhibit their portraits as pictures of perfect and harmonious beauty. In other words, we can breed cows and pigs precisely because we cannot really criticize cows and pigs. We cannot judge them from the point of view of the Cow Concept or the Pig Ideal. Therefore we cannot, and do not, criticize them in the way in which we criticize our fellow creatures . . . when we call them feeble-minded; or when we betray our own feeble-mindedness by calling them unfit. . . . Nobody would call a cow fit without naturally adding what she was fit for. Nobody would call up the insanely isolated vision of the Unfit Pig in the abstract. But when we talk about human beings, we are bound to break off the sentence in the middle; we are bound to call them unfit in the abstract. For we know how varied, how complex, and how controversial are the questions that arise about the functions for which they should be fitted.

—Avowals, 58–59

Play

It is not only possible to say a great deal in praise of play; it is really possible to say the highest things in praise of it. It might reasonably be maintained that the true object of all human life is play. Earth is a task garden; heaven is a playground. To be at last in such secure innocence that one can juggle with the universe and the stars, to be so good that one can treat everything as a joke—that may be, perhaps, the real end and final holiday of human souls.

—ATC, 72

Pleasure

... the man who finds most pleasure for himself is often the man who least hunts for it.

—TT, 84

Poetic Ignorance (Beauty of)

It is well sometimes to half understand a poem in the same manner that we half understand the world. One of the deepest and strangest of all human moods, is the mood which will suddenly strike us perhaps in a garden at night, or deep in sloping meadows, the feeling that every flower and leaf has just uttered something stupendously direct and important, and that we have by a prodigy of imbecility not heard or understood it. There is a certain poetic value, and that a genuine one, in this sense of having missed the full meaning of things. There is beauty, not only in wisdom, but in this dazed and dramatic ignorance.

—RB, 158

Poetry

Poetry is not a selection of the images which will express a particular thought; it is rather an analysis of the thoughts which are evoked by a certain image.

—HA, 103

... poetry is not an ornamental and indirect way of stating philosophy but a perfectly simple and direct way of stating something that is outside philosophy. There are fleeting and haphazard sights of nature that are words out of an unknown dictionary: every sunset might have founded a separate creed.

—HA, 105

Poetry deals with primal and conventional things—the hunger for bread, the love of woman, the love of children, the desire for immortal life. If men really had new sentiments, poetry could not deal with them. If, let us say, a man did not feel a bitter craving to eat bread; but did, by way of substitute, feel a fresh, original craving to eat brass fenders or mahogany tables, poetry could not express him. If a man, instead of falling in love with a woman, fell in love with a fossil or a sea-anemone, poetry could not express him.

—*RB,* 99

Poetry deals entirely with those great eternal and mainly forgotten wishes which are the ultimate despots of existence. Poetry presents things as they are to our emotions, not as they are to any theory, however plausible, or any argument, however conclusive. If love is in truth a glorious vision, poetry will say that it is a glorious vision, and no philosophers will persuade poetry to say that it is the exaggeration of the instinct of sex.

—*RB,* 184

Ethics is the science of actions, but poetry is the science of motives.

—*RB,* 185

Prose can only use a large and clumsy notation; it can only say that a man is miserable, or that a man is happy; it is forced to ignore that there are a million diverse kinds of misery and a million diverse kinds of happiness. Poetry alone, with the first throb of its metre, can tell us whether the depression is the kind of depression that drives a man to suicide, or the kind of depression that drives him to the Tivoli. Poetry can tell us whether the happiness is the happiness that sends a man to a restaurant, or the much richer and fuller happiness that sends him to church.

—*RB,* 185

Poetry (Modern)

Poetry has become more than normally individualistic. The individualist can write a song; but not a song with a chorus.

—*S*, 213

Poetry (of Childhood)

There really is no sense or meaning, in this continuous tribute of the poets to the poetry of early childhood, unless it be, as Treherne says, that the world of sin comes between us and something more beautiful or, as Wordsworth says, that we came first from God who is our home.

—*RLS*, 166

Poets

A poet is a man who mixes up heaven and earth unconsciously.

—*Blake*, 4

The poet makes men realize how great are the great emotions which they, in a smaller way, have already experienced.

—*C*, 20

The great poet exists to show the small man how great he is. A man does not learn from Hamlet a new method of psycho-analysis, or the proper treatment of lunatics. What he learns is not to despise the soul as small; even when rather feminine critics say the will is weak. As if the will were ever strong enough for the tasks that confront it in this world! The great poet is alone strong enough to measure that broken strength we call the weakness of man.

—*C*, 20–21

. . . generally speaking, a poet cannot be properly appreciated if we separate one of his functions from the rest. Poets represent to a greater degree than any other men the conception of the unity of things. The poet includes the theologian, but he also includes the butcher, the baker, and the candlestick-maker. It is one of the curses of the criticism of poetry that it tends to detach the ideas of a poet from the forms by which he expresses them, which is like detaching the abstract idea of vegetation from all conceivable forms of vegetables.

—HA, 91

Poetry is only the algebra of life; passion is its arithmetic. If we recall to ourselves any deep sentiment; if we think of a dead friend or a primitive attachment, it is a hundred to one that we shall not think of any poetic images, stars, or thrones, or angels, but of something utterly trivial and ugly—a railing, a door-knocker, a lost umbrella. Men talk foolishly of these things not rising into poetry; on the contrary, it is poetry that falters feebly behind and does not rise to the graphic passion of these things. But scarcely any poet has come nearer to these queer memories, the veritable rag-bag of passion, than Browning in the incomparable realism of his love-poems.

—HA, 94

A poet who has lost his gods must always be like a lover who has lost his love and has married a sensible woman.

—HA, 160

The poet is right. The poet is always right. Oh, he has been here from the beginning of the world, and seen wonders and terrors that are all round our path, and only hiding behind a bush or a stone.

—MWKTM, 298–299

. . . the poet has passions like great unearthly appetites; and the world has always judged more gently of his sins.

—MWKTM, 335

The philosopher may sometimes love the infinite; the poet always loves the finite. For him the great moment is not the creation of light, but the creation of the sun and the moon.

— Thursday, 183

Poets (and Critics)

The poet, like the priest, should bear the ancient title of the builder of the bridge. His claim is exactly that he can really cross the chasm between the world of unspoken and seemingly unspeakable truths to the world of spoken words. His triumph is when the bridge is completed and the word is spoken; above all when it is heard. The literary middleman is the man who always stops the building of the bridge by trying to meet the builder half-way. A great idea or image grows in the shadow and often exists long before it is fit for the daylight.

—S, 230

Poets (and Mathematicians)

It is the very difference between the artistic mind and the mathematical that the former sees things as they are in a picture, some nearer and larger, some smaller and further away: while to the mathematical mind everything, every unit in a million, every fact in a cosmos, must be of equal value. That is why mathematicians go mad; and poets scarcely ever do.

—GFW, 35

Poets (and Prophets)

We have all heard of prophets and poets being unpopular; and also of unpopularity as a thing that may purify the soul. But there is this further and rather odd fact—that every great man must go through a period of unpopularity, not while he is alive, but shortly after he is dead. That after eclipse is essential because in that is settled the difference between

262

temporary and eternal oblivion. The prophet and the quack are alike admired for a generation, and admired for the wrong reasons. Then they are both forgotten, for no reason at all. But if the man is a mere quack he never returns. If he is a great man he returns, and he returns for the right reasons.

—HA, 107

Poets (Art and Convention)

Unless he is describing an emotion which others share with him, his labours will be utterly in vain. If a poet really had an original emotion; if, for example, a poet suddenly fell in love with the buffers of a railway train, it would take him considerably more time than his allotted three-score years and ten to communicate his feelings.

—RB, 98

Poets (Modern)

The fierce poet of the Middle Ages wrote, "Abandon hope all ye who enter here," over the gates of the lower world. The emancipated poets of today have written it over the gates of this world.

—CD, 18

Poets (Traditional)

Each taught in an individual way; 'with a perpetual slight novelty,' as Aristotle said; but they were not a series of separate lunatics looking at separate worlds. One poet did not provide a pair of spectacles by which it appeared that the grass was blue; or another poet lecture on optics to teach people to say that the grass was orange; they both had the far harder and much more heroic task of teaching people to feel that the grass is green. And because they continue their heroic task, the world, after every epoch of doubt and despair, always grows green again.

—C, 22

Poland

Poland is the Catholic culture thrust like a sort of long sword-blade between the Byzantine tradition of Muscovy and the materialism of Prussia. That is what Poland is; and that is infinitely the most real, practical, determining and important thing that she is.

—EA, 122

Most of our people actually do not know of the existence of Poland. An educated Englishman wrote to a Pole the other day and addressed his letter "So-and-so, Warsaw, Russia." I feel a deep and glowing thankfulness in being able to say that the Pole replied by addressing his letter "So-and-so, Esq., London, Germany."

—EA, 141

Poland (and the Bolshevist Threat)

If Bolshevism really is such a danger, if it really is any sort of danger, then there is no doubt at all about what is the real protection against that danger. It is Poland; and the time may come when the protector must be protected.

—EA, 137

Police

When the detective in a police romance stands alone, and somewhat fatuously fearless amid the knives and fists of a thieves' kitchen, it does certainly serve to make us remember that it is the agent of social justice who is the original and poetic figure. . . . The romance of the police force is thus the whole romance of man. . . . It reminds us that the whole noiseless and unnoticeable police management by which we are ruled and protected is only a successful knight-errantry.

—D, 123

"The work of the philosophical policeman," replied the man in blue, "is at once bolder and more subtle than that of the ordinary detective. The ordinary detective goes to pot-houses to arrest thieves; we go to artistic tea-parties to detect pessimists. The ordinary detective discovers from a ledger or a diary that a crime has been committed. We discover from a book of sonnets that a crime will be committed. We have to trace the origin of those dreadful thoughts that drive men on at last to intellectual fanaticism and intellectual crime."

— Thursday, 42

Politeness

Politeness has indeed about it something mystical; like religion, it is everywhere understood and nowhere defined.

— Five Types, 64

Political Campaigns (Rules for)

The rules for canvassers . . . are printed on the little card which you carry about with you and lose. There is a statement, I think, that you must not offer a voter food or drink. However hospitable you may feel to him in his own house, you must not carry his lunch about with you. You must not produce a veal cutlet from your tail-coat pocket. You must not conceal poached eggs about your person. You must not, like a kind of conjurer, produce baked potatoes from your hat. In short, the canvasser must not feed the voter in any way. . . . But there are voters who might find it worth while to discover if there is any law against bribing a canvasser. They might bribe him to go away.

—ATC, 29–30

The second veto for canvassers which was printed on the little card said that you must not persuade any one to personate a voter. I have no ideas what it means. To dress up as an average voter seems a little vague. There is no well-recognised uniform, as far as I know, with civic waistcoat and patriotic whiskers.

—ATC, 30

The third injunction on the card was one which seemed to me, if interpreted exactly and according to its words, to undermine the very foundations of our politics. It told me that I must not "threaten a voter with any consequence whatever." No doubt this was intended to apply to threats of a personal and illegitimate character; as, for instance, if a wealthy candidate were to threaten to raise all the rents, or to put up a statue of himself. But as verbally and grammatically expressed, it certainly would cover those general threats of disaster to the whole community which are the main matter of political discussion. When a canvasser says that if the opposition candidate gets in the country will be ruined, he is threatening the voters with certain consequences. . . . What is the use of being a politician . . . at all if one cannot tell the people that if the other man gets in, England will be instantly invaded and enslaved, blood be pouring down the Strand, and all the English ladies carried off into harems.

—ATC, 31

Politicians

It seemed somehow that politicians were very important. And yet, anything seemed important about them except their politics.

—FBO, 55

When men tell us that the old Liberal politicians of the type of Gladstone cared only for ideals, of course, they are talking nonsense—they cared for a great many other things, including votes.

—H, 254

266

You Politicians are such ingrained demagogues that even when you have a despotism you think of nothing but public opinion.

—NNH, 140

The politicians know nothing of politics, which is their own affair: they know nothing of religion, which is certainly not their affair: it may legitimately be said that they have to do with nothing; they have reached that low and last level where a man knows as little about his own claim, as he does about his enemies.

—VA, 210

Politicians and the Media

For fear of the newspapers politicians are dull, and at last they are too dull even for the newspapers.

—ATC, 129

Politicians (Modern)

. . . modern politicians have no ideas.

—EA, 22

Politicians (Practical)

For us a practical politician really means a man who can be thoroughly trusted to do nothing at all; that is where his practicality comes in.

—CD, 166

Politicians (Progressive)

Politicians have to be progressive; that is, they have to live in the future, because they know that they have done nothing but evil in the past.

—Avowals, 212

Politics

.... politics are a fugitive thing in the face of history.

—Irish, 93

Politics (American vs. English)

All good Americans wish to fight the representatives they have chosen. All good Englishmen wish to forget the representatives they have chosen.... [Americans] arm the President with the powers of a King, that he may be a nuisance in politics. We deprive the King even of the powers of a President, lest he should remind us of a politician.

—Amer, 121

Politics (Modern)

In most modern politics, unfortunately, it may truly be said that those who make history never know history.

—EA, 38

Half modern politics consists of rich men blackmailing people.

—FBO, 742

Pomposity

... pomposity is only the failure of pomp.

—HA, 207

Wherever there is pomp there is some peril of pomposity. But it is only fair to remember that most rebels against it have not ultimately avoided pomposity, even when they avoided pomp.

—Rome, 147

The Poor

What is quite evident is that if a logical praise of the poor man is pushed too far, and if a logical distress about him is pushed too far, either will involve wreckage to the central paradox of reform. If the poor man is made too admirable he ceases to be pitiable; if the poor man is made too pitiable he becomes merely contemptible. There is a school of smug optimists who will deny that he is a poor man. There is a school of scientific pessimists who will deny that he is a man.

—CD, 194

When humanity is going to hell, the poor are always nearest to heaven.

—VA, 81

Most educators of the poor seem to think that they have to teach the poor not to drink. I should be quite content if they teach him to drink; for it is mere ignorance about how to drink and when to drink that is accountable for most of his tragedies.

—WW, 277

The Poor (and the Rich)

The honest poor can sometimes forget poverty. The honest rich can never forget it.

—ATC, 11

You've got that eternal idiotic idea that if anarchy came, it would come from the poor. Why should it? The poor have been rebels, but they have never been anarchists; they have more interest than anyone else in there being some decent government. The poor man really has a stake in the country. The rich man hasn't; he can go away to New Guinea in a yacht. The poor have sometimes objected to being governed badly; the rich have always objected to being governed at all.

— Thursday, 132

Popularity or Publicity?

There is no real test, in an American atmosphere, where the best-seller is only a tribute to the best salesman.

—S, 249

Population Control

Scrooge utters all the sophistries by which the age of machinery has tried to turn the virtue of charity into a vice.... He belongs not only to the hard times of the middle of the nineteenth century, but to the harder times of the beginning of the twentieth century; the yet harder times in which we live. Many amiable sociologists will say, as he said, "Let them die and decrease the surplus population." The improved proposal is that they should die before they are born.

—GKC, 152

Pornography

There is such a thing as pornography; as a system of deliberate erotic stimulants. That is not a thing to be argued about with one's intellect, but to be stamped on with one's heel. But the point about it to be noted for our purpose is that this form of excess is separated from the other two by the fact that the nature of it *must* be bad. If a man tries to excite a sex instinct which is too strong already, and that in its meanest form, he *must* be a scoundrel. He is either taking money to degrade his kind or else he is acting on that mystical itch of the evil man to make others evil, which is the strangest secret in hell.

—CM, 126–127

Power

... power can only make ugliness uglier.

—RB, 123

Pragmatism

Pragmatism is a matter of human needs; and one of the first of human needs is to be something more than a pragmatist. Extreme pragmatism is just as inhuman as the determinism it so powerfully attacks. The determinist (who, to do him justice, does not pretend to be a human being) makes nonsense of the human sense of actual choice. The pragmatist, who professes to be specially human, makes nonsense of the human sense of actual fact.

—O, 64–65

The Pragmatist sets out to be practical, but his practicality turns out to be entirely theoretical.

—STA, 157

Precedenters

... there are others whom I may call the Precedenters, who flourish particularly in Parliament. They are best represented by the solemn official who said the other day that he could not understand the clamour against the Feeble-Minded Bill as it only extended the principles of the old Lunacy Laws. To which again one can only answer "Quite so. It only extends the principles of the Lunacy Laws to persons without a trace of lunacy." This lucid politician finds an old law, let us say, about keeping lepers in quarantine. He simply alters the word "lepers" to "long-nosed people," and says blandly that the principle is the same.

—Evils, 21

Predestination

Of the idea of Predestination there are broadly two views; the Calvinist and the Catholic; and it would make a most uncommon difference to *my* comfort, if I held the former instead of the latter. It is the difference between believing that God knows, as a fact, that I choose to go to the devil; and believing that God has given me to the devil, without my having any choice at all.

— Thing, 58–59

Prejudice and Dogma

There are two things and two things only, for the human mind, a dogma and a prejudice. . . . A doctrine is a definite point; a prejudice is a direction. That an ox may be eaten, while a man should not be eaten, is a doctrine. That as little as possible of anything should be eaten is a prejudice.

—WW, 21

The Present Generation (and Catch Phrases)

What the present generation knows is a number of catch phrases taken from one particular theory, which happens to be the last theory, and which will therefore be blown to bits by the next theory.... It has learnt for instance, to use the phrase "Inferiority Complex" to describe what Christians used to call Modesty and gentlemen good manners. But if you stop somebody who has just used the phrase "Inferiority Complex," and ask him whether there is such a thing as "Superiority Complex," he will gape and gobble and gurgle unmeaning sounds and his legs will give way beneath him. His inferiority complex, anyhow, will be instantly and appallingly apparent. For he has never thought about the phrase he uses; he has only seen it in the newspapers. The new phrase is not in the newspapers; and he has never heard of it. But the much older and much more profound Psychology of the Christian Religion was founded on the very ancient discovery that a superiority complex was the beginning of all evil.

—S, 55–56

Press

My friends in Manchester are in a terrible state of excitement about the powers of brewers and the dangers of admitting them to public office. But at least, if a man has controlled politics through beer, people generally know it: the subject of beer is too fascinating for anyone to miss such personal peculiarities. But a man may control politics through journalism, and no ordinary English citizen know that he is controlling them at all.

—ATC, 123

Surely the art of reporting speeches is in a strange state of degeneration. We should not object, perhaps, to the reporter's making the speeches much shorter than they are; but we do object to his making all the speeches much worse than they are.

—ATC, 126

For the journalist, having grown accustomed to talking down to the public, commonly talks too low at last, and becomes merely barbaric and unintelligible. By his very efforts to be obvious he becomes obscure.

—ATC, 130

...misrepresentation of speeches is only a part of a vast journalistic misrepresentation of all life as it is. Journalism is popular, but it is popular mainly as fiction. Life is one world, and life seen in the newspapers another; the public enjoys both, but it is more or less conscious of the difference.... But the people know in their hearts that journalism is a conventional art like any other, that it selects, heightens, and falsifies. Only its Nemesis is the same as that of other arts: if it loses all care for truth it loses all form likewise. The modern who paints too cleverly produces a picture of a cow which might be the earthquake at San Francisco. And the journalist who reports a speech too cleverly makes it mean nothing at all.

—ATC, 132

The point about the Press is that it is not what it is called. It is not the "popular Press".... It is not an organ of public opinion. It is a conspiracy of a very few millionaires, all sufficiently similar in type to agree on the limits of what this great nation (to which we belong) may know about itself and its friends and enemies. The ring is not quite complete; there are old-fashioned and honest papers: but it is sufficiently near to completion to produce on the ordinary purchaser of news the practical effects of a corner and a monopoly. He received all his political information and all his political marching orders from what is by this time a sort of half-conscious secret society, with very few members, but a great deal of money.

—UU, 202–203

Press (Eulogies of the Modern)

... the moderns have invented a much subtler and more poisonous kind of eulogy. The modern method is to take the prince or rich man, to give a credible picture of his type of personality, as that he is business-like, or a sportsman, or fond of art, or convivial or reserved; and then enormously exaggerate the value and importance of these natural qualities.... The journalists who write about Mr. Pierpont Morgan do not say that he is as beautiful as Apollo; I wish they did. What they do is to take the rich man's superficial life and manner, clothes, hobbies, love of cats, dislike of doctors or what not; and then with the assistance of this realism make the man out to be a prophet and a saviour of his kind, whereas he is merely a private and stupid man who happens to like cats or to dislike doctors.

—*ATC,* 133–134

Press (Irresponsibility of)

For my part I do feel very strongly about the frivolity and irresponsibility of the press. It seems impossible to exaggerate the evil that can be done by a corrupt and unscrupulous press.... bad journalism does directly ruin the nation, considered as a nation; it acts on the corporate national will and sways the common national decision. It may force a decision in a few hours that will be an incurable calamity for hundreds of years.

—*FVF,* 97

Press (Modern)

... the whole modern world, or at any rate the whole modern Press, has a perpetual and consuming terror of plain morals. Men always attempt to avoid condemning a thing upon merely moral grounds. If I beat my grandmother to death to-morrow in the middle of Battersea Park, you may be perfectly certain that people will say everything about it except the simple and fairly obvious fact that it is wrong.... But of this simple moral explanation modern journalism has, as I say, a standing fear. It will

275

call the action anything else—mad, bestial, vulgar, idiotic, rather than call it sinful.

—ATC, 110–111

Press (Reform)

... I would make a law, if there is none such at present by which an editor, proved to have published false news without reasonable verification, should simply go to prison. This is not a question of influences or atmospheres; the thing could be carried out as easily and as practically as the punishment of thieves and murderers. Of course there would be the usual statement that the guilt was that of a subordinate. Let the accused editor have the right of proving this if he can; if he does, let the subordinate be tried and go to prison. Two or three good rich editors and proprietors properly locked up would take the sting out of the Yellow Press....

—ATC, 118

... I would do my best to introduce everywhere the practice of signed articles. Those who urge the advantages of anonymity are either people who do not realise the special peril of our time or they are people who are profiting by it. It is true, but futile, for instance, to say that there is something noble in being nameless when a whole corporate body is bent on a consistent aim: as in an army or men building a cathedral. The point of modern newspapers is that there is no such corporate body and common aim; but each man can use the authority of the paper to further his own private fads and his own private finances.

—ATC, 119–120

I should like it to be a fixed thing that the name of the proprietor as well as the editor should be printed upon every paper.... If (as is far more common in this singularly undemocratic age) it is owned by one man, let that one man's name be printed on the paper, if possible in large red letters. Then, if there are any obvious interests being served, we shall know that they are being served.

—ATC, 123

Press (Yellow)

. . . the Yellow Press is exaggerative, over-emotional, illiterate, and anarchical, and a hundred other long words; whereas the only objection to it is that it tells lies.

—ATC, 115

Pride

. . . for pride is not only (as the modern world fails to understand) a sin to be condemned; it is also (as it understands even less) a weakness to be very much commiserated.

—CD, 28

If I had only one sermon to preach, it would be a sermon against Pride. The more I see of existence, and especially of modern practical and experimental existence; the more I am convinced of the reality of the old religious thesis, that all evil began with some attempt at superiority; some moment when, as we might say, the very skies were cracked across like a mirror, because there was a sneer in Heaven.

—CM, 246

Pride consists in a man making his personality the only test, instead of making the truth the test. It is not pride to wish to do well, or even to look well, according to a real test. It is pride to think that a thing looks ill, because it does not look like something characteristic of oneself.

—CM, 254

The weakness of pride lies after all in this; that oneself is a window. It can be a coloured window, if you will; but the more thickly you lay on the colours the less of a window it will be. The two things to be done with a window are to wash it and then forget it. So the truly pious have always said the two things to do personally are to cleanse and to forget oneself.

—GKC, 19

... the one kind of pride which is wholly damnable is the pride of the man who has something to be proud of. The pride which ... does not hurt the character, is the pride in things which reflect no credit on the person at all. Thus it does a man no harm to be proud of his country. . . . It does him more harm to be proud of having made money, because in that he has a little more reason for pride. It does him more harm still to be proud of what is nobler than money — intellect. And it does him most harm of all to value himself for the most valuable thing on earth — goodness. The man who is proud of what is really creditable to him is the Pharisee, the man whom Christ Himself could not forbear to strike.

—H, 168

And it is always the humble man who talks too much; the proud man watches himself too closely.

— Thursday, 12

It can be maintained that the evil of pride consists in being out of proportion to the universe.

—TT, 3

Privacy

... there is a third class of things on which the best civilisation does permit privacy, does resent all inquiry or explanation. This is in the case of things which need not be explained, because they cannot be explained, things too airy, instinctive, or intangible — caprices, sudden impulses, and the more innocent kind of prejudice. A man must not be asked why he is talkative or silent for the simple reason that he does not know. . . . A man must take his own road through a wood, and make his own use of a holiday. . . . If you like to put it so he must act on the impulse because the impulse is not worth a moment's thought. All these fancies men feel should be private; and even Fabians have never proposed to interfere with them.

—ATC, 89

Production (Modern)

Big Business is not business-like; it is not enterprising; it is not favourable to science and invention. By the very nature of its monopoly of machinery and mass production, it works entirely the other way. Millions are sunk into plants that cannot be changed or brought up-to-date. Machinery is made so that it must be used, even when it is useless. Things are made badly so that they must be mended. Things are even made badly so that they may be mended badly; and therefore mended again.

—S, 245

Profanity

Profanity is now more than an affectation—it is a convention. The curse against God is Exercise I. in the primer of minor poetry.

—D, 2

Profound and the Prosaic

A man warmly concerned with any large theories has always a relish for applying them to any triviality.

—FBO, 233

Progress

Human history is so rich and complicated that you can make out a case for any course of improvement or retrogression.

—ATC, 162

But in all cases progress means progress only in some particular thing. Have you ever noticed that strange line of Tennyson, in which he confesses, half consciously, how very *conventional* progress is? —

"Let the great world spin for ever down the ringing grooves of change."

Even in praising change, he takes for a simile the most unchanging thing. He calls our modern change a groove. And it is a groove; perhaps there was never anything so groovy.

—ATC, 163

... there are only two things that really progress; and they both accept accumulations of authority. . . . they have steadily advanced in a certain definable direction; they are the only two things, it seems, that ever *can* progress. The first is strictly physical science. The second is the Catholic Church.

—BC, 146–147

Progress, in the sense of the progress that has progressed since the sixteenth century, has upon every matter persecuted the Common Man; punished the gambling he enjoys and permitted the gambling he cannot follow . . . silenced the political quarrels that can be conducted among men and applauded the political stunts and syndicates that can only be conducted by millionaires; encouraged anybody who had anything to say against God, if it was said with a priggish and supercilious accent; but discouraged anybody who had anything to say in favour of Man, in his common relations to manhood and motherhood and the normal appetites of nature. Progress has been merely the persecution of the Common Man.

—CM, 4–5

Progress, in the good sense, does not consist in looking for a direction in which one can go on indefinitely. For there is no such direction, unless it be in quite transcendental things, like the love of God. It would be far truer to say that true progress consists in looking for the place where we can stop.

—FVF, 193

But it is clear that no political activity can be encouraged by saying that progress is natural and inevitable; that is not a reason for being active, but rather a reason for being lazy. If we are bound to improve, we need not trouble to improve. The pure doctrine of progress is the best of all reasons for not being progressive.

—O, 204

Prohibition

If a man says, "I wish to abolish beer because I am a temperance man," his remark conveys no meaning to my mind. It is like saying, "I wish to abolish roads because I am a moderate walker."

—ATC, 142

The upholders of Prohibition, strangely enough, seem to be quite proud of the fact that many are buying motor-cars instead of wine or beer. For my part, I think it rather more foolish merely to rush from one place to another and back again, and pay money for wind (not to mention dust) than to pay money for wine, with its not quite extinct accompaniment of wit.

—S, 32

After a careful study of the operations of prohibition in America, I have come to the conclusion that one of the best things that the Government could do would be to prohibit everything.

—S, 92

I know an American university where practically every one of the professors brews his own beer; some of them experimenting in two or three different kinds. But what is especially delightful is this: that with this widespread revival of the old human habit of home-brewing, much of that old human atmosphere that went with it has really reappeared. The professor of the higher metaphysics will be proud of his strong ale; the professor of the lower mathematics (otherwise known as high finance) will allege something more subtle in his milder ale; the professor of moral theology (whose ale I am sure is the strongest of all) will offer to drink all the other dons under the table without any ill effect on the health. Prohibition has to that extent actually worked the good, in spite of so malignantly and murderously willing the evil. And the good is this: the restoration of legitimate praise and pride for the creative crafts of the home.

—S, 94

Let Congress or Parliament pass a law not only prohibiting fermented liquor, but practically prohibiting everything else. Let the Government forbid bread, beef, boots, hats and coats; let there be a law against anybody indulging in chalk, cheese, leather, linen, tools, toys, tales, pictures or newspapers. Then, it would seem by serious sociological analogy, all human families will begin vigorously to produce all these things for themselves; and the youth of the world will really return.

—S, 95

Prohibition (and Bootlegging)

It is intolerable that crime should end merely in comedy. And there is added to all the rest the crowning and capering comedy that the criminals are among the few people who are still in favour of legislation against the crime. It would seem an extraordinary thing to say of any community that nearly all the citizens were Communists, and nobody approved of private property except the burglars. It is really true to say, of many parts of the American community, that most of the citizens are drinkers, and that nobody approves of Prohibition except the bootleggers.

—S, 110

Prohibition (and the Cocktail)

The reason why the American millionaire does not drink wine or beer with his meals, like all poorer and better Christians, is simple if not dignified. It was summed up admirably by an American in an excellent cartoon in *Life;* a cartoon entitled "Henpecked." He prefers to be a Prohibitionist on public occasions; especially those highly important public occasions when he meets his wife. Hence arose, originally, the habit of the males of the party consuming hurried, secret and very potent drinks before they assembled at the table. It was necessary that the sort of drink should be one that could be gulped down quickly; it was necessary that it should be very strong for its size; and it was natural that it should be made a sort of separate science of luxury in itself. Later, of course, the case was complicated by other modern movements, and some sections of feminine society becoming fast society. But that was what determined the novelty and the nature of this remarkable sort of refreshment. It was, quite simply, a tippling husband hiding from a nagging wife. It is not a very noble origin even for a modern mode.

−S, 36–37

Prohibitionists

The honest men among them definitely gave up drink for the good of their country. Practical politicians among them, on the other hand, forbade drink to their country and went on cheerfully drinking themselves. These are the only sort that now remain, and even they are tending more and more to an open avowal of their contempt for Prohibition. They are described, with considerable restraint, as Political Drys; instead of being described as greasy humbugs and dirty cowards, as they would be among truthful people.

−S, 102

Property

Property is merely the art of democracy. It means that every man should have something that he can shape in his own image, as he is shaped in the image of heaven.

—WW, 58

Prussian Organization

Because Prussians always stand in rows to commit their crimes, it was obvious to every solid sensible man that they could not be really criminal. Because they always marked out the land they had just stolen from somebody else with a neat row of black and white posts (all of them, mark you, at exactly the same number of inches apart), it became obvious to reasonable men that there was no possibility of any further stealing.

—EA, 157

Psycho-analysis

I do not know anything about psycho-analysis, except that it demands a great deal more than the Confessional was always abused for demanding.

—Come, 52

Psychologists

We may tolerate the dentist, who passes from the curing of toothache to the universal pulling out of teeth. We need not tolerate the psychologist, whose only cure for a headache is cutting off the head. It will be some time before the psychologist can provide an artificial head, as the dentist can provide an artificial set of teeth.

—Avowals, 187

Psychology

"Don't you know what psychology means?" asked Flambeau with friendly surprise. "Psychology means being off your chump."

—*FBO,* 103

If successive cults and cultures, one older than another, all lead back to one idea that man held happiness on a condition, and is unhappy through breaking that condition, I think they lead a long way nearer the truth of human psychology than the little bustling journeys of popular science.

—*Lands,* 140

If we read a passionate and heart-searching modern novel (which God forbid) we may open any page and come on a sentence like this: "Maurice fascinated Daphne by his exquisite understanding of her psychology." This is exactly as if I were to say: "I should like to meet Maurice and give him a good hearty kick in the physiology." So indeed I should; but I should not express my just and natural aspiration in such illogical terms. Physiology is not his body, but the study of his body; and Psychology is not his mind, but the study of his mind.

—*S,* 54–55

... somebody will say, in a more scholarly work: "The Psychology of Atilla, the Hun, has never been scientifically studied." Which is like saying his Geology has never been adequately studied. The Hun, happy fellow, had no Psychology and no Geology. He could lay waste the earth without asking what it was made of and enjoy himself without asking what he himself was made of. Many human beings, without being Huns, have in the past managed to enjoy themselves a great deal without bothering about Psychology. Still, if a whole human generation is going to bother and bewilder itself with Psychology, it might as well know something about it. The present generation knows nothing about it.

—*S,* 95

Psychology (Modern)

Determinists in my youth bullied us all about the urgent necessity of choosing a philosophy which would prove the impossibility of choosing anything. No doubt the new psychology will somehow enable us to know what we are doing about all that we do without knowing it.

—FVF, 27

Public Opinion

When the public mood is not mere indifference, it is a rapidly alternating series of likes and dislikes, or what Matthew Arnold truly called hot fits and cold fits; all of them arising from certain hasty impressions about our own advantage or disadvantage; and none of them founded on anything but newspaper stories, which are very often stories in the nursery rather than the newspaper sense.

—EA, 54

Public Opinion (Predicting)

. . . guesses about the fashions of the future are generally quite wide of the mark, because they are founded on a very obvious fallacy. They always imply that public taste will continue to progress in its present direction; which is, in truth, the only thing we know that it will not do.

—RLS, 141

Publicity (Modern)

. . . all modern publicity and popularization consist of concentrating a book into a paragraph or a chapter into a sentence.

—FFF, 229

Puritans

Since the Puritan was content to cry with the Moslem: 'God is Great,' so the descendent of the Puritan is always a little inclined to cry with the Nietzschean: 'Greatness is God.'

—RLS, 89

The Puritan substituted a God who wished to damn people for a God who wished to save them.

—S, 146

Q

Quackery

Quackery is false science; it is everywhere apparent in cheap and popular science; and the chief mark of it is that men who begin by boasting that they have cast away all dogmas go on to be incessantly, imprudently, and quite irrationally dogmatic. . . . It is all the worse because the dogmas are generally concerned with domestic and very delicate human relations . . . and everything that can be coloured by the pompous and pretentious polysyllables of Psychology and Education. . . . these dogmas always directly attack fathers and wives and children, without offering either credentials or evidence. The general rule is that nothing must be accepted on any ancient or admitted authority, but everything must be accepted on any new or nameless authority or accepted even more eagerly on no authority at all.

—*AIG*, 130–131

Quarrel

I object to a quarrel because it always interrupts an argument.

—*Magic*, 61

R

Racketeering

It seems, for some mysterious reason, to be applied especially to Beauty Parlours, which are now very nearly the national industry of America. . . . I cannot quite understand why it is not done everywhere. But anyhow, it is another step outside the self-contained society of mutual murder and as such regretable. A member of the F.F.C.K., or First Families of Chicago Killers, should not stoop to associate with people who run beauty parlours. As a mere matter of romance and sentiment, I should be relieved if most of the beauty parlours were blown up; but I draw the line when there are people inside them. Perhaps people are blown up in the very act of being beautified. It would lend a new and impressive meaning to face-lifting.

—*S,* 98–99

Rationalism

When a child looks out of the nursery window and sees anything, say the green lawn of the garden, what does he actually know; or does he know anything? There are all sorts of nursery games of negative philosophy played round this question. A brilliant Victorian scientist delighted in declaring that the child does not see any grass at all; but only a sort of green mist reflected in the tiny mirror of the human eye. This piece of rationalism has always struck me as almost insanely irrational. If he is not sure of the existence of the grass, which he sees through the glass of the

289

window, how on earth can he be sure of the existence of the retina which he sees through the glass of the microscope?

—STA, 165

A Reactionary

A reactionary is one in whom weariness itself has become a form of energy.

—Rome, 232

Reading

There is a great deal of difference between the eager man who wants to read a book, and the tired man who wants a book to read. A man reading a Le Queux mystery wants to get to the end of it. A man reading the Dickens novel wished that it might never end.

—CD, 73

Real Politik

As a matter of fact, it is an almost insanely unreal politik. It is always stubbornly and stupidly repeating that men fight for material ends without reflecting for a moment that the material ends are hardly ever material to the men who fight. In any case no man will die for practical politics, just as no man will die for pay. . . . Does anybody in the world believe that a soldier says, 'My leg is nearly dropping off, but I shall go on till it drops; for after all I shall enjoy all the advantages of my government obtaining a warm-water port in the Gulf of Finland'. . . . Whatever starts wars, the thing that sustains wars is something in the soul; that is something akin to religion.

—EM, 162–163

Realism

Realism is simply Romanticism that has lost its reason. This is so not merely in the sense of insanity but of suicide. It has lost its reason; that is its reason for existing.

—Alarms, 6

Realism, Idealism and Art

Mr. Gill says, "Look inside you, for the wonderful plastic powers that God has given you." Ruskin said, "Look outside you, for the wonderful sea and birds that God has made." But is it so absolutely certain that the sea and birds are outside you? Are not the sea and birds you really look at, when you recall them artistically, things already soaked in your own mystical nature, reshaped and simplified by your own instinct for symbol and design; so that being true to that truth is not merely photographic, but something which quacks call psychological and sensible men call spiritual.

—HA, 187

Realists

The realists, who overlook so many details, have never quite noticed where lay the falsity of their method; it lay in the fact that so long as it was materialistic, it could not really be realistic. For it could not be psychological. If toys and trifles can make people happy, that happiness is not a trifle and certainly cannot be a trick.

—RLS, 68

Reason (Age of)

There is nothing very much the matter with the age of reason; except, alas, that it comes before the age of discretion.

—Cobbett, 106

Reason (and the Church)

. . . Reason is always reasonable, even in the last limbo, in the lost border-land of things. I know that people charge the Church with lowering reason, but it is just the other way. Alone on earth, the Church makes reason really supreme. Alone on earth, the Church affirms that God himself is bound by reason.

—FBO, 18–19

Reason (Thomism vs. Lutheranism)

It was the very life of the Thomist teaching that Reason can be trusted: it was the very life of the Lutheran teaching that Reason is utterly untrustworthy.

—STA, 33

Reason vs. Authority

Modern people talk of "Reason versus Authority"; but authority itself involves reason, or its orders would not even be understood. If you say to your valet, "Look after the buttons on my waistcoat," he may do it, even if you throw a boot at his head. But if you say to him, "Look after the buttons on my top hat," he will not do it, though you empty a bootshop over him.

—Evils, 170

Rebels

. . . the new rebel is a sceptic, and will not entirely trust anything. . . . And the fact that he doubts everything really gets in his way when he wants to denounce anything. For all denunciation implies a moral doctrine of some kind; and the modern revolutionist doubts not only the institution he denounces, but the doctrine by which he denounces it. Thus he writes one book complaining that imperial oppression insults the purity of women, and then he writes another book (about the sex problem) in which he insults it himself.... As a politician, he will cry out that war is a waste of life, and then, as a philosopher, that all life is a waste of time.

—O, 73-74

Each generation of rebels in turn is remembered by the next, not as the pioneers who began the march, or started to break away from the old conventions; but as the old convention from which only the very latest rebels have dared to break away.

—Survey, 173

Reform

For reform implies form. It implies that we are trying to shape the world in a particular image; to make it something that we see already in our minds. Evolution is a metaphor from mere automatic unrolling. Progress is a metaphor from merely walking along a road—very likely the wrong road. But reform is a metaphor for reasonable and determined men: it means that we see a certain thing out of shape and we mean to put it into shape. And we know what shape.

—O, 104-105

The Reformation

The Reformation is always described as a protest against the power of the Pope. I should rather describe it as a protest against the impotence of the Pope. It did not come in a time like that of Innocent III, when the Pope was really powerful. It came at the end of a long trail of tragi-comedy and bathos, in which the central power, so far from being too central, had been hopelessly decentralized and divided. It was not until people had had the absurd experience of having three Popes that they completed the absurdity by having three or four religions.

—Rome, 106

It is perfectly true that we can find real wrongs, provoking rebellion, in the Roman Church just before the Reformation. What we cannot find is one of those real wrongs that the Reformation reformed.

— Thing, 66

Reformers

His triumph is a religious triumph; it rests upon his perpetual assertion of the value of the human soul and of human daily life. It rests upon his assertion that human life is enjoyable because it is human. And he will never admit, like so many compassionate pessimists, that human life ever ceases to be human. He does not merely pity the lowness of men; he feels an insult to their elevation.

— CD, 196–197

There does exist, then, this strange optimistic reformer; the man whose work begins with approval and yet ends with earthquake. Jesus Christ was destined to found a faith which made the rich poorer and the poor richer; but even when He was going to enrich them, He began with the phrase, "Blessed are the poor." The Gissings and Gorkys say, as an universal literary motto, "Cursed are the poor."

— CD, 198

The more modern type of reformer goes gaily up to it and says, "I don't see the use of this; let us clear it away." To which the more intelligent type of reformer will do well to answer: "If you don't see the use of it, I certainly won't let you clear it away. Go away and think. Then, when you can come back and tell me that you *do* see the use of it, I may allow you to destroy it."

— Thing, 27

Relativity

The Victorian agnostics waited hopefully for science to give them a working certainty about life. The new physicist philosophers are in no way different, except that they wait hopelessly instead of hopefully. For they know very well the real meaning of relativity; that their own views may pass from being relatively right to being relatively wrong.

—*Well,* 58

Religion

The present writer will not, in so important a matter, pretend to the absurd thing called impartiality; he is personally quite convinced that if every human being lived a thousand years, every human being would end up either in utter pessimistic scepticism or in the Catholic creed.

—*Blake,* 208

For religion all men are equal, as all pennies are equal, because the only value in any of them is that they bear the image of the King.

—*CD,* 9

It has often been said, very truly, that religion is the thing that makes the ordinary man feel extraordinary; it is an equally important truth that religion is the thing that makes the extraordinary man feel ordinary.

—*CD,* 9

Religion has had to provide that longest and strangest telescope—the telescope through which we could see the star upon which we dwelt. For the mind and eyes of the average man this world is as lost as Eden and as sunken as Atlantis.

—*D,* 3

I have heard modern people talk of the needlessness of all the old rituals and reliquaries and the need for a simple religion of the heart. But their demand is rather dangerous, especially to themselves. If we really had a simple religion of the heart we should all be loaded with relics, and rituals would be going on all day long. If our creed were only of the higher emotions, it would talk of nothing else but special shrines, sacred spots, indispensable gestures, and adorable rags and bones. In short, a religion of pure good feeling would be a positive orgy of superstition. This seems to me excessive; I prefer a little clean theology to keep the thing within bounds.

—HA, 69

Above all, it must be remembered that when the interests of an age are mainly religious they must be universal. Nothing can be more universal than the universe.

— St. Francis, 69

Religion and Superstition

Religion is a rare and definite conviction of what this world of ours really is. Superstition is only the commonsense acceptation of what it obviously is. Sane peasants, healthy hunters, are all superstitious; they are superstitious because they are healthy and sane. They have a reasonable fear of the unknown; for superstition is only the creative side of agnosticism. The superstitious man sees quite plainly that the universe is a thing to be feared. The religious man maintains paradoxically that the universe is a thing to be trusted. The awe is certainly the obvious thing. . . . The fear of the Lord is the beginning of wisdom—but not the end.

—HA, 141–142

Religion (Comparative)

Comparative religion has indeed allowed us to compare religions—and to contrast them. Fifty years ago, it set out to prove that all religions were much the same; generally proving, alternately, that they were all equally worthy and that they were all equally worthless.

—STA, 114

Religion (Cosmic)

The essence of all pantheism, evolutionism, and modern cosmic religion is really in this proposition: that Nature is our mother. Unfortunately, if you regard Nature as a mother, you discover that she is a stepmother. The main point of Christianity was this: that Nature is not our mother: Nature is our sister. We can be proud of her beauty, since we have the same father; but she has no authority over us; we have to admire, but not to imitate.

—O, 207

Religion (Enemies of)

For the enemies of religion cannot leave it alone. They laboriously attempt to smash religion. They cannot smash religion; but they do smash everything else. With your queries and dilemmas you have made no havoc in faith; from the first it was a transcendental conviction; it cannot be made any more transcendental than it was. But you have (if that is any comfort to you) made a certain havoc in common morals and commonsense.

—L & L, 191

Religion, Materialism and Science

Of course, the real truth is that science has introduced no new principle into the matter at all. A man can be a Christian to the end of the world, for the simple reason that a man could have been an Atheist from the beginning of it. The materialism of things is on the face of things; it does not require any science to find it out. A man who has lived and loved falls down dead and the worms eat him. That is Materialism if you like. That is Atheism if you like. If mankind has believed in spite of that, it can believe in spite of anything. But why our human lot is made any more hopeless because we know the names of all the worms who eat him, or the names of all the parts of him that they eat, is to a thoughtful mind somewhat difficult to discover.

—ATC, 142

Religion (Root of)

It is the root of all religion that a man knows that he is nothing in order to thank God that he is something.

—Rome, 80

Religions

And it is generally true, in religions especially, that the real enthusiasm or even fanaticism is to be found in the rank and file. In all intense religions it is the poor who are more religious and the rich who are more irreligious. It is certainly so with the creeds and causes that come to a collision in Jerusalem.

—NJ, 133

Religious Persecution

... the essence of religious persecution is this: that the man who happens to have material power in the State, either by wealth or by official position, should govern his fellow-citizens not according to their religion or philosophy, but according to his own.... These people ask the poor to accept in practice what they know perfectly well that the poor would not accept in theory. That is the very definition of religious persecution.

—ATC, 6–7

Religious Views (Progressive)

Some statements I disagree with; others I do not understand. . . . If a man says, "I am not a Trinitarian," I understand. But if he says (as a lady once said to me), "I believe in the Holy Ghost in a spiritual sense," I go away dazed. In what other sense could one believe in the Holy Ghost? . . . What can people mean when they say that science has disturbed their view of sin? What sort of view of sin can they have had before science disturbed it? Did they think that it was something to eat? When people say that science has shaken their faith in immortality, what do they mean? Did they think that immortality was a gas?

—ATC, 141–142

Religious War

But it certainly is the fact that religious war is in itself much more rational than patriotic war. I for one have often defended and even encouraged patriotic war, and should always be ready to defend and encourage patriotic passion. But it cannot be denied that there is more of mere passion, of mere preference and prejudice, in short of mere personal accident, in fighting another nation than in fighting another faith. The Crusader is in every sense more rational than the modern conscript or professional soldier. He is more rational in his object, which is the intelligent and intelligible object of conversion; where the modern militarist has an object much more confused by momentary vanity and one-sided satisfaction.

—NJ, 220–221

The Renaissance

The Renaissance was, as much as anything, a revolt from the logic of the Middle Ages. We speak of the Renaissance as the birth of rationalism; it was in many ways the birth of irrationalism. It is true that the Medieval Schoolmen, who had produced the finest logic that the world has ever seen, had in later years produced more logic than the world can ever be expected to stand. They had loaded and lumbered up the world with libraries of mere logic; and some effort was bound to be made to free it from such endless chains of deduction. Therefore, there was in the Renaissance a wild touch of revolt, not against religion but against reason.

—C, 218–219

It is true, for instance, that the Renaissance had expanded the exploration of the earth; and in that sense, I have spoken of its artists inhabiting a wider and a wilder world. But in some other respects, they inhabited a world which, though certainly wilder, was not so wide. It was very exciting to discover that there were Red Indians or Yellow Chinamen; but it did not increase the old Roman and philosophical sense of the broad brotherhood of the *humanum genus:* the human race. Rather it raised new problems about it; problems which produced all sorts of horrible things, from slavery to anthropology.

—C, 228

It was, after all, one of the supreme examples of Roman civilization possessing this power of resurrection; and resurrection is not material, but mystical; not a result of doubt but rather of faith; not a mere contempt of the past, but rather an invocation; a sort of wild veneration for the dead.

—Rome, 21

Responsibility

Responsibility, a heavy and cautious responsibility of speech, is the easiest thing in the world; anybody can do it. That is why so many tired, elderly, and wealthy men go in for politics. They are responsible, because they have not the strength of mind left to be irresponsible.

—ATC, 4

Revolution

The man who said that revolutions are not made with rose-water was obviously inexperienced in practical human affairs. Men like Rousseau and Shelley do make revolutions, and do make them with rose-water; that is, with a too rosy and sentimental view of human goodness. Figures that come before and create convulsion and change (for instance, the central figure of the New Testament) always have the air of walking in an unnatural sweetness and calm. They give us their peace ultimately in blood and battle and division; not as the world giveth give they unto us.

—*CD*, 195

The real case against Revolution is this; that there always seems to be so much more to be said against the old *regime* than in favour of the new *regime*.

—*S*, 191

Revolutions turn into institutions; revolts that renew the youth of old societies in their turn grow old; and the past which was full of new things, of splits and innovations and insurrections, seems to us a single texture of tradition.

—*STA*, 47–48

Perhaps there is really no such thing as a revolution recorded in history. What happened was always a Counter-Revolution. Men were always rebelling against the last rebels; or even repenting against the last rebellion.

—*STA*, 76

You cannot see a wind; you can only see that there is a wind. So, also, you cannot see a revolution; you can only see that there is a revolution. And that there never has been in the history of the world a real revolution, brutally active and decisive, which was not preceded by unrest and new dogma in the reign of invisible things. All revolutions begin by

301

being abstract. Most revolutions begin by being quite pedantically abstract.

—TT, 91

All true revolutions are reversions to the natural and the normal. A revolutionist who breaks with the past is a notion fit for an idiot.

—Types, 268

Revolution (Communist)

They hardly realize how much of educational and philanthropic reform has been kidnapping on a large scale. That is, it has shown an increasing disregard for the privacy of the private citizen, considered as a parent. I have called it a revolution; and at bottom it is really a Bolshevist revolution. For what could be more purely and perfectly Communist than to say that you regard other people's children as if they were your own?

—Survey, 5

The Rich

These men only surrender the things that bind them to other men. Go and dine with a temperance millionaire and you won't find he's abolished the *hors d'oeuvres* or the five courses or even the coffee. What he's abolished is the port and sherry, because poor men like that as well as rich. . . . But you will find he boasts of early rising, because sleep is a thing poor men can still enjoy. . . . Nobody ever heard of a modern philanthropist giving up petrol or typewriting or troops of servants. No, no! What he gives up must be some simple and universal thing. He will give up beef or beer or sleep—because these pleasures remind him that he is only a man.

—Flying, 179–180

Rich

But among the very rich you will never find a really generous man even by accident. They may give their money away, but they will never give themselves away; they are egoistic, secretive, dry as old bones. To be smart enough to get all that money you must be dull enough to want it.

—*MM*, 143

A man like Rockefeller is praised as a sort of pagan stoic for his early rising or his unassuming dress. His "simple" meals, his "simple" clothes, his "simple" funeral, are all extolled as if they were creditable to him. They are disgraceful to him: exactly as disgraceful as the tatters and vermin of the old miser were disgraceful to *him*. To be in rags for charity would be the condition of a saint, to be in rags for money was that of a filthy old fool. . . . Of the two [Rockefeller and the miser] I have more respect for the old miser, gnawing bones in an attic: if he was not nearer to God, he was at least a little nearer to men. His simple life was a little more like the life of the real poor.

—*MM*, 143–144

All but the hard-hearted must be torn with pity for this pathetic dilemma of the rich man, who has to keep the poor man just stout enough to do the work and just thin enough to have to do it.

—*UU*, 40

Rights

To have a right to do a thing is not at all the same as to be right in doing it.

—*England*, 120

Ritualism

All reasonable men believe in symbol; but some reasonable men do not believe in ritualism; by which they mean, I imagine, a symbolism too complex, elaborate, and mechanical. But whenever they talk of ritualism they always seem to mean the ritualism of the Church. Why should they not mean the ritualism of the world? It is much more ritualistic. The ritual of the Army, the ritual of the Navy, the ritual of the Law Courts, the ritual of Parliament are much more ritualistic. The ritual of a dinner-party is much more ritualistic. . . . There is much more *fuss* about symbols in the world than in the Church.

—ATC, 204–205

Romance

. . . romance is a very real part of life and perhaps the most real part of youth.

—CD, 228

In history itself there is a school which may be called anti-romantic; and it is perpetually occupied in trying to explain away the many romances that have really happened.

—Glass, 56

Posting a letter and getting married are among the few things left that are entirely romantic; for to be entirely romantic a thing must be irrevocable.

—H, 35

. . . nearly all people I have ever met in this western society in which I live would agree to the general proposition that we need this life of practical romance; The combination of something that is strange with something that is secure. We need so to view the world as to combine an idea of wonder and an idea of welcome. We need to be happy in this wonderland without once being merely comfortable.

—O, 16

No genuine criticism of romance will ever arise until we have grasped the fact that romance lies not upon the outside of life, but absolutely in the centre of it. The centre of every man's existence is a dream.

—Types, 162

Rome

I do not mean that it is a place where the mind can dreamily return to the past. I mean it is a place where the past can actually return to the present. I do not mean that it amuses me to imagine certain conditions that were there a few thousand years ago. I mean that I can quite well imagine some such conditions there a few thousand years hence. I mean that it has a sort of access to its own origins, and a power upon its own vanished youth, which is what is really meant by calling it The Eternal City.

—Rome, 15

A Round Table

The idea of a round table is not merely universality but equality.

—England, 27

Ruskin, John

We do not disagree with Ruskin as we disagree with the great decisive philosophers who are our decisive opponents or offer to us decisive alternatives. We do not disagree with Ruskin as we might disagree with Lucretius or with Calvin or with Mahomet or with Professor Haeckel. We disagree with Ruskin as we disagree with a friend gone wrong; with a man who ought to understand and does not; or (in some cases I think) who does understand but will not. For the irritation against an enemy is a sudden and exceptional passion; but the irritation against a friend is a thing that grows and bears fruit like a living orchard. It is possible to be content with our enemies; it is not possible to be content with our friends. Our irritation against a friend always arises, I think, from the good he has suggested and has not fulfilled; and this is exactly the feeling which a modern man has about Ruskin.

—*HA,* 149

S

Saints

Alone of all superiors, the saint does not depress the human dignity of others. He is not conscious of his superiority to them; but only more conscious of his inferiority than they are.

—England, 14

Saints and Socialists

"What do you call a man who wants to embrace the chimney-sweep?"

"A saint," said Father Brown.

"I think," said Sir Leopold, with a supercilious smile, "that Ruby means a socialist."

—FBO, 71

Santa Claus

Personally, of course, I believe in Santa Claus; but it is the season of forgiveness, and I will forgive others for not doing so.

—TT, 134

Satanism

The worst is always very near the best; there is something much worse than Atheism which is Satanism; otherwise known as Being God.

—Poet, 122

Satire

To write great satire, to attack a man so that he feels the attack and half acknowledges its justice, it is necessary to have a certain intellectual magnanimity which realizes the merits of the opponent as well as his defects.

— Five Types, 21–22

We might be angry at the libel, but not at the satire: for a man is angry at a libel because it is false, but at a satire because it is true.

— Types, 53

Scandal

... there'd be a lot less scandal if people didn't idealize sin and pose as sinners.

—FBO, 830

Scepticism

It is assumed that the sceptic has no bias; whereas he has a very obvious bias in favour of scepticism.

—ATC, 155

I saw an almost startling example of this essential frivolity in the professor of final scepticism, in a paper the other day. A man wrote to say that he accepted nothing but Solipsism, and added that he had often wondered it was not a more common philosophy. Now Solipsism simply means that a man believes in his own existence, but not in anybody or anything else. And it never struck this simple Sophist, that if his philosophy was true, there obviously were no other philosophers to profess it.

—STA, 148

Most fundamental sceptics appear to survive, because they are not consistently sceptical and not at all fundamental. They will first deny everything and then admit something, if for the sake of argument—or often rather of attack without argument.

—STA, 148

I suppose it is true in a sense that a man can be a fundamental sceptic, but he cannot be anything else; certainly not even a defender of fundamental scepticism. If a man feels that all the movements of his own mind are meaningless, then his mind is meaningless, and he is meaningless; and it does not mean anything to attempt to discover his meaning.

—STA, 148

Heavens! to think of the dull rut of the sceptics who go on asking whether we possess a future life. The exciting question for real scepticism is whether we possess a past life. What is a minute ago, rationalistically considered, except a tradition and a picture?

—TT, 37–38

Scepticism and Certainty

... the whole argument worked out ultimately to this: that the question is whether a man can be certain of anything at all. I think he can be certain, for if (as I said to my friend, furiously brandishing an empty bottle) it is impossible intellectually to entertain certainty, what is this certainty which it is impossible to entertain? If I have never experienced such a thing as certainty I cannot even say that a thing is not certain.

—TT, 34

Sceptics

If you are merely a sceptic, you must sooner or later ask yourself the question, "Why should *anything* go right; even observation and deduction? Why should not good logic be as misleading as bad logic? They are both movements in the brain of a bewildered ape?" The young sceptic says, "I have a right to think for myself." But the old sceptic, the complete sceptic, says, "I have no right to think for myself. I have no right to think at all."

—O, 58

Science

. . . the world of science and evolution is far more nameless and elusive and like a dream than the world of poetry and religion; since in the latter images and ideas remain themselves eternally, while it is the whole idea of evolution that identities melt into each other as they do in a nightmare.

—BC, 1

So far the result would painfully appear to be that whereas men in the earlier times said unscientific things with the vagueness of gossip and legend, they now say unscientific things with the plainness and the certainty of science.

—GFW, 22

Science in the modern world has many uses; its chief use, however, is to provide long words to cover the errors of the rich. The word "Kleptomania" is a vulgar example of what I mean. It is on a par with that strange theory, always advanced when a wealthy or prominent person is in the dock, that exposure is more of a punishment for the rich than for the poor. . . . An enormous amount of modern ingenuity is expended on finding defenses for the indefensible conduct of the powerful.

—H, 170–171

But if we look at the progress of our scientific civilization we see a gradual increase everywhere of the specialist over the popular function. Once men sang together round a table in chorus; now one man sings alone, for the absurd reason that he can sing better. If scientific civilization goes on (which is most improbable) only one man will laugh, because he can laugh better than the rest.

—H, 229

The rest is all cant and repetition ... the baseless dogmatism about science forbidding men to believe in miracles; as if *science* could forbid men to believe in something which science does not profess to investigate. Science is the study of the admitted laws of existence; it cannot prove a universal negative about whether those laws could ever be suspended by something admittedly above them.

—Thing, 205

Science (and Original Sin)

How could physical science prove that man is not depraved? You do not cut a man open to find his sins. You do not boil him until he gives forth the unmistakable green fumes of depravity. How could physical science find any traces of a moral fall? What traces did the writer expect to find? Did he expect to find a fossil Eve with a fossil apple inside her? Did he suppose that the ages would have spared for him a complete skeleton of Adam attached to a slightly faded fig-leaf? ... I am honestly bewildered as to the meaning of such passages as this, in which the advanced person writes that because geologists know nothing about the Fall, therefore any doctrine of depravity is untrue. Because science has not found something which obviously it could not find, therefore something entirely different— the psychological sense of evil—is untrue. ... To me it is all wild and whirling; as if a man said—"The plumber can find nothing wrong with our piano; so I suppose that my wife does love me."

—ATC, 140–141

Science (and Philosophy)

Physical science is like simple addition: it is either infallible or it is false. To mix science up with philosophy is only to produce a philosophy that has lost all its ideal value and a science that has lost all its practical value. I want my private physician to tell me whether this or that food will kill me. It is for my private philosopher to tell me whether I ought to be killed.

—ATC, 138

Science (and Religion)

... unfortunately, nineteenth-century scientists were just as ready to jump to the conclusion that any guess about nature was an obvious fact, as were seventeenth-century sectarians to jump to the conclusion that any guess about Scripture was the obvious explanation. Thus, private theories about what the Bible ought to mean, and premature theories about what the world ought to mean, have met in loud and widely advertised controversy, especially in the Victorian time; and this clumsy collision of two very impatient forms of ignorance was known as the quarrel of Science and Religion.

—STA, 88

Science (Modern)

So far from being knowledge, it's actually suppression of what we know. It's treating a friend as a stranger, and pretending that something familiar is really remote and mysterious. It's like saying that a man has a proboscis between the eyes, or that he falls down in a fit of insensibility once every twenty-four hours.

—FBO, 639

What I complain of is a vague popular philosophy which supposes itself to be scientific when it's really nothing but a sort of new religion and an uncommonly nasty one. When people talked about the fall of man they knew they were talking about a mystery, a thing they didn't understand. Now that they talk about the survival of the fittest they think they do understand it, whereas they have not merely no notion, they have an elaborately false notion of what the words mean. The Darwinian movement has made no difference to mankind, except that, instead of talking unphilosophically about philosophy, they now talk unscientifically about science.

— Queer, 241

Science of Human Beings

Science can analyse a pork-chop, and say how much of it is phosphorous and how much is protein; but science cannot analyse any man's wish for a pork-chop, and say how much of it is hunger, how much custom, how much nervous fancy. . . . The man's desire for the pork-chop remains literally as mystical and ethereal as his desire for heaven. All attempts, therefore at a science of any human things, at a science of history, a science of folk-lore, a science of sociology, are by their nature not merely hopeless, but crazy.

— H, 143

Scientific Culture

Only the modern, advanced, progressive scientific culture is unreasonably incomplete. It is, as Stevenson said, "a dingy ungentlemanly business; it leaves so much out of a man."

— Avowals, 25–26

The Scientific Eye

To the scientific eye all human history is a series of collective movements, destructions or migrations, like the massacre of flies in winter or the return of birds in spring.

—FBO, 233–234

Scientists

When the scientist talks about a type, he never means himself, but always his neighbour; probably his poorer neighbour.

—FBO, 639

The man of science has always been much more of a magician than the priest; since he would "control the elements" rather than submit to the spirit who is more elementary than the elements.

—STA, 69

The Scotsman

It might be maintained that the best effect of the Scotsman's religious training was teaching him to do without his religion.

—RLS, 86

Scott, Sir Walter

It is said that Scott is neglected by modern readers; if so, the matter could be more appropriately described by saying that modern readers are neglected by Providence. The ground of this neglect, in so far as it exists, must be found, I suppose, in the general sentiment that, like the beard of Polonius, he is too long.

— Types, 160

Séance

But my correspondent . . . charges me with actually ignoring the value of communication (if it exists) between this world and the next. I do not ignore it. But I do say this—That a different principle attaches to investigation in this spiritual field from investigation in any other. If a man baits a line for fish, the fish will come, even if he declares there are no such things as fishes. If a man limes a twig for birds, the birds will be caught, even if he thinks it superstitious to believe in birds at all. But a man cannot bait a line for souls. A man cannot lime a twig to catch gods. All wise schools have agreed that this latter capture depends to some extent on the faith of the capturer. So it comes to this: if you have no faith in the spirits your appeal is in vain; and if you have—is it needed?

—ATC, 151–152

Secularist Hypocrisy

In all ages the world has rightly satirised religious hypocrisy. But in our age the world suffers terribly from something that can only be called secular hypocrisy. The cant is not only secular, it is even secularist. It acts on a fixed theory that religious motives, in national and international things, need not be calculated and must not even be mentioned.

—EA, 121

It is not a question of liking or disliking any of the religions, or of having any religion at all. It is simply a taboo of tact or convention, whereby we are free to say that a man does this or that because of his nationality, or his profession, or his place of residence, or his hobby, but not because of his creed about the very cosmos in which he lives.

—EA, 121–122

Self-analysis

When studying ourselves, we are looking at a fresco with a magnifying glass. Consequently, these early impressions which great men have given of themselves are nearly always slanders upon themselves, for the strongest man is weak to his own conscience, and Hamlet flourished to a certainty even inside Napoleon.

—*RB*, 42

Self-sacrifice

If man has self-sacrifice and God has none, then man has in the Universe a secret and blasphemous superiority. And this tremendous story of a Divine jealousy Browning reads into the story of the Crucifixion. If the Creator had not been crucified He would not have been as great as thousands of wretched fanatics among His own creatures.

—*RB*, 178–179

Sentimentalists

The Sentimentalist, roughly speaking, is the man who wants to eat his cake and have it. He has no sense of honour about ideas; he will not see that one must pay for an idea as for anything else. He will not see that any worthy idea, like any honest woman, can only be won on its own terms, and with its logical chain of loyalty.... This is the essence of the Sentimentalist; that he seeks to enjoy every idea without its sequence, and every pleasure without its consequence.

—*Alarms*, 213–214

If those called free-thinkers are sentimentalists, those called free-lovers are open and obvious sentimentalists. We can always convict such people of sentimentalism by their weakness for euphemism.... They talk of free love when they mean something quite different, better defined as free lust.... They insist on talking about Birth Control when they mean less birth and no control. We could smash them to atoms, if we could be as indecent in our language as they are immoral in their conclusions. And as it is with morals, so it is with religion. The general notion that science establishes agnosticism is a sort of mystification produced by talking Latin and Greek instead of plain English. Science is the Latin for knowledge. Agnosticism is the Greek for ignorance.

— Thing, 45–46

Servile State

The thesis of the book is that the Socialist movement does not lead to Socialism. This is partly because of compromise and cowardice; but partly also because men have a dim indestructible respect for property, even in its disgusting disguise of modern monopoly. Therefore, instead of the intentional result, Socialism, we shall have the unintentional resultant: Slavery.

—Bio, 307

For the heathen state is a Servile State. And no one has more of this view of the state than the state socialists. The official Labour Politician ... would be the first to say in practice that it is the poor and ignorant who must be regulated. Doubtless it is one thing to be regulated and another to be tortured. But when once the principle is admitted broadly, the progress towards torture may proceed pretty briskly.

—FVF, 106–107

Sex

Every man feels the need of some element of purity in sex; perhaps they can only typify purity as the absence of sex.

—BC, 153

"Why cannot we discuss sex cooly and rationally anywhere?" is a tired and unintelligent question. It is like asking, "Why does not a man walk on his hands as well as on his feet?" It is silly. If a man walked systematically on his hands, they would not be hands but feet. And if love or lust were things that we could all discuss without any possible emotion they would not be love or lust, they would be something else—some mechanical function or abstract natural duty which may or may not exist in animals or in angels, but which has nothing at all to do with the sexuality we are talking about ... And all that we mean when we speak of "sex" is involved in the fact that it is not an unconscious or innocent thing, but a special and violent emotional stimulation at once spiritual and physical. A man who asks us to have no emotion in sex is asking us to have no emotion in emotion. ... It may be said of him, in the strict meaning of the words, that he does not know what he is talking about.

—*CM*, 125–126

The moment sex ceases to be a servant it becomes a tyrant. There is something dangerous and disproportionate in its place in human nature, for whatever reason; and it does really need a special purification and dedication. The modern talk about sex being free like any other sense, about the body being beautiful like any tree or flower, is either a description of the Garden of Eden or a piece of thoroughly bad psychology, of which the world grew weary two thousand years ago.

—*St. Francis*, 41

The Sexes

Of the two sexes the woman is in the more powerful position. For the average woman is at the head of something with which she can do as she likes; the average man has to obey orders and do nothing else.

—*ATC*, 77–78

. . . A lot of men, especially careless men . . . could go on saying for days that something ought to be done, or might as well be done. But if you convey to a woman that something ought to be done, there is always a dreadful danger that she will suddenly do it.

—FBO, 704

There is one real difference between men and women; that women prefer to talk in twos, while men prefer to talk in threes.

—TT, 270

The Sexes (Inequality of)

Wherever there is no element of variety, wherever all the items literally have an identical aim, there is at once and of necessity inequality. A woman is only inferior to man in the matter of being not so manly; she is inferior in nothing else. Man is inferior to woman in so far as he is not a woman; there is no other reason. And the same applies in some degree to all genuine differences.

—CD, 179

Shakespeare, William

For my part, I feel there is something national, something wholesomely symbolic, in the fact that there is no statue of Shakspere [sic]. There is, of course, one in Leicester Square; but the very place where it stands shows that it was put up by a foreigner for foreigners. There is surely something modest and manly about not attempting to express our poet in the plastic arts in which we do not excel. We honor Shakspere [sic] as the Jews honour God—by not daring to make of him a graven image. Our sculpture, our statues, are good enough for bankers and philanthropists, who are our curse: not good enough for him, who is our benediction.

—ATC, 63

319

When all is said, there is something a little sinister in the number of mad people there are in Shakespeare. We say that he uses his fools to brighten the dark background of tragedy; I think he sometimes uses them to darken it. Somewhere on that highest of human towers there is a tile loose. There is something that rattles rather crazily in the high wind of the highest of mortal tragedies. What is felt faintly even in Shakespeare is felt far more intensely in the other Elizabethan and Jacobean dramatists; they seem to go in for dancing ballets of lunatics and choruses of idiots, until sanity is the exception rather than the rule.

—C, 221–222

Shaw, George Bernard

Mr. Bernard Shaw's philosophy is exactly like black coffee—it awakens but it does not really inspire.

—Blake, 99

In these days, when Mr. Bernard Shaw is becoming gradually, amid general applause, the Grand Old Man of English letters, it is perhaps ungracious to record that he did once say there was nobody, with the possible exception of Homer, whose intellect he despised so much as Shakespeare's. He has since said almost enough sensible things to outweigh even anything so silly as that.

—C, 19

He can write the most energetic and outspoken of propaganda plays; but he cannot rise to a problem play. He cannot really divide his mind and let the two parts speak independently to other. He has never, so to speak, actually split his head in two; though I dare say there are many other people who are willing to do it for him.

—GBS, 176–177

The whole force and triumph of Mr. Bernard Shaw lie in the fact that he is a thoroughly consistent man. He puts the Shaw test rapidly and rigorously to everything that happens in heaven or earth. His standard never varies. You may attack his principles, as I do; but I do not know of any instance in which you can attack their application. If he dislikes lawlessness, he dislikes the lawlessness of socialists as much as that of individualists. . . . If he laughs at the authority of priests, he laughs louder at the pomposity of men of science.

—H, 50

He has pleased all the Bohemians by saying that women are equal to men; but he has infuriated them by suggesting that men are equal to women.

—H, 51

Mr. Shaw's old and recognized philosophy was . . . in brief, that conservative ideals were bad, not because they were conservative, but because they were ideals. Every ideal prevented men from judging justly the particular case; every moral generalization oppressed the individual; the golden rule was there was no golden rule.

The saying that "the golden rule is that there is no golden rule," can, indeed, be simply answered by being turned around. That there is no golden rule is itself a golden rule, or rather it is much worse than a golden rule. It is an iron rule; a fetter on the first movement of man.

—H, 54–55

No man has any right whatever merely to enjoy the work of Mr. Bernard Shaw; he might as well enjoy the invasion of his country by the French. Mr. Shaw writes either to convince or to enrage us.

—H, 294

The truth is, of course, that Mr. Shaw is cruelly hampered by the fact that he cannot tell any lie unless he thinks it is the truth.

—O, 17

... there is some truth in his own theory that the Americans are especially interested in him because he abuses Americans and will not come to America. It is not surprising, I say, that they should be intensely interested in Bernard Shaw; what is extraordinary is that they should be so intensely interested in me in connexion with Bernard Shaw. They seem to suppose that I am his brother or his keeper; though I admit that, if we travelled together, there might be a dispute among the schools as to which was the keeper and which the lunatic. Sometimes I am almost tempted to think that Shaw and I are the only Britishers they have heard of; or perhaps because one of us is thin and the other fat we figure as buffoons in an eternal dust and dance.... By this time I am driven to go about declaring that I am Bernard Shaw; the difference is a mere matter of two disguises: of alternative cushions and a beard. And that as I point out, is the real reason why Bernard Shaw cannot come to America.

—S, 112–113

Shaw has frequently compared himself with Shakespeare; Shakespeare was so unfortunate as to have few opportunities of comparing himself with Shaw. This was perhaps what some of the Shavians have meant by saying that Shakespeare wrote under the disadvantage of his age.

—S, 234

Shelley, Percy Bysshe

Few men in the world's history had more faith than Shelley. He had faith in the end of the most earthquake speculations, in the license of the most confounding passions. Indeed, he could bring himself to have faith in anything except in the faiths of everybody else.

—HA, 85

Sherlock Holmes

... the fact remains that Mr. Conan Doyle's hero is probably the only literary creation since the creations of Dickens which has really passed into the life and language of the people, and become a being like John Bull or Father Christmas.

—HA, 168

The stories of Sherlock Holmes are very good stories; they are perfectly graceful and conscientious works of art. The thread of irony which runs through all the solemn impossibilities of the narrative gives it the position of a really brilliant addition to the great literature of nonsense. The notion of the greatness of an intellect, proved by its occupation with small things instead of with great, is an original departure; it constitutes a kind of wild poetry of the commonplace.

—HA, 169

Sherlock Holmes would have been a better detective if he had been a philosopher, if he had been a poet, nay, if he had been a lover. It is remarkable to notice (I assume that you are as intimate with Dr. Watson's narratives as you should be)—it is remarkable to notice that the very same story in which the biographer describes Holmes's inaccessibility to love and such emotions, and how necessary it was to the clear balance of his logic, is the very same story in which Holmes is beaten by a woman because he does not know whether a certain man is her fiancé or her lawyer. If he had been in love he might have known well enough.

—HA, 172

Short Story (the Modern)

The moderns, in a word, describe life in short stories because they are possessed with the sentiment that life itself is an uncommonly short story, and perhaps not a true one.

—CD, 63

323

Our modern attraction to short stories is not an accident of form; it is the sign of a real sense of fleetingness and fragility; it means that existence is only an impression, and, perhaps, only an illusion. A short story of today has the air of a dream; it has the irrevocable beauty of a falsehood; we get a glimpse of grey streets of London or red plains of India, as in an opium vision; we see people—arresting people, with fiery and appealing faces. But when the story is ended, the people are ended. We have no instinct of anything ultimate and enduring behind the episodes.

—CD, 63

Silence

Complaint always comes back in an echo from the ends of the world; but silence strengthens us.

—FBO, 710

Similarity

As competition means always similarity, it is equally true that similarity always means inequality. If everything is trying to be green, some things will be greener than others; but there is an immortal and indestructible equality between green and red.

—CD, 180

Simplicity

The more simple an idea is, the more it is fertile in variations.

—ATC, 206

Men rush toward complexity; but they yearn toward simplicity.

—RLS, 160

Simplification

The simplification of anything is always sensational.

—Types, 126

Sin

If I get drunk I shall forget dignity; but if I keep sober I may still desire drink. Virtue has the heavy burden of knowledge; sin has often something of the levity of sinlessness.

—Glass, 145

Sin (Origins of)

... it was a product of spiritual conviction; it had nothing to do with remote physical origins. Men thought mankind wicked because they felt wicked themselves. If a man feels wicked, I cannot see why he should suddenly feel good because somebody tells him that his ancestors once had tails. Man's primary purity and innocence may have dropped off with his tail, for all anybody knows; the only thing we all know about that primary purity and innocence is that we have not got it. Nothing can be, in the strictest sense of the word, more comic than to set so shadowy a thing as the conjectures made by the vaguer anthropologists about primitive man against so solid a thing as the human sense of sin. By its nature the evidence of Eden is something that one cannot find. By its nature the evidence of sin is something that one cannot help finding.

—ATC, 141

Slander and Truth

... truth is still half an hour behind the slander; and nobody can be certain when or where it will catch up with it.

—FBO, 831

Sleep

I am always expecting to hear that a scientific campaign has been opened against sleep. Sooner or later the prohibitionists will turn their attention to the old tribal traditional superstition of sleep; and they will say that the sluggard is merely encouraged by the cowardice of the moderate sleeper. There will be tables of statistics, showing how many hours of output are lost . . . in which men have contracted the habit of sleep. . . . there will be all the scientific facts, except one scientific fact. And that is the fact that if men do not have sleep, they go mad. It is also a fact that if men do not have solitude, they go mad. You can see that, by the way they go on, when the poor miserable devils only have society.

—*Well*, 101–102

Snobs and Prigs

I am no more awed by the flying fashions among prigs than I am by the flying fashions among snobs. Snobs say they have the right kind of hat; prigs say they have the right kind of head. But, in both cases I should like some evidence beyond their own habit of staring at themselves in the glass.

—*Diversity*, 91

Social Life (the Ideal)

The reactionary wishes to return to what he would call 'the morning of the world.' But the revolutionist is quite equally prone to talk about waiting for the daybreak, about songs before sunrise, and about the dawn of a happier day. He does not seem to think so much about the noon of that day. And one mode in which this morning spirit is expressed is the return to the child.

—*RLS*, 160–161

Social Reform

If we are to save the oppressed, we must have two apparently antagonistic emotions in us at the same time. We must think the oppressed man intensely miserable, and, at the same time, intensely attractive and important. We must insist with violence upon his degradation; we must insist with the same violence upon his dignity. For if we relax by one inch the one assertion, men will say he does not need saving. And if we relax by one inch the other assertion, men will say he is not worth saving. The optimists will say that reform is needless. The pessimists will say that reform is hopeless. We must apply both simultaneously to the same oppressed man; we must say that he is a worm and a god; and we must thus lay ourselves open to the accusation (or the compliment) of transcendentalism. This is, indeed, the strongest argument for the religious conception of life.

—CD, 194

Socialism

I am myself primarily opposed to Socialism, or Collectivism or Bolshevism or whatever we call it, for a primary reason not immediately involved here: the ideal of property. I say the ideal and not merely the idea; and this alone disposes of the moral mistake in the matter. It disposes of all the dreary doubts of the Anti-Socialists about men not yet being angels, and all the yet drearier hopes of the Socialists about men soon being supermen. I do not admit that private property is a concession to baseness and selfishness; I think it is a point of honour. I think it is the most truly popular of all points of honour.

—Evils, 207–208

Those of us who study the papers and the parliamentary speeches with proper attention must have by this time a fairly precise idea of the nature of the evil of Socialism. It is a remote Utopian dream impossible of fulfilment and also an overwhelming practical danger that threatens us at every moment.

—Outline, 48

So long as the Trust State is fairly humane and works steadily, there is nothing to fight about; but there is precious little to sing about. For Business Government has neither authority nor liberty. Whether or no this explanation be right, it is certainly a paradox that this patchy isolation of the mind should exist under social conditions of almost inhuman sameness and centralization. But the paradox is in any case a very practical part of the tragedy. Wilde, in The Soul of Man Under Socialism, unconsciously uttered a very profound warning—against Socialism. It was the warning that even under Socialism the soul might have a tragedy like that of Wilde. Under the Servile State the soul will be yet more horribly free. There will be nothing to prevent a man losing his soul, as long as he does not lose his time or his ticket or his place in the bread queue.

−S, 214−215

Socialism vs. Capitalism

There is less difference than many suppose between the ideal Socialist system, in which the big businesses are run by the State, and the present Capitalist system, in which the State is run by the big businesses. They are much nearer to each other than either is to my own ideal; of breaking up the big businesses into a multitude of small businesses.

−Come, 13

Socialists

"A radical does not mean a man who lives on radishes," remarked Crook, with some impatience; "and a Conservative does not mean a man who preserves jam. Neither, I assure you, does a Socialist mean a man who desires a social evening with the chimney-sweep. A Socialist means a man who wants all the chimneys swept and all the chimney-sweeps paid for it."

"But who won't allow you," put in the priest in a low voice, "to own your own soot."

−FBO, 71

Societal Change

The changes that pass over great societies are often too big to be seen. That is they are too big to be summarized under a public name; but it is a gross mistake to suppose that each of them is not felt as a private fact. Every man feels the faith or the sin; but every man feels it as something peculiar to himself. It is the most secret part of every separate man that makes up a real social movement. The general philosophy is drawn not from what everybody says, but rather from what everybody does not say, but feels the more. Public opinion is made up of all the most peculiarly private opinions. Hence we always find a paradox in the fashion of speech and thought. The changes which men in any age are always talking about are never the changes that are really going on. The changes that are really going on are not those which men pompously applaud when they get together, but those which they vigorously promote when they get by themselves.

—HA, 157

Society

The existing and general system of society, subject in our own age and industrial culture to very gross abuses and painful problems, is nevertheless a normal one. It is the idea that the commonwealth is made up of a number of small kingdoms, of which a man and a woman become the king and queen and on which they exercise a reasonable authority, subject to the commonsense of the commonwealth, until those under their care grow up to found similar kingdoms and exercise similar authority. This is the social structure of mankind, far older than all its records and more universal than any of its religions; and all attempts to alter it are mere talk and tomfoolery.

— Thing, 32–33

Sociologists

The trouble with most sociologists, criminologists, etc., is that while their knowledge of their own details is exhaustive and subtle, their knowledge of man and society, to which these are to be applied, is quite exceptionally superficial and silly. They know everything about biology, but almost nothing about life. Their ideas of history, for instance, are simply cheap and uneducated.

—Alarms, 82

Socrates

If the Death of Socrates were condensed into a journalistic paragraph, there would be no room for the remarks on immortality, and not much even for the cup of hemlock; but only a special mention of a request to somebody to buy a cock—perhaps turned by the report into a cocktail.

—AIWS, 5

Soldiers

Soldiers have many faults, but they have one redeeming merit: they are never worshippers of force. . . . No soldier could possibly say that his own bayonets were his authority. No soldier could possibly say that he came in the name of his own bayonets. It would be as absurd as if a postman said that he came inside his bag.

—ATC, 103

. . . the soldier is always, by the nature of things, loyal to something. And as long as one is loyal to something one can never be a worshipper of mere force. For mere force, violence in the abstract, is the enemy of anything we love. To love anything is to see it at once under lowering skies of danger. Loyalty implies loyalty in misfortune; and when a soldier has accepted any nation's uniform he has already accepted its defeat.

—ATC, 104

330

The Soul

The soul does not die by sin but by impenitence.

—Rome, 230

State (Modern)

It comes back to the fundamental truth of the modern state. Our commercialism does not punish the vices of the poor, but the virtues of the poor. It hampers the human character at its best and not merely at its worst; and makes impossible even the merits that it vainly recommends. Capitalism has prevented the poor man from saving more than it has prevented him from spending. It has restrained him from respectable marriage more than from casual immorality. It may be that Socialism threatens to destroy domesticity; but it is capitalism that destroys it. This is doubtless what is meant by saying that capitalism is the more practical of the two.

—Cobbett, 47

Statesmen (English)

The English statesman is bribed not to be bribed. He is born with a silver spoon in his mouth, so that he may never afterwards be found with the silver spoons in his pocket.

—WW, 50

Stevenson, Robert Louis

I do not quite see why he should be covered with cold depreciation merely because he could put into a line what other men put into a page; why he should be regarded as superficial because he saw more in a man's walk or profile than the moderns can dig out of his complexes and his subconsciousness; why he should be called artificial because he sought (and found) the right word for a real object; why he should be thought shallow because he went straight for what was significant, without wading towards it through wordy seas of insignificance; or why he should be treated as a liar because he was not ashamed to be a story-teller.

—RLS, 103

Stevenson's Dr. Jekyll and Mr. Hyde

The point of the story is not that a man *can* cut himself off from his conscience, but that he cannot.

—RLS, 50

You will find twenty allusions to Jekyll and Hyde in a day's newspaper reading. You will also find that all such allusions suppose the two personalities to be equal, neither caring for the other. Or more roughly, they think the book means that man can be cloven into two creatures, good and evil. The whole stab of the story is that man *can't:* because while evil does not care for good, good must care for evil. Or, in other words, man cannot escape from God, because good is the God in man; and insists on omniscience. This point, which is good psychology and also good theology and also good art, has missed its main intention merely because it was also good story-telling.

—VA, 246–247

Stories (Modern)

A detective story generally describes six living men discussing how it is that a man is dead. A modern philosophic story generally describes six dead men discussing how any man can possibly be alive.

—MM, 235

Strength and Levity

Moderate strength is shown in violence, supreme strength is shown in levity.

— Thursday, 171

Style

A man who loves all men enough to use them rightly is a democrat. A man who loves all words enough to use them rightly is a stylist. Style comes out, as the fraternal human sentiment comes out, pre-eminently and most definitely in dealing with coarse or everyday things.

—HA, 130

Subtle Distinctions

The subtle distinctions have made the simple Christians; all the men who think drink right and drunkenness wrong; all the men who think marriage normal and polygamy abnormal; all the men who think it wrong to hit first and right to hit back; and . . . all the men who think it right to carve statues and wrong to worship them. These are all, when one comes to think of it, very subtle theological distinctions.

—Rome, 64

Success

To begin with, of course, there is no such thing as Success. Or, if you like to put it so, there is nothing that is not successful. That a thing is successful merely means that it is; a millionaire is successful in being a millionaire and a donkey in being a donkey. Any live man has succeeded in living; any dead man may have succeeded in committing suicide.

—ATC, 17

The old sense of honour taught men to suspect success; to say, 'This is a benefit; it may be a bribe.' The new nine-times-accursed nonsense about Making Good teaches men to identify being good with making money.

—FBO, 891

Success (Books on)

They are much more wild than the wildest romances of chivalry and much more dull than the dullest religious tract. Moreover, the romances of chivalry were at least about chivalry; the religious tracts are about religion. But these things are about nothing; they are about what is called Success. On every bookstall, in every magazine, you may find works telling people how to succeed. They are books showing men how to succeed in everything; they are written by men who cannot even succeed in writing books.

—ATC, 17

...I really think that the people who buy these books (if any people do buy them) have a moral, if not a legal, right to ask for their money back. Nobody would dare to publish a book about electricity which literally told one nothing about electricity; no one would dare to publish an article on botany which showed that the writer did not know which end of a plant grew in the earth. Yet our modern world is full of books about Success and successful people which literally contain no kind of idea, and scarcely any kind of verbal sense.

—ATC, 18

Suffragettes

The popular papers always persisted in representing the New Woman or the Suffragette as an ugly woman, fat, in spectacles, with bulging clothes, and generally falling off a bicycle. As a matter of plain external fact there was not a word of truth in this. The leaders of the movement of female emancipation are not at all ugly; most of them are extraordinarily good-

334

looking. . . . Yet the popular instinct was right. For the popular instinct was that in this movement, rightly or wrongly, there was an element of indifference to female dignity, of a quite new willingness of women to be grotesque. These women did truly despise the pontifical quality of woman. . . . For the two things that a healthy person hates most between heaven and hell are a woman who is not dignified and a man that is.

—ATC, 15–16

If she were being burned alive as a witch, if she then looked up in unmixed rapture and saw a ballot-box descending out of heaven, then I should say that the incident, though not conclusive, was frightfully impressive. It would not prove logically that she ought to have the vote, or that anybody ought to have the vote. But it would prove this: that there was, for some reason, a sacramental reality in the vote, that the soul could take the vote and feed on it; that it was in itself a positive and overpowering pleasure, capable of being pitted against positive and overpowering pain.

—ATC, 84

Suicide

Not only is suicide a sin, it is the sin. It is the ultimate and absolute evil, the refusal to take an interest in existence; the refusal to take the oath of loyalty to life. The man who kills a man, kills a man. The man who kills himself, kills all men; as far as he is concerned he wipes out the world. . . . When a man hangs himself on a tree, the leaves might fall off in anger and the birds fly away in fury: for each has received a personal affront. . . . There is a meaning in burying the suicide apart. The man's crime is different from other crimes—for it makes even crimes impossible.

—O, 131–132

Supernatural

... it's natural to believe in the supernatural. It never feels natural to accept only natural things.

—FBO, 529

Supernatural (Denial of)

Surely we cannot take an open question like the supernatural and shut it with a bang, turning the key of the mad-house on all the mystics of history. To call a man mad because he has seen ghosts is in a literal sense religious persecution. It is denying him his full dignity as a citizen because he cannot be fitted into your theory of the cosmos.... you are setting your own theory of things inexorably against the sincerity or sanity of human testimony. Such dogmatism at least must be quite as impossible to anyone calling himself an agnostic as to anyone calling himself a spiritualist. You cannot take the region called the unknown and calmly say that though you know nothing about it, you know that all the gates are locked.... that was the whole fallacy of Herbert Spencer and Huxley when they talked about the unknowable instead of about the unknown. An agnostic like Huxley must concede the possibility of a gnostic like Blake. We do not know enough about the unknown to know that is it unknowable.

—Blake, 73–74

Superstition

A Puritan may think it blasphemous that God should become a wafer. A Moslem thinks it blasphemous that God should become a workman in Galilee. And he is perfectly right, from his point of view; and given his primary principle. But if the Moslem has a principle, the Protestant has only a prejudice. That is, he has only a fragment; a relic; a superstition. If it be profane that the miraculous should descend to the plane of matter, then certainly Catholicism is profane; and Protestantism is profane; and Christianity is profane. Of all human creeds or concepts, in that sense, Christianity is the most utterly profane. But why a man should accept a

Creator who was a carpenter, and then worry about holy water, why he should accept a local Protestant tradition that God was born in some particular place mentioned in the Bible, merely because the Bible had been left lying about in England, and then say it is incredible that a blessing should linger on the bones of a saint, why he should accept the first and most stupendous part of the story of Heaven on Earth, and then furiously deny a few small but obvious deductions from it—that is a thing I do not understand; I never could understand; I have come to the conclusion that I shall never understand. I can only attribute it to Superstition.

—Thing, 160

Symbols (Worldly)

And yet (strangely enough) though men fuss more about the worldly symbols, they mean less by them. It is the mark of religious forms that they declare something unknown. But it is the mark of worldly forms that they declare something which is known, and which is known to be untrue. When the Pope in an Encyclical calls himself your father, it is a matter of faith or of doubt. But when the Duke of Devonshire in a letter calls himself yours obediently, you know that he means the opposite of what he says. Religious forms are, at the worst, fables; they might be true. Secular forms are falsehoods; they are not true.

—ATC, 205

T

Tastes

. . . there is always a difference between the eccentricity of an elderly man who defies the world and the enthusiasm of a younger man who hopes to alter it. The old gentleman may be willing, in a sense, to stand on his head; but he does not hope, as the boy does, to stand the world on its head.

—Bow, 89–90

Taverns

I believe that if by some method the local public-house could be as definite and isolated a place as the local post-office or the local railway station, if all types of people passed through it for all types of refreshments, you would have the same safeguard against a man behaving in a disgusting way in a tavern that you have at present against his behaving in a disgusting way in a post-office: simply the presence of his ordinary sensible neighbours. In such a place the kind of lunatic who wants to drink an unlimited number of whiskies would be treated with the same severity with which the post-office authorities would treat an amiable lunatic who had an appetite for licking an unlimited number of stamps. It is a small matter whether in either case a technical refusal would be officially employed. . . . At least, the postmistress would not dangle a strip of tempting sixpenny stamps before the enthusiast's eyes as he was being dragged away with his tongue out.

—ATC, 172–173

Teachers (Bad)

If I were an examiner appointed to examine all examiners (which does not at present appear probable), I would not only ask the teachers how much knowledge they had imparted; I would ask them how much splendid and scornful ignorance they had erected, like some royal tower in arms.

—ATC, 53

Teaching

But there is something to be said for the idea of teaching everything to somebody, as compared with the modern notion of teaching nothing, and the same sort of nothing, to everybody.

—Survey, 50

Teetotalism and Vegetarianism (Parallels of)

. . . their only apparent point of union is that they . . . come from the East. Thus a modern vegetarian is generally also a teetotaler, yet there is certainly no obvious intellectual connection between consuming vegetables and not consuming fermented vegetables. A drunkard, when lifted labouriously out of the gutter, might well be heard huskily to plead that he had fallen there through excessive devotion to a vegetable diet. On the other hand, a man might well be a practised and polished cannibal and still be a strict teetotaler. A subtle parallelism might doubtless be found; but the only quite obvious parallelism is that vegetarianism is Buddhist and teetotalism is Mahometan.

—Blake, 201–202

Teetotallers

The teetotaller has chosen a most unfortunate phrase for the drunkard when he says that the drunkard is making a beast of himself. The man who drinks ordinarily makes nothing but an ordinary man of himself. The man who drinks excessively makes a devil of himself. But nothing connected with a human and artistic thing like wine can bring one nearer to the brute life of nature. The only man who is, in the exact and literal sense of the words, making a beast of himself is the teetotaller.

−CD, 156

Temperance

Mr. Aldous Huxley remarked, in a brilliant article the other day, that those who are now pursuing pleasure are not only fleeing from boredom, but are acutely suffering from it. It is no longer a question of A Good Time Coming; for The Good Times have gone with the arrival of A Good Time All the Time.

−S, 58

"Temperance Reformers"

But "temperance reformers" are like a small group of vegetarians who should silently and systematically act on an ethical assumption entirely unfamiliar to the mass of the people. They would always be giving peerages to greengrocers. They would always be appointing Parliamentary Commissions to enquire into the private life of butchers. Whenever they found a man quite at their mercy, as a pauper or a convict or a lunatic, they would force him to add the final touch to his inhuman isolation by becoming a vegetarian. All the meals for school children will be vegetarian meals. All the state public houses will be vegetarian public houses. There is a very strong case for vegetarianism as compared with teetotalism. Drinking one glass of beer cannot by any philosophy be drunkenness; but killing one animal can, by this philosophy, be murder.

−ATC, 6−7

Tennyson, Alfred

His religious range was very much wider and wiser than his political; but here also he suffered from treating as true universality a thing that was only a sort of a lukewarm local patriotism. Here also he suffered by the very splendour and perfection of his poetical powers. He was quite the opposite of the man who cannot express himself; the inarticulate singer who dies with all his music in him. He had a great deal to say; but he had much more power of expression than was wanted for anything he had to express. He could not think up to the height of his own towering style.

—VA, 164–165

Terror

Fear is of the body, perhaps; but terror is only of the soul. The body runs with fear: it is only the soul that stands still with it.

—L & L, 157

Testimony

... the more we study it the more queer the whole question of human evidence becomes. There is not one man in twenty who really observes things at all. There is not one man in a hundred who observes them with real precision; certainly not one in a hundred who can first observe, then remember and finally describe.

—FBO, 522–523

Teutons, Christians and Europe

... the historical theory which Froude and Freeman and others shared with Carlyle, the theory of a Teutonic root of all the real greatness of Europe, has been criticised by saner historians, with a broader outlook which the Victorians never imagined, and often with a number of new facts which the Victorians could not be expected to know. To-day, no

341

well-informed person has any right to be ignorant of the part really played, not by the Germanic chaos, but by the Roman order and the Catholic faith, in the making of everything civilised or half-civilised, including Germany.

—EA, 67

Thanksgiving

The Americans have established a Thanksgiving Day to celebrate the fact that the Pilgrim Fathers reached America. The English might very well establish another Thanksgiving Day; to celebrate the happy fact that the Pilgrim Fathers left England.

—S, 160

Theatre

For what is the theatre? First and last, and above all things, it is a festival. . . . The theatre is nothing if it is not joyful; the theatre is nothing if it is not sensational; the theatre is nothing if it is not theatrical.

—L & L, 39–40

Theologians (Liberal)

The Catholic Church believed that man and God both had a sort of spiritual freedom. Calvinism took away the freedom from man, but left it to God. Scientific materialism binds the Creator Himself; it chains up God as the Apocalypse chained the devil. It leaves nothing free in the universe. And those who assist this process are called the "liberal theologians."

—O, 237

Theological Distinctions

Theological distinctions are fine but not thin. In all the mess of modern thoughtlessness, that still calls itself modern thought, there is perhaps nothing so stupendously stupid as the common saying, "Religion can never depend on minute disputes about doctrine." It is like saying that life can never depend on minute disputes about medicine.

—Rome, 61–62

Theological Terms

. . . I have known some people of very modern views driven by their distress to the use of theological terms to which they attached no doctrinal significance, merely because a drawer was jammed tight and they could not pull it out.

—ATC, 27

Theology

Theology is only thought applied to religion.

—NJ, 110

But theology is only the element of reason in religion; the reason that prevents it from being a mere emotion.

—Thing, 146

Theology and Philosophy

Men talk of philosophy and theology as if they were something specialistic and arid and academic. But philosophy and theology are not only the only democratic things, they are democratic to the point of being vulgar, to the point, I was going to say, of being rowdy. They alone admit all matters; they alone lie open to all attacks. All other sciences may, while

343

studying their own, laugh at the rag-tag and bobtail of other sciences. An astronomer may sneer at animalculae, which are very like stars; an entomologist may scorn the stars, which are very like animalculae. Physiologists may think it dirty to grub about in the grass; botanists may think it dirtier to grub about in an animal's inside. But there is nothing that is not relevant to these more ancient studies. There is no detail, from buttons to kangaroos, that does not enter into the gay confusion of philosophy. There is no fact of life, from the death of a donkey to the General Post Office, which has not its place to dance and sing in, in the glorious Carnival of theology.

—GFW, 74–75

Theory and Practice

Some of the best men in the world—Dr. Johnson, for instance—have been specially remarkable for being conventional in theory and unconventional in practice. But if once a man is unconventional in theory, then the situation is atrocious. It almost certainly means either that a man has no morals or that he has no brains. The type of man does exist who says clearly and deliberately that he does not want to observe the little laws that surround him, that he is proud of being absent-minded, that he is proud of his disdain of detail. Whenever this occurs it certainly arises in another and most literal sense from absence—of Mind.

—HA, 173

Things (New and Old)

And in the darkest of the books of God there is written a truth that is also a riddle. It is of the new things that men tire—of fashions and proposals and improvements and change. It is the old things that startle and intoxicate. It is the old things that are young. There is no sceptic who does not feel that many have doubted before. There is no worshipper of change who does not feel upon his neck the vast weight of the weariness of the universe. But we who do the old things are fed by nature with a perpetual infancy. No man who is in love thinks that any one has been in love before. No woman who has a child thinks that there have been such things

344

as children. . . . Yes, oh dark voice, the world is always the same, for it is always unexpected.

—NNH, 191–192

Things (Undying)

It is not merely true that all old things are already dead; it is also true that all new things are already dead; for the only undying things are the things that are neither new nor old.

—CD, 206

Thinkers (Modern)

A modern "thinker" will find it easier to make up a hundred problems than to make up one riddle. For in the case of the riddle he has to make up the answer.

—Diversity, 74

Thinkers (Original)

If a man has some fierce or unfamiliar point of view, he must, even when he is talking about his cat, begin with the origin of the cosmos; for his cosmos is as private as his cat. . . . This explains the extraordinary air of digression and irrelevancy which can be observed in some of the most direct and sincere minds. It explains the bewildering allusiveness of Dante; the galloping parentheses of Rabelais; the gigantic prefaces of Mr. Bernard Shaw. The brilliant man seems more lumbering and elaborate than anyone else, because he has something to say about everything. The very quickness of his mind makes the slowness of his narrative. For he finds sermons in stones, in all the paving stones of the street he plods along. . . . Because he is original he is always going back to the origins.

—Blake, 126–129

There is only one moment, at most, of triumph for the original thinker; while his thought is an originality and before it becomes merely an origin. News spreads quickly; that is, it grows stale quickly; and though we may call a work wonderful, we cannot easily put ourselves in the position of those for whom it was a cause of wonder, in the sense of surprise.

—*RLS,* 70

We talk of looking back with gratitude to innovators or the introducers of new ideas; but in fact nothing is more difficult to do, since for us they are now necessarily old ideas.

—*RLS,* 70

The Thomistic Revolution

There really was a new reason for regarding the senses, and the sensations of the body, and the experiences of the common man, with a reverence at which great Aristotle would have stared, and no man in the ancient world could have begun to understand. The Body was no longer what it was when Plato and Porphyry and the old mystics had left it for dead. It had hung upon a gibbet. It had risen from a tomb. It was no longer possible for the soul to despise the senses, which had been the organs of something that was more than man. Plato might despise the flesh; but God had not despised it. The senses had truly become sanctified; as they are blessed one by one at a Catholic baptism.

—*STA,* 118

After the Incarnation had become the idea that is central in our civilisation, it was inevitable that there should be a return to materialism, in the sense of the serious value of matter and the making of the body. When once Christ had risen, it was inevitable that Aristotle should rise again.

—*STA,* 118–119

Thought (Free)

I have pointed out that mere modern free-thought has left everything in a fog, including itself. The assertion that thought is free led first to the denial that will is free; but even about that there was no real determination among the Determinists. In practice, they told men that they must treat their will as free though it was not free. In other words, Man must live a double life; which is exactly the old heresy of Siger Brabant about the Double Mind.

—STA, 164–165

Thought (Modern)

We talk, by a sort of habit, about Modern Thought, forgetting the familiar fact that moderns do not think. They only feel, and that is why they are so much stronger in fiction than in facts; why their novels are so such better than their newspapers.

—AIG, 240

Another savage trait of our time is the disposition to talk about material substances instead of about ideas. The old civilisation talked about the sin of gluttony or excess. We talk about the Problem of Drink—as if drink could be a problem. When people have come to call the problem of human intemperance the Problem of Drink, and to talk about curing it by attacking the drink traffic, they have reached quite a dim stage of barbarism. The thing is an inverted form of fetish worship; it is no sillier to say that a bottle is a god than to say that a bottle is a devil. . . . In a little while we shall have them calling the practice of wife-beating the Problem of Pokers; the habit of housebreaking will be called the Problem of the Skeleton-Key Trade; and for all I know they may try to prevent forgery by shutting up all the stationers' shops by Act of Parliament.

—ATC, 167

Have you ever seen a fellow fail at the high jump because he had not gone far enough back for his run? That is Modern Thought. It is so confident of where it is going to that it does not know where it comes from.

—Diversity, 83

Thrift

Thrift by derivation means thriving; and the miser is the man who does not thrive. The whole meaning of thrift is making the most of everything; and the miser does not make anything of anything.

—AIWS, 160

To-day

For though to-day is always to-day and the moment is always modern, we are the only men in all history who fell back upon bragging about the mere fact that to-day is not yesterday.

—Survey, 11

Tolstoian Rules

But the greatest error of all lies is the mere act of cutting up the teaching of the New Testament into five rules. It precisely and ingeniously misses the most dominant characteristic of the teaching—its absolute spontaneity. The abyss between Christ and all His modern interpreters is that we have no record that He ever wrote a word, except with His finger in the sand. The whole is the history of one continuous and sublime conversation. Thousands of rules have been deduced from it before these Tolstoian rules were made, and thousands will be deduced afterwards. It was not for any pompous proclamation, it was not for any elaborate output of printed volumes; it was for a few splendid and idle words that the cross was set up on Calvary, and the earth gaped, and the sun was darkened at noonday.

—Types, 144

Tolstoy, Leo

The work of Tolstoy has another and more special significance. It represents the re-assertion of a certain awful common sense which characterised the most extreme utterances of Christ. It is true that we cannot turn the cheek to the smiter; it is true that we cannot give our cloak to the robber; civilisation is too complicated, too vain-glorious, too emotional. The robber would brag, and we should blush; in other words, the robber and we are alike sentimentalists. The command of Christ is impossible, but it is not insane; it is rather sanity preached to a planet of lunatics.

— Types, 134

Torture

. . . the most atrocious of all tortures, which is called caprice.

—NJ, 117

This is, first and last, the frightful thing we must remember. In so far as we grow instructed and refined we are not (in any sense whatever) naturally moving away from torture. We may be moving towards torture. We must know what we are doing, if we are to avoid the enormous secret cruelty which has crowned every historic civilisation.

— TT, 259

There is nothing particularly nasty about being a relic of barbarism. Dancing is a relic of barbarism. Man is a relic of barbarism. Civilisation is a relic of barbarism.

But torture is not a relic of barbarism at all. In actuality it is simply a relic of sin; but in comparative history it may well be called a relic of civilisation.

— TT, 258–259

Totalitarian State

The Totalitarian State is now making a clean sweep of all our old notions of liberty, even more than the French Revolution made a clean sweep of all the old ideas of loyalty. It is the Church that excommunicates; but, in that very word, implies that a communion stands open for a restored communicant. It is the State that exterminates; it is the State that abolishes absolutely and altogether; whether it is the American State abolishing beer, or the Fascist State abolishing parties, or the Hitlerite State abolishing almost everything but itself.

—Well, 247

Tradition

Indeed the vulgar rumor is nearly always much nearer the historical truth than the "educated" opinion of today; for tradition is truer than fashion.

—England, 67

The truth is that the things that meet to-day in Jerusalem are by far the greatest things that the world has yet seen. If they are not important nothing on this earth is important, and certainly not the impressions of those who happen to be bored by them. But to understand them it is necessary to have something which is much commoner in Jerusalem than in Oxford or Boston; that sort of living history which we call tradition.

—NJ, 110

I have never been able to understand where people got the idea that democracy was in some way opposed to tradition. It is obvious that tradition is only democracy extended through time. It is trusting to a consensus of common human voices rather than to some isolated or arbitrary record.

—O, 84

Tradition may be defined as an extension of the franchise. Tradition means giving votes to the most obscure of all classes, our ancestors. It is the democracy of the dead. Tradition refuses to submit to the small and arrogant oligarchy of those who merely happen to be walking about. All democrats object to men being disqualified by the accident of birth; tradition objects to their being disqualified by the accident of death. . . . I, at any rate, cannot separate the two ideas of democracy and tradition; it seems evident to me that they are the same idea. . . . The ancient Greeks voted by stones; these shall vote by tombstones. It is all quite regular and official; for most tombstones, like most ballot papers are marked with a cross.

—O, 85–86

Tragedy

. . . tragedy is that point when things are left to God and men can do no more.

—HA, 65

Tragedy (Literary)

. . . great tragedy is only great when it describes loss so as to increase value, and not to decrease it.

—S, 246

The Tragic and the Comic

There are two things in which all men are manifestly unmistakably equal. They are not equally clever or equally muscular or equally fat, as the sages of the modern reaction (with piercing insight) perceive. But this is a spiritual certainty, that all men are tragic. And this, again, is an equally sublime spiritual certainty, that all men are comic. No special and private sorrow can be so dreadful as the fact of having to die. And no freak or deformity can be so funny as the mere fact of having two legs. Every man is important if he loses his life; and every man is funny if he loses his hat, and has to run after it. And the universal test everywhere of whether a thing is popular, of the people, is whether it employs vigorously these extremes of the tragic and the comic.

−CD, 175

Trains (How to Catch)

The only way of catching a train I have ever discovered is to be late for the one before.

−TT, 260

Traitors

Judas Iscariot was one of the very earliest of all possible early Christians. And the whole point about him was that his hand was in the same dish; the traitor is always a friend, or he could never be a foe.

−NJ, 286

Trinity (Doctrine of)

In the days of my youth the Religion of Humanity was a term commonly applied to Comtism, the theory of certain rationalists who worshipped corporate mankind as a Supreme Being. Even in the days of my youth, I remarked that there was something slightly odd about despising and dismissing the doctrine of the Trinity as a mystical and even maniacal contradiction; and then asking us to adore a deity who is a hundred million persons in one God, neither confounding the persons nor dividing the substance.

−EM, 83

Truth

In one sense truth alone can be exaggerated; nothing else can stand the strain.

—CD, 134

Truth, of course, must of necessity be stranger than fiction, for we have made fiction to suit ourselves.

—H, 53–54

The Twentieth Century

As the eighteenth century thought itself the Age of Reason, and the nineteenth century thought itself the Age of Common Sense, the twentieth century cannot as yet even manage to think itself anything but the Age of Uncommon Nonsense.

—STA, 25

Tyranny

Tyranny is the opposite of authority. For authority simply means right; and nothing is authoritative except what somebody has a right to do, and therefore is right in doing. . . . Tyranny means too little authority; for though, of course, an individual may use wrongly the power that may go with it, he is in that act disloyal to the law of right, which should be his own authority.

—AIWS, 158–159

Modern tyranny can find its prototype in the torturing of heathen slaves in two fundamental respects. First, that the modern world has returned to the test of the heathen world, that of considering service to the state and not justice to the individual. And second, that the modern world, like the heathen world, is here inflicting it chiefly on subordinate and submerged classes of society; on slaves or those who are almost slaves.

—*FVF,* 106

Tyrants

For the worst tyrant is not the man who rules by fear; the worst tyrant is he who rules by love and plays on it as on a harp.

—*RB,* 74

U

Umbrellas

I could never reconcile myself to carrying an umbrella; it is a pompous Eastern business, carried over the heads of despots in the dry hot lands. Shut up, an umbrella is an unmanageable walking stick; open, it is an inadequate tent.

—MM, 193

Uniqueness

Lord! what a strange world in which a man cannot remain unique even by taking the trouble to go mad.

—NNH, 172

Unity

... the problem of the Christian is not merely to unite all things, but to unite union with disunion. The differences are not indifferent; and the problem is to let things differ while they agree. In short, the Western man seeks after Liberty, which is a real mystery. Compared with that unity is a platitude.

—Survey, 99

Universality

Universality is a contradiction in terms. You cannot be everything if you are anything. If you wish to be white all over, you must austerely resist the temptation to have green spots or yellow stripes. If you wish to be good all over, you must resist the spots of sin or the stripes of servitude. It may be great fun to be many-sided; but however many sides one has there cannot be one of them which is complete and rounded innocence. A polygon can have an infinite number of sides; but no one of its sides can be a circle.

—HA, 146

Utopia

Utopia always seems to me to mean regimentation rather than emancipation; repression rather than expansion. It is generally called a Republic and it always is a Monarchy. It is a Monarchy in the old and exact sense of the term; because it is really ruled by one man: the author of the book. He may tell us that all the characters in the book spontaneously delight in the beautiful social condition; but somehow we never believe him. His ideal world is always the world that he wants; and not the world that the world wants.

—Gen S, 30–31

V

Vandalism

Vandalism is of two kinds, the negative and the positive; as in the Vandals of the ancient world, who destroyed buildings, and the Vandals of the modern world who erect them.

—CM, 181

Vanity

Vanity is not only not the same thing as self-consciousness, it is very often the opposite of it. When a man becomes self-conscious he very often becomes painfully and abominably humble. But so long as a man is healthily unconscious he is almost certain to be healthily vain. He will take a delight, without a moments *arrière pensée,* in any of his own powers or characteristics.

—HA, 41

The literature of candour unearths innumerable weaknesses and elements of lawlessness which is called romance. It perceives superficial habits like murder and dipsomania, but it does not perceive the deepest of sins—the sin of vanity—vanity which is the mother of all day-dreams and adventures, the one sin that is not shared with any boon companion, or whispered to any priest.

— Types, 162–163

357

Vice (as Poetical)

The general claim that vices are poetical is largely unfounded; and this is an excellent example of how unpoetical is the vice of profanity. Blasphemy is not wild; blasphemy is in its nature prosaic. It consists in regarding in a commonplace manner something which other and happier people regard in a rapturous and imaginative manner. This is well exemplified in poor Blake and his Gnostic heresy about Jesus. In holding that Christ was weakened by being crucified he was certainly a pedant, and certainly not a poet. If there is one point on which the spirit of poets and the poetic soul in all peoples is on the side of Christianity, it is exactly this one point on which Blake is against Christianity—"was crucified, dead and buried." The spectacle of a God dying is much more grandiose than the spectacle of a man living for ever; the former suggests that awful changes have really entered the alchemy of the universe; the latter is only vaguely reminiscent of hygienic octogenarians.

—Blake, 178–179

Victoria, Queen

She had an inspired genius for the'familiarising virtues; her sympathy and sanity made us feel at home even in an age of revolutions. That indestructible sense of security which for good and evil is so typical of our nation, that almost scornful optimism which, in the matter of ourselves, cannot take peril or even decadence seriously, reached by far its highest and healthiest form in the sense that we were watched over by one so thoroughly English in her silence and self-control, in her shrewd trustfulness and her brilliant inaction.

— Types, 226

The Victorian Age

The real vice of the Victorians was that they regarded history as a story that ended well—because it ended with the Victorians.

—C, 28

This is the last essential of the Victorian. Laugh at him as a limited man, a moralist, conventionalist, an opportunist, a formalist. But remember also that he was really a humorist; and may still be laughing at you.

—*VA*, 155

The Victorian Age made one or two mistakes, but they were mistakes that were really useful; that is, mistakes that were really mistaken. They thought that commerce outside a country must extend peace: it has certainly often extended war. They thought that commerce inside a country must certainly promote prosperity; it has largely promoted poverty. But for them these were experiments; for us they ought to be lessons. If *we* continue the capitalist use of the populace—if *we* continue the capitalist use of external arms, it will lie heavy on the living. The dishonor will not be on the dead.

—*VA*, 250–251

Villains

The villain is not in the story to be a character; he is there to be a danger—a ceaseless, ruthless, and uncompromising menace, like that of wild beasts or the sea. For the full satisfaction of the sense of combat, which everywhere and always involves a sense of equality, it is necessary to make the evil thing a man; but it is not always necessary, it is not even always artistic, to make him a mixed and probable man. In any tale, the tone of which is at all symbolic, he may quite legitimately be made an aboriginal and infernal energy. He must be a man only in the sense that he must have a wit and will to be matched with the wit and will of the man chiefly fighting. The evil may be inhuman, but it must not be impersonal, which is almost exactly the position occupied by Satan in the theological scheme.

—*CD*, 204–205

Virtues

Let us then, by all means, be proud of the virtues that we have not got; but let us not be too arrogant about the virtues that we cannot help having. It may be that a man living on a desert island has a right to congratulate himself upon the fact that he can meditate at his ease. But he must not congratulate himself on the fact that he is on a desert island, and at the same time congratulate himself on the self-restraint he shows in not going to a ball every night.

—ATC, 42

Men imagine their own virtues much more universal than they really are.

—S, 131

Virtue is not the absence of vices or the avoidance of moral dangers; virtue is a vivid and separate thing, like pain or a particular smell.

—TT, 14

Vivisection

Now, it always seems to me that this is the weak point in the ordinary vivisectionist argument, "Suppose your wife were dying." Vivisection is not done by a man whose wife is dying. If it were it might be lifted to the level of the moment, as would be lying or stealing bread, or any other ugly action. But this ugly action is done in cold blood, at leisure, by men who are not sure that it will be of any use to anybody—men of whom the most that can be said is that they may conceivably make the beginnings of some discovery which may perhaps save the life of someone else's wife in some remote future. That is too cold and distant to rob an act of its immediate horror. That is like training a child to tell lies for the sake of some great dilemma that may never come to him. You are doing a cruel thing, but not with enough passion to make it a kindly one.

—ATC, 214–215

Vows

The Man who makes a vow makes an appointment with himself at some distant time or place. . . . And in modern times this terror of one's self, of the weakness and mutability of one's self, has perilously increased, and is the real basis of the objection to vows of any kind.

—D, 20

The idea, or at any rate the ideal, of the thing called a vow is fairly obvious. It is to combine the fixity that goes with finality with the self-respect that only goes with freedom.

—Div, 95

Vows and Marriage

The civilisation of vows was broken up when Henry the Eighth broke his own vow of marriage. . . . Marriage not only became less of a sacrament but less of a sanctity. It threatened to become not only a contract, but a contract that could not be kept.

—Div, 97

W

War

The only defensible war is a war of defence. And a war of defence, by its very definition and nature, is one from which a man comes back battered and bleeding and only boasting that he is not dead.

—Bio, 253

The refined people seem to think that there is something unpleasant and profane about making a war religious. I should say that there ought to be no war except religious war. If war is irreligious, it is immoral. No man ought ever to fight at all unless he is prepared to put his quarrel before that invisible Court of Arbitration with which all religion is concerned. Unless he thinks he is vitally, eternally, cosmically in the right, he is wrong to fire off a pocket-pistol.

—Glass, 72

The curse of war is that it does lead to more international imitation; while in peace and freedom men can afford to have national variety.

—NJ, 45

War and Peace

But in bald fact religion does not involve perpetual war in the East, any more than patriotism involves perpetual war in the West. What it does involve in both cases is a defensive attitude; a vigilance on the frontiers. There is no war; but there is an armed peace.

—NJ, 109

War and Slavery

War is, in the main, a dirty, mean inglorious business, but it is not the dirtiest calamity that can befall a people. There is one worse state at least: the state of slavery.

—EA, 202–203

Weapons

. . . we still for some reason admit the tools of destruction to be nobler than the tools of production, because decorative art is expended on the one and not on the other. The sword has a golden hilt; but no plough has golden handles. There is such a thing as a sword of state; there is no such thing as a scythe of state. Men come to court wearing imitation swords; few men come to court wearing imitation flails.

—Blake, 46–49

The Welfare State

This modern notion about the State is a delusion. It is not founded on the history of real States, but entirely on reading about unreal or ideal States, like the Utopias of Mr. Wells. The real State, though a necessary human combination, always has been and always will be, far too large, loose, clumsy, indirect and even insecure, to be the "home" of the human young who are to be trained in the human tradition. If mankind had not been organised into families, it would never have had the organic power to be organized into commonwealths. Human culture is handed down in the customs of countless households; it is the only way in which human culture can remain human. The households are right to confess a common loyalty or federation under some king or republic. But the king cannot be the nurse in every nursery; or even the government become the governess in every schoolroom.

—*S,* 79

Wilde, Oscar

His philosophy (which was vile) was a philosophy of ease, of acceptance, and luxurious illusion; yet, being Irish, he could not help putting it in pugnacious and propagandist epigrams. He preached his softness with hard decisions; he praised pleasure in the words most calculated to give pain. This armed insolence, which was the noblest thing about him, was also the Irish thing; he challenged all comers.

—*GBS,* 28

Wilde knew how to say the precise thing which, whether true or false, is irresistible. As, for example, "I can resist everything but temptation."

—*HA,* 144

This irritating duplication of real brilliancy with snobbish bluff runs through all his three comedies. "Life is much too important to be taken seriously"; that is the true humourist. "A well-tied tie is the first serious step in life"; that is the charlatan. "Man can believe the impossible, but man can never believe the improbable"; that is said by a fine philosopher. "Nothing is so fatal to a personality as the keeping of promises, unless it be telling the truth"; that is said by a tired quack. "A man can be happy with any woman so long as he does not love her"; that is wild truth. "Good intentions are invariably ungrammatical"; that is tame trash.

—*HA,* 145–146

Will

You can discuss whether a man's act in jumping over a cliff was directed towards happiness; you cannot discuss whether it was derived from will. Of course it was. You can praise an action by saying that it is calculated to bring pleasure or pain to discover truth or to save the soul. But you cannot praise an action because it shows will; for to say that is merely to say that it is an action. By this praise of will you cannot really choose one course as better than another. And yet choosing one course as better than another is the very definition of the will you are praising.

—*O*, 69

All the will-worshippers, from Nietzsche to Mr. Davidson, are really quite empty of volition. They cannot will, they can hardly wish. And if any one wants a proof of this, it can be found quite easily. It can be found in this fact: that they always talk of will as something that expands and breaks out. But it is quite the opposite. Every act of will is an act of self-limitation. To desire action is to desire limitation. . . . When you choose anything, you reject everything else. . . . Every act is an irrevocable selection and exclusion. Just as when you marry one woman you give up all the others, so when you take one course of action you give up all other courses.

—*O*, 70-71

. . . . He who wills to reject nothing, wills the destruction of will; for will is not only the choice of something, but the rejection of almost everything.

—*O*, 77

There is, and has long been, pouring upon the world, mostly in an immediate sense from the Germans and the Slavs, probably in an ultimate sense from the dark philosophies of Asia, a sort of doctrine of mystical helplessness that takes a hundred forms; and that recognises everything in the world except will. It denies the will of God and it does not believe even in the will of man. It does not believe in one of the most glorious manifestations of the will of man, which is the act of creative choice essential to art.

—RLS, 134

Wit

But wit is a more manly exercise than fiddling or fooling; wit requires an intellectual athleticism, because it is akin to logic. A wit must have something of the same running, working, and staying power as a mathematician or metaphysician. Moreover, wit is a fighting thing and a working thing. A man may enjoy humour all by himself; he may see a joke when no one else sees it; he may see the point and avoid it. But wit is a sword; it is meant to make people feel the point as well as see it. All honest people saw the point of Mark Twain's wit. Not a few dishonest people felt it.

—HA, 11

Women

I should favour anything that would increase the present enormous authority of women and their creative action in their own homes. The average woman, as I have said, is a despot; the average man is a serf.

—ATC, 80

. . . they refuse to be emotional at emotional moments.

—BC, 365

For wisdom, first and last, is the characteristic of women. They are often silly, they are always wise. Commonsense is uncommon among men; but commonsense is really and literally a common sense among women. And the sagacity of women, like the sagacity of saints, or that of donkeys, is something outside all questions of ordinary cleverness and ambition. The whole truth of the matter was revealed to Mr. Rudyard Kipling when the spirit of truth suddenly descended on him and he said: "Any woman can manage a clever man; but it requires a rather clever woman to manage a fool."

—HA, 163–164

Little Women was written by a woman for women—for little women. Consequently it anticipated realism by twenty or thirty years; just as Jane Austen anticipated it by at least a hundred years. For women are the only realists; their whole object in life is to pit their realism against the extravagant, excessive, and occasionally drunken idealism of men.

—HA, 164

A man's good work is effected by doing what he does, a woman's by being what she is.

—RB, 44

The Modern Girl with the lipstick and the cocktail is as much a rebel against the Woman's Rights Woman of the '80's, with her stiff stick-up collars and strict teetotalism, as the latter was a rebel against the Early Victorian lady of the languid waltz tunes and the album full of quotations from Byron; or as the last, again, was a rebel against a Puritan mother to whom the waltz was a wild orgy and Byron the Bolshevist of his age.

—STA, 76–77

Women (and Worrying)

If my correspondent can find any way of preventing women from worrying, he will indeed be a remarkable man. . . . Theoretically, I suppose, every one would like to be freed from worries. But nobody in the world would always like to be freed from worrying occupations. I should very much like . . . to be free from the consuming nuisance of writing this article. But it does not follow that I should like to be free from the consuming nuisance of being a journalist. Because we are worried about a thing, it does not follow that we are not interested in it. The truth is the other way. If we are not interested, why on earth should we be worried? Women are worried about housekeeping, but those that are most interested are the most worried. Women are still more worried about their husbands and their children. And I suppose if we strangled the children and poleaxed the husbands it would leave woman free for higher culture. That is, it would leave them free to begin to worry about that. For women would worry about higher culture as much as they worry about everything else.

—ATC, 76–77

Women (Liberated)

I wonder how long liberated woman will endure the invidious ban which excludes her from being a hangman. Or rather, to speak with more exactitude a hangwoman. The very fact that there seems something vaguely unfamiliar and awkward about the word, is but a proof of the ages of sex oppression that have accustomed us to this sex privilege.

—FVF, 54

Women (Modern)

The tragedy of the modern woman is not that she is not allowed to follow man, but that she follows him far too slavishly.

—VA, 148

Words

What is the good of words if they aren't important enough to quarrel over? Why do we choose one word more than another if there isn't any difference between them? If you called a woman a chimpanzee instead of an angel, wouldn't there be a quarrel about a word? If you're not going to argue about words, what are you going to argue about? Are you going to convey your meaning to me by moving your ears? The Church and the heresies always used to fight about words, because they are the only things worth fighting about.

—BC, 96

...every word we use comes to us coloured from all its adventures in history, every phase of which has made at least a faint alteration.

—Blake, 1

What's the good of words?...If you try to talk about a truth that's merely moral, people always think it's merely metaphorical. A real live man with two legs once said to me: 'I only believe in the Holy Ghost in a spiritual sense.' Naturally, I said: 'In what other sense could you believe it?' And *then* he thought I meant he needn't believe in anything except evolution, or ethical fellowship, or some bilge....

—FBO, 638

It is strange how you people worship words and are satisfied with words. What difference does it make to a thing that you now call it telepathy, as you once called it tomfoolery? If a man climbs into the sky on a mango-tree, how is it altered by saying it is only levitation, instead of saying it is only lies? If a mediaeval witch waved a wand and turned me into a blue baboon, you would say it was only atavism.

—FBO, 688

Work Songs (Decline of)

If there are songs for all the separate things that have to be done in a boat, why are there not songs for all the separate things that have to be done in a bank?...And the more I thought about the matter the more painfully certain it seemed that the most important and typical modern things could not be done with a chorus. One could not, for instance, be a great

369

financier and sing; because the essence of being a great financier is that you keep quiet. You could not even in many modern circles be a public man and sing; because in those circles the essence of being a public man is that you do nearly everything in private. Nobody would imagine a chorus of money-lenders. Every one knows the story of the solicitors' corps of volunteers who, when the Colonel on the battlefield cried "Charge!" all said simultaneously, "Six-and-eightpence." And at the end of my reflections I had really got no further than the sub-conscious feeling . . . that there is something spiritually suffocating about our life. . . .

$-TT$, 239–243

World

It is a curious and perhaps melancholy truth that the world is imitating our worst, our weariness and our dingy decline, when it did not imitate our best and the high moment of our morning.

$-NJ$, 102

World (Modern)

The modern world is materialistic, but it isn't solid. It isn't hard or stern or ruthless in pursuit of its purpose, or all the things that the newspapers and novels say it is; and sometimes actually praise it for being. Materialism isn't like stone; it's like mud, and liquid mud at that.

$-Bow$, 154

The modern world is insane, not so much because it admits the abnormal as because it cannot recover the normal.

$-Evils$, 31

The modern world is full of the old Christian virtues gone mad. The virtues have gone mad because they have been isolated from each other and are wandering alone. Thus some scientists care for truth; and their

370

truth is pitiless. Thus some humanitarians only care for pity; and their pity (I am sorry to say) is often untruthful.

—O, 53

Worldly Wisdom

Nothing in this universe is so unwise as that kind of worship of worldly wisdom.

—H, 13

Worrying

I am afraid that the maxim that the smallest worries are the worst is sometimes used or abused by people, because they have nothing but the very smallest worries.

—TT, 50

Writing

In the end it will not matter to us whether we wrote well or ill; whether we fought with flails or reeds. It will matter to us greatly on what side we fought.

—ATC, 8

Writing Badly

Writing badly anyone can understand who writes at all; I for one do it perpetually. Writing badly is the definition of journalism; writing badly is almost in such cases the definition of living honestly. But writing badly on such an enormous scale; writing badly with such immense ambition of design; writing badly with such immense industry of words and pages; and writing so badly as Dumas did—these things are the marks of no common mind. It requires a great man to write so badly as that. It is as courageous as building an ugly Cathedral, and staring at it as it sits triumphant in the sky. It is as bold as building the Great Wall of China, and deliberately building it wrong. If Dumas was futile it was almost in the same sense that Napoleon was futile.

—*HA,* 202–203

X Y Z

Yes and No

... a thing cannot be and not be. Henceforth, in common or popular language, there is a false and true. ... This is the dilemma that many sceptics have darkened the universe and dissolved the mind, solely in order to escape. They are those who maintain that there is something that is both Yes and No. I do not know whether they pronounce it Yo.

—STA, 167

Youth

The current phrase ... that everything must be done for youth, that the rising generation is all that matters, is in sober fact a piece of pure sentimentalism. It is also, within reason, a perfectly natural piece of sentiment. All healthy people like to see the young enjoying themselves; but if we turn that pleasure into a principle, we are sentimentalists. If we desire the greatest happiness of the greatest number, it will be obvious that the greatest number, at any given moment, are rather more likely to be between twenty-five and seventy than to be between seventeen and twenty-five.

—Thing, 45

Zionist Problem

. . . for the Zionist problem is complicated by a real quarrel in the Ghetto about Zionism. The old religious Jews do not welcome the new national-ist Jews; it would sometimes be hardly an exaggeration to say that one party stands for the religion without the nation, and the other for the nation without the religion.

—NJ, 125

Zola and Ibsen

. . . all the Zola heredity and Ibsen heredity that has been written in our time affects me as not merely evil, but as essentially ignorant and retrogressive. This sort of science is almost the only thing that can with strict propriety be called reactionary. Scientific determinism is simply the primal twilight of all mankind; and some men seem to be returning to it.

—ATC, 167

BIBLIOGRAPHY OF G.K. CHESTERTON WORKS
CITED WITH SYMBOLS

AIG	*All Is Grist.* New York: Dodd, Mead and Co., 1932.
AIWS	*As I Was Saying.* London: Methuen, 1936.
Alarms	*Alarms and Discursions.* London: Library Press, The Minerva Edition.
Amer	*What I Saw in America.* London: Hodder and Stoughton, 1922.
ATC	*All Things Considered.* New York: Sheed and Ward, 1956.
Avowals	*Avowals and Denials.* New York: Dodd, Mead and Co., 1935.
BC	*The Ball and the Cross.* New York: John Lane Co., 1910.
Bio	*The Autobiography of G. K. Chesterton.* New York: Sheed and Ward, 1936.
Blake	*William Blake.* London: Duckworth and Co.
Bow	*Tales of the Long Bow.* New York: Sheed and Ward, 1956.
C	*Chaucer.* New York: Sheed and Ward, 1956.
CCC	*The Catholic Church and Conversion.* New York: Macmillan Co., 1951.
CD	*Charles Dickens: Last of the Great Men.* New York: Press of the Reader's Club, 1942.
Cobbett	*Cobbett.* New York: Dodd, Mead and Co., 1926.
CM	*The Common Man.* New York: Sheed and Ward, 1950.
Come	*Come to Think of It.* London: Methuen, 1930.
Crimes	*The Crimes of England.* New York: John Lane Co., 1916.
D	*The Defendant.* New York: Dodd, Mead and Co., 1902.
Div	*The Superstition of Divorce.* New York: John Lane Co., 1920.
Diversity	*The Uses of Diversity.* London: Library Press, The Minerva Edition.

Don Q	*The Return of Don Quixote.* New York: Dodd, Mead and Co., 1927.
EA	*The End of the Armistice.* New York: Sheed and Ward, 1936.
EM	*The Everlasting Man.* New York: Dodd, Mead and Co., Apollo Edition.
England	*A Short History of England.* London: New Phoenix Library, 1951.
Evils	*Eugenics and Other Evils.* New York: Dodd, Mead and Co., 1927.
FBO	*The Father Brown Omnibus.* New York: Dodd, Mead and Co., 1951.
FFF	*Four Faultless Felons.* New York: Dodd, Mead and Co., 1930.
Five Types	*Five Types.* London: Henry Holt and Co., 1911.
Flying	*The Flying Inn.* New York: John Lane Co., 1914.
FVF	*Fancies Versus Fads.* New York: Dodd, Mead and Co., 1923.
GBS	*George Bernard Shaw.* London: John Lane-The Bodley Head, 1910.
Gen S	*Generally Speaking.* New York: Dodd, Mead and Co., 1929.
GFW	*G. F. Watts.* London: Duckworth, 1975.
GKC	*G. K. C. as M.C.* London: Methuen and Co., 1929.
Glass	*The Glass Walking Stick.* London: Methuen and Co., 1955.
H	*Heretics.* New York: Devin Adair, 1950.
HA	*A Handful of Authors: Essays on Books and Writers,* New York: Sheed and Ward, 1953.
Irish	*Irish Impressions.* New York: John Lane Co., 1920.
Judgement	*The Judgement of Dr. Johnson.* London: Sheed and Ward. (Foreword by C. C. Martindale, S.J.)
Lands	*The Coloured Lands.* New York: Sheed and Ward, 1938.
L & L	*Lunacy and Letters.* New York: Sheed and Ward, 1958.
Magic	*Magic.* London: Martin Secker, 1926.
Manalive	*Manalive.* London: Thomas Nelson and Sons, 1912.

MM	*A Miscellany of Men.* London: Methuen and Co., 1912.
Mr. Pond	*The Paradoxes of Mr. Pond.* New York: Dodd, Mead and Co., 1945.
MWKTM	*The Man Who Knew Too Much.* New York: Al Burt Co., 1922.
NJ	*The New Jerusalem.* London: Hodder and Stoughton.
NNH	*The Napoleon of Notting Hill.* New York: Paulist Press, 1978.
O	*Orthodoxy.* New York: Dodd, Mead and Co., 1954.
Outline	*The Outline of Sanity.* London: Methuen and Co., 1926.
Poet	*The Poet and the Lunatics.* New York: Dodd, Mead and Co., 1929.
Queer	*The Club of Queer Trades.* New York and London: Harper and Brothers, 1905.
RB	*Robert Browning.* London: Macmillan Co., 1914.
RLS	*Robert Louis Stevenson.* New York: Sheed and Ward, 1955.
Rome	*The Resurrection of Rome.* New York: Dodd, Mead and Co., 1930.
S	*Sidelights on New London and Newer New York.* New York: Dodd, Mead and Co., 1932.
STA	*Saint Thomas Aquinas.* Garden City: Doubleday and Co., 1956.
St. Francis	*St. Francis of Assisi.* Garden City: Doubleday and Co., 1954.
Surprise	*The Surprise.* New York: Sheed and Ward, 1953.
Survey	*All I Survey.* London: Methuen and Co., 1934.
Thing	*The Thing: Why I Am a Catholic.* New York: Dodd, Mead and Co., 1946.
Thursday	*The Man Who Was Thursday.* New York: Dodd, Mead and Co., 1935.
TT	*Tremendous Trifles.* New York: Dodd, Mead and Co., 1917.
Types	*Varied Types.* New York: Dodd, Mead and Co., 1908.
Tyranny	*The Appetite of Tyranny.* New York: Dodd, Mead and Co., 1915.
UU	*Utopia of Usurers.* New York: Boni and Liveright, 1917.

VA   *The Victorian Age in Literature*. New York: Henry Holt and Co., 1913.

Well   *The Well and the Shallows*. New York: Sheed and Ward, 1935.

WW   *What's Wrong with the World*. New York: Dodd, Mead and Co., 1910.

381

INDEX OF TOPICS

This index includes only those topics in an excerpt other than the topic under which that excerpt is listed in the text.

385

386

George J. Marlin, a Vice President of the Marine Midland Bank, N.A., is a specialist in municipal finance. Mr. Marlin received his undergraduate degree from Iona College in political science and philosophy. He did graduate work in government at New York University. Born in New York City in 1952, Mr. Marlin now resides in Highland Mills, New York.

Richard P. Rabatin, a professional musician, resides in Stony Brook, New York. Born in 1950, Mr. Rabatin received his undergraduate degree in political science from the State University of New York at Stony Brook. He received his Masters Degree at Fordham University in political science and he also studied musical composition at Berkley College of Music in Boston.

John L. Swan is a partner in the community relations firm Institutional Planning and Development Corporation. He was formerly associated with the National Broadcasting Corporation and the American Cancer Society. Mr. Swan attended Manhattan College and is a lifelong resident of New York City.

Joseph Sobran is a long time senior editor for the *National Review* and a contributing editor for the *Human Life Review.* He is also a nationally syndicated columnist and a regular commentator for CBS radio.